International Monetary Fund (IMF)

International Monetary Fund (IMF)

Fourth Edition

Annamaria Viterbo

This book was originally published as a monograph in the International Encyclopaedia of Laws/Intergovernmental Organizations.

Founding Editor: Roger Blanpain†
General Editor: Frank Hendrickx
Volume Editor: Jan Wouters

Wolters Kluwer

Published by:
Kluwer Law International B.V.
PO Box 316
2400 AH Alphen aan den Rijn
The Netherlands
E-mail: lrs-sales@wolterskluwer.com
Website: www.wolterskluwer.com/en/solutions/kluwerlawinternational

Sold and distributed by:
Wolters Kluwer Legal & Regulatory U.S.
920 Links Avenue
Landisville, PA 17538
United States of America
E-mail: customer.service@wolterskluwer.com

ISBN 978-94-035-0156-7

e-Book: ISBN 978-94-035-0166-6
web-PDF: ISBN 978-94-035-0176-5

This title is available on www.kluwerlawonline.com

The Author

Annamaria Viterbo is Full Professor of International Law at the Law Department of the University of Torino, Italy, Fellow of the Collegio Carlo Alberto and non-resident Fellow with the Global Economic Governance Initiative at the Boston University Global Development Policy Center. She obtained a PhD in International Economic Law from Bocconi University, Milan. She was an intern at the ECB Legal Department, a Jean Monnet Fellow at the European University Institute and a visiting professor at the IMF Legal Department. She has published two well-received monographs: *International Economic Law and Monetary Measures* (2012) and *Sovereign Debt Restructuring: The Role and Limits of Public International Law* (2020). Her research interests mainly involve issues of international economic law, and she has published works on the IMF, the World Bank, sovereign debt, sovereign wealth funds, financial regionalism, investment protection, the European monetary union and the ECB. The author is thankful to Prof. Erik Denters of VU University, Amsterdam, for his precious contribution to previous editions of this work.

The Author

Table of Contents

List of Abbreviations

AREAER	IMF Annual Reports on Exchange Arrangements and Exchange Restrictions
BIS	Bank for International Settlements
CACs	Collective Action Clauses
CCRT	Catastrophe Containment and Relief Trust
CES	Country Engagement Strategies
CFMs	Capital Flow Management Measures
CPD	Climate Policy Diagnostic
CPIA	Country Policy and Institutional Assessment
DSA	Debt Sustainability Analysis
DSSI	Debt Service Suspension Initiative
ECB	European Central Bank
ECF	Extended Credit Facility
ECOSOC	UN Economic and Social Council
ECU	European Currency Unit
EFF	Extended Fund Facility
EMS	European Monetary System
EMU	European Economic and Monetary Union
ESM	European Stability Mechanism
EU	European Union
EWG	Eurogroup Working Group
FCL	Flexible Credit Line
FCSs	Fragile and Conflict-Affected States
FSAP	Financial Sector Assessment Program
FSB	Financial Stability Board
FSF	Financial Stability Forum
FSSA	Financial System Stability Assessment
G-	Intergovernmental Groups (G-7, G-10, G-20, G-24)
GAB	General Arrangements to Borrow
GATS	General Agreement on Trade in Services

List of Abbreviations

GATT	General Agreement on Tariffs and Trade
GDP	Gross Domestic Product
GFSN	Global Financial Safety Net
GFSR	Global Financial Stability Report
GRA	General Resources Account
HIPC	Heavily Indebted Poor Countries
IBRD	International Bank for Reconstruction and Development
ICESCR	International Covenant on Economic, Social and Cultural Rights
ICJ	International Court of Justice
ICMA	International Capital Market Association
ICSID	International Centre for Settlement of Investment Disputes
IDA	International Development Association
IEO	Independent Evaluation Office
IFC	International Finance Corporation
IMF	International Monetary Fund
IMFC	International Monetary and Financial Committee
ITO	International Trade Organisation
JMAP	Joint Management Action Plan
LIC	Low-Income Country
LIC DSF	Debt Sustainability Framework for Low-Income Countries
MDGs	Millennium Development Goals
MDRI	Multilateral Debt Relief Initiative
MEFP	Memorandum on Economic and Financial Policies
MIGA	Multilateral Investment Guarantee Agency
MONA	Monitoring of Fund Arrangements
MoU	Memorandum of Understanding
NAB	New Arrangements to Borrow
NGO	Non-governmental Organisation
OECD	Organisation for Economic Co-operation and Development
PLL	Precautionary and Liquidity Line
PMB	Staff-Monitored Program with Board Involvement
PRGS	Poverty Reduction and Growth Strategy
PRGT	Poverty Reduction and Growth Trust
QPCs	Quantitative Performance Criteria
RCF	Rapid Credit Facility
RFAs	Regional Financing Arrangements
RFI	Rapid Financing Instrument
ROSCs	Reports on the Observance of Standards and Codes

RSF	Resilience and Sustainability Facility
RST	Resilience and Sustainability Trust
SBA	Stand-By Arrangement
SCF	Standby Credit Facility
SCIMF	Subcommittee on the IMF
SDDS	Special Data Dissemination Standard
SDGs	Sustainable Development Goals
SDRM	Sovereign Debt Restructuring Mechanism
SDRs	Special Drawing Rights
SMP	Staff Monitored Program
SRDSF	Sovereign Risk and Debt Sustainability Framework for Market Access Countries
TFEU	Treaty on the Functioning of the European Union
TMU	Technical Memorandum of Understanding
UN	United Nations
UNDP	UN Development Programme
VTA	Voluntary Trading Agreement
WEO	World Economic Outlook
WTO	World Trade Organization

List of Abbreviations

Introduction

1. The International Monetary Fund (IMF) is the only international organisation that administers and supervises monetary relations between States. Its primary purpose is to ensure the stability of the international monetary system, but the Fund also promotes monetary cooperation, facilitates international trade, promotes employment and sustainable economic growth, and provides financial and technical assistance to its member countries. As a result, the Fund is expected to positively contribute to creating the conditions and providing the resources for national and international prosperity.

2. Since its establishment, the IMF has witnessed considerable changes in the global economic landscape. The process of decolonisation, a growing membership and the emergence of capital markets have created a new environment. More recently, the Fund has been confronted with multiple crises (the global financial crisis of 2008–2009, the European debt crisis of 2009–2014, the crisis triggered by the COVID-19 pandemic in 2020–2021, the increased debt vulnerability of low- and middle-income countries in recent years) and is expected to address new risks, such as those arising from climate change. However, the Fund's purposes have not been redefined, and despite pressures to shift its orientation towards the promotion of economic growth and the safeguarding of financial stability, it remains primarily a monetary institution. To date, the few amendments to the Articles of Agreement that have been adopted mostly refer to the methods by which the Fund is mandated to pursue its objectives. Even if its mandate has not been updated, the IMF has developed the continuous capacity to change and adapt to circumstances, proving capable of responding to unprecedented challenges.

3. The activities of the IMF are complex, technical and versatile. They are reflected in a myriad of policies, decisions and guidelines. Within the framework of the *International Encyclopaedia of Laws*, there is only limited space to outline the key activities of the Fund, without going into extensive detail. Chapter 1 discusses the Fund's genesis and historical development. Chapter 2 describes the IMF's membership and institutional structure. Chapters 3 and 4 respectively analyse the IMF's lending and other activities. Chapter 5 discusses the Fund in the global context.

4. For further reading, there is a wealth of literature available. The most important author on the Fund's legal and institutional aspects is the late Sir Joseph Gold, who was the General Counsel and Director of the legal department from 1960 to 1979. Gold published dozens of articles and books that explain the purposes and powers of the IMF. Another important source is the historical studies published by the IMF, which cover five periods: 1945–1965 (by J. Keith Horsefield), 1966–1971 and 1972–1978 (by Margaret Garritsen de Vries) as well as 1979–1989 and 1990–1999 (by James M. Boughton); these volumes are published by the IMF and include a chronological overview of policy development and the Fund's corpus juris and practice. The IMF published two other useful series of volumes on banking and finance: *Current Legal Issues Affecting Central Banks* (Volumes I–V) and *Current Developments in Monetary and Financial Law* (Volumes 1–6).

5. Legal documents are published in the *Selected Decisions and Selected Documents of the IMF*. This publication contains decisions of the Executive Board, resolutions of the Board of Governors and agreements with other international organisations, such as the United Nations, the World Bank and the World Trade Organization (WTO). Documents on the internal functioning of the IMF are published in the 'By-Laws, Rules and Regulations of the International Monetary Fund'.

6. For keeping track with current developments, the biweekly periodical *IMF Survey* and the *Annual Reports of the Executive Board* are useful sources. In addition, the Fund maintains a comprehensive website (www.imf.org) that publishes documents and economic data from the Fund and its membership. The IMF Archives provide public access to primary resources and documentary materials. Sources and documents discussed in this monograph are available on the Fund's website.

Chapter 1. Genesis and Historical Development

§1. The Bretton Woods Conference and the Par Value System

7. Towards the end of World War II, a renewed interest in multilateral cooperation developed within the international community. States that had experienced the horrors of the war were ready to cooperate to establish a new system of international relations to promote orderly economic and financial conditions and ensure the maintenance of peace and security.

8. In July 1944 (when the war was at its height, but not yet over), the United Nations Monetary and Financial Conference was convened in the town of Bretton Woods (New Hampshire, US) to negotiate the Articles of Agreement of the IMF and the Articles of Agreement of the International Bank for Reconstruction and Development (IBRD). Interestingly, the United States invited several Third-World countries to participate in the conference (both colonies and non-colonies) even though the United Kingdom opposed this initiative.

9. The creation of the IMF was essentially an American-British undertaking. Two economists – Harry Dexter White for the US Treasury and Sir John Maynard Keynes for the British government – were the leading negotiators among the representatives of the forty-four allied governments that gathered at the Conference. Their 'Joint Statement by Experts on the Establishment of an International Monetary Fund' formed the basis for negotiations. The Plan was a merger of White's proposal of an 'International Stabilisation Fund' and Keynes's idea of an 'International Currency (or Clearing) Union'. Both proposals addressed the same issue: providing a lending mechanism to help countries address balance of payments shortfalls. However, while the stabilisation fund proposal sought adjustment for balance of payments problems mostly from debtor countries, the clearing union proposal introduced provisions to put pressure on both creditor and debtor countries to share the responsibility for balanced international payments. The final proposal was clearly dominated by White's ideas.

10. The founding fathers of the Bretton Woods Institutions shared a common vision: in order to avert a new phase of economic instability of a gravity comparable to the Great Depression of the early 1930s, they sought to create a rules-based multilateral framework – a system of international treaties, institutions and decision-making procedures – to regulate economic relations among States and the international monetary system. The new multilateral framework was intended to impose clear obligations on the contracting parties, prohibiting the adoption of protectionist and beggar-thy-neighbour policies. In fact, during the interwar period, trade protectionism, exchange restrictions, multiple exchange rates and competitive exchange rate manipulations (especially devaluations) had become widespread. They were used as tools of economic warfare, discouraging cross-border trade and investment flows. Many observers believed that the recurring economic crises and the failure of international cooperation had contributed to the outbreak of the war in 1939. To avoid repetition of the ruinous policies of the interwar period, a new – internationally negotiated – economic order would be established. There was indeed a broad consensus that achieving peace and economic stability required both collective action at the international level and the creation of specialised institutions designed to promote interstate cooperation.

11. Despite considerable problems in achieving consensus on issues such as the conditions for the use of Fund's resources and the location of its headquarters, the Bretton Woods Conference successfully established a permanent institutional and legal framework that required the firm commitment of States to manage their currencies for the benefit of international monetary stability. Of the forty-four countries that had taken part in the negotiations (Germany, Italy and Japan were not represented at the Conference), twenty-nine ratified the IMF Articles of Agreement as original members. China and Iran were among the original members, while the Russian Federation took part in the negotiations but only joined in 1992. The Articles entered into force on 27 December 1945, followed a few days later by the Articles of Agreement of the IBRD, the first organisation of what would later evolve into the World Bank Group. Both organisations became specialised agencies of the United Nations (UN) in 1947.

12. The term 'Bretton Woods system' became synonymous with the international monetary regime that emerged at the end of World War II and lasted until 1971. A key feature of the post-war monetary system was that, in order to maintain monetary stability, the IMF would oversee a system of exchange rates based on par values. The keystone of the system was the convertibility of the US dollar into gold at the fixed rate of USD 35 per ounce (as set by Franklin Delano Roosevelt in 1934). The currencies of all the other IMF Member States were to be fixed against the dollar at an official exchange rate (i.e., their par value). This value had to be expressed in terms of gold as a common denominator or in US dollars. Central banks were required to contain exchange rate fluctuations and maintain the exchange rate of their currency within a band of ±1% around the central parity.

13. In order to guarantee 'stability without rigidity', a member was permitted to change the par value of its currency only to correct a 'fundamental disequilibrium' in its balance of payments. To make such a modification, authorisation of the IMF was required. If a member adjusted its par value in spite of objections by the Fund, that member would not be breaching the Fund's Articles, but the Fund would cease providing balance of payments support to the country making the unauthorised change. Regrettably, the notion of fundamental disequilibrium was not explicitly defined in the IMF Articles of Agreement, and this led to abuse: States would often change their exchange rates and par values without consulting the Fund or would fail to declare a par value, choosing instead to let their currency float, while still maintaining full access to IMF resources. In addition, many States failed to meet the commitment to maintain the ±1% range around their par value.

14. At the end of the 1960s, the US monetary gold stock had fallen from USD 22.9 billion in 1951 to USD 10.9 billion in 1968. Confidence in the convertibility of

US dollars into gold started to fade, and France increased its demands to exchange its US dollar reserves into gold. The par value system collapsed in August 1971, when US President Richard Nixon 'temporarily' suspended the external convertibility of the dollar into gold. In December 1971, under the so-called Smithsonian Agreement, the countries of the Group of Ten (G-10) negotiated a devaluation of the US dollar against gold and a realignment of their currencies. The new structure of parities lasted until 1973 when, during the first oil crisis, a wave of speculation hit the European currencies, which started to float independently against one another. In 1978, when the Second Amendment to the IMF Articles entered into force, the Bretton Woods system of fixed exchange rates was formally terminated (on amendments *see infra*, paragraphs 118 ff.).

15. The Second Amendment introduced a new purpose clause within IMF Article IV, and the title of the provision was changed from 'Par-Values of Currencies' into 'Obligations Regarding Exchange Arrangements'. The Fund's close control over members' exchange rates was substituted with a high degree of deregulation. IMF members were allowed to choose the form of exchange arrangement they preferred, subject to one exception: the use of gold as a denominator was explicitly forbidden. All the other categories of exchange arrangements were – and still are – available: free or managed floating; a peg to another currency or a basket of currencies; the adoption of the currency of another country as legal tender; and participation in a monetary area or a currency union.

16. The firm obligations related to the functioning of the par value system were replaced by the obligation 'to collaborate with the Fund and other members to assure orderly exchange arrangements and to promote a stable system of exchange rates' (IMF Article IV, section 1 as amended). Accordingly, the Fund's responsibilities were reduced from being a dedicated custodian of the par value system to being a supervisor of members' exchange rate policies, with IMF lending remaining a tool of last resort to support members facing balance of payments difficulties.

§2. The IMF as One of the Three Pillars of the Post-War International Economic Order

17. Before studying the IMF in depth, it is useful to have a clear understanding of the triangular relationship between the IMF, the IBRD and the proposed International Trade Organisation (ITO). These organisations were intended to constitute the three pillars of the post-war international economic order, forming an integrated framework, with the common objective of promoting prosperity, either directly or indirectly, by fostering the growth of international trade and investment.

I. The IMF and the IBRD: Monetary Stability and Economic Development

18. The IMF and the IBRD were created with complementary purposes. The original mission of the Bank, as devised by the second working commission of the

Bretton Woods Conference, consisted of fostering economic development, assisting in the reconstruction of war-torn Europe and favouring the transition to a peacetime economy. The decision to include the word 'development' in the Bank's mandate was made at the last minute, following a request from representatives of Third World countries. This addition was intended to ensure that the Bank's activities extended beyond the West to also address the needs of 'economically backward countries'. Shortly after its foundation, though, due to the US bilateral aid programme for Western Europe (the European Recovery Program launched in 1948), the IBRD shifted its focus to the provision of project financing and adjustment loans to developing countries.

19. Soon it became clear that the poorest countries could not afford to borrow capital at the near-market conditions set by the IBRD. To overcome this problem, in 1960, the International Development Association (IDA) was established to provide interest-free long-term loans and grants to the poorest countries. Together, the IBRD and the IDA are officially referred to as the 'World Bank'. The 'World Bank Group', however, also comprises three other legally and financially independent international organisations: the International Finance Corporation (IFC), which was established in 1956 to finance and promote sustainable private sector investments in developing countries; the International Centre for Settlement of Investment Disputes (ICSID), set up in 1966 to provide the institutional and procedural framework for the conciliation and arbitration of disputes between foreign investors and States; and the Multilateral Investment Guarantee Agency (MIGA), created in 1988 with a mandate to promote foreign direct investment in developing countries, offering political risk insurance to investors and lenders.

20. The Articles of Agreement of the IBRD stipulate that among the organisation's purposes there is the promotion of 'the long-range balanced growth of international trade and the maintenance of equilibrium in balances of payments' (Article I). To this end, the IBRD promotes economic and social progress through project lending and support for private foreign investments. A major characteristic, therefore, is the IBRD's focus on development by addressing microeconomic constraints to growth. By contrast, no reference is made to the promotion of economic development in the IMF Articles of Agreement.

21. Whereas the IMF focuses on balance of payments, exchange rate stability, and currency convertibility, and assists members in implementing macroeconomic reforms, the IBRD stimulates long-term investment in priority areas of a member's economy. While the Fund makes short-term loans available to Member States facing balance of payments problems, the IBRD provides loans, guarantees, risk management products and advisory services to middle-income and creditworthy low-income countries (LICs).

II. The IMF and the WTO: Liberalisation of Current Payments and Trade

22. Even the relationship between the IMF and the ITO was expected to be of a complementary nature, with both institutions working to promote international economic stability and trade. However, the ITO Charter adopted in March 1948 at the Havana Conference on Trade and Employment never came into effect because ratification by the United States proved impossible for political reasons. After the failure of the ITO, the General Agreement on Tariffs and Trade (GATT) became the principal multilateral trade treaty until the foundation of the WTO in 1994 (on the relationship between the IMF and the WTO *see also infra*, paragraphs 400 ff.).

23. The IMF/WTO complementarity in facilitating economic exchange stems from the dual nature of trade, which involves two primary transactions: the transfer of goods and services and payments. Trade and payments are two sides of the same coin. On the one side, the WTO administers multilateral trade agreements, such as the GATT that is 'directed to the substantial reduction of tariffs and other barriers of trade and to the elimination of discriminatory treatment in international trade relations'. On the other side, in order to facilitate 'the expansion and balanced growth of international trade', the IMF promotes, *inter alia*, the removal of restrictions on international payments for current transactions (Article I). Payments for current transactions include 'all payments due in connection with foreign trade' (Article XXX). In short, the IMF administers rules that ensure that international trade payments can be made freely.

24. The above suggests that for the smooth functioning of the international trading system, it is imperative that States become members of both the WTO and the IMF. The argument is that trade cannot be liberalised unless States fully accept the obligations of both institutions. WTO members cannot fully comply with the rules set forth by the GATT and other multilateral trade agreements if they maintain exchange restrictions on current payments. This explains why there is substantial overlap in membership: practically all WTO members are also IMF members. By contrast, an IMF member can fulfil its obligations even if it does not accept those arising from WTO law. In this case, no conflict seems to exist, as current payments can be liberalised independently of the WTO's requirements to liberalise trade.

Chapter 2. Institutional Framework

§1. The IMF's Purposes

I. Purposes Explained

25. The purposes of the Fund are outlined in Article I. While amendments have led to significant changes in the Fund's mandate and activities, they have resulted in only minor revisions to the text of Article I. The IMF's purposes are described in Article I as follows:

26. '(i) To promote international monetary cooperation through a permanent institution which provides the machinery for consultation and collaboration on international monetary problems.' This purpose underlines the monetary nature of the IMF and creates a platform for both consultation and collaboration with Member States. It is important to note that the IMF is mandated to deal principally with international monetary problems, which may be considered a subset of manifold problems in international economic relations. Key provisions to fulfil this purpose are to be found throughout the IMF Articles.

27. '(ii) To facilitate the expansion and balanced growth of international trade, and to contribute thereby to the promotion and maintenance of high levels of employment and real income and to the development of the productive resources of all members as primary objectives of economic policy.' This purpose refers to international trade, employment and real income. The expansion and balanced growth of these factors are supposed to be primary objectives of all the Member States but not necessarily of the IMF per se. A note of caution must be added to the interpretation of this purpose: 'facilitate' is not equivalent to 'promote'. The Fund's task is to create an enabling environment – i.e., a stable monetary system – that removes obstacles to economic growth rather than directly promoting growth, which would constitute a more straightforward obligation. Moreover, 'to contribute thereby' underlines that high levels of employment and development of productive resources are merely desired consequences of monetary stability.

28. '(iii) To promote exchange stability, to maintain orderly exchange arrangements among members, and to avoid competitive exchange depreciation.' Three objectives are mentioned here. The promotion of exchange stability indicates that the Fund has to play an active role in promoting exchange rate stability. Further, the obligations 'to maintain' orderly exchange arrangements among members and 'to avoid' competitive exchange depreciations imply that the Fund may exercise certain supervisory tasks over its membership. This purpose still bears the imprint of the Bretton Woods system of par values but was maintained, nonetheless, after its official abrogation by the Second Amendment in 1978. As we will see, IMF Article IV provides instruments through which the Fund exercises surveillance over its members (*see infra*, paragraphs 235 ff.).

29. '(iv) To assist in the establishment of a multilateral system of payments in respect of current transactions between members and in the elimination of foreign exchange restrictions which hamper the growth of world trade.' The Fund 'assists' in the establishment of a payments system and the elimination of foreign exchange restrictions. In practice, however, little contribution has been made to the creation of a payments system. Cross-border payments are administered through domestic and regional arrangements such as the Federal Reserve Wire Network (FEDWIRE) and the Trans-European Automated Real-time Gross Settlement Express Transfer system (TARGET2). Nevertheless, the Fund has made a considerable contribution to the elimination of exchange restrictions by urging members to avoid restrictions on their current payments and to restore full current account convertibility. The Fund administers the elimination of exchange restrictions under Article VIII, subject to the transitional arrangements of Article XIV (*see infra*, paragraphs 273 ff.).

30. '(v) To give confidence to members by making the general resources of the Fund temporarily available to them under adequate safeguards, thus providing them with opportunity to correct maladjustments in their balance of payments without resorting to measures destructive of national or international prosperity.' Whereas balance of payment support (i.e., IMF financial assistance or lending) was originally conceived as one of the tools to promote stability alongside the par value system, it has now overshadowed other activities of the IMF. 'To give confidence' should be understood in the light of the original Articles. As was explained above, under the Bretton Woods system, members were expected to maintain a stable exchange rate, with the IMF giving members confidence that they could maintain their par value – even in times of monetary distress – by providing balance of payments support. The 'adequate safeguards' requirement has been used to justify the IMF's so-called conditionality (*see infra*, paragraphs 174 ff.). Conditionality, in fact, assures the Fund that the country will be able to repay its loan, thus ensuring that the IMF's resources remain available to other countries. At the same time, conditionality helps countries address their balance of payments problems 'without resorting to measures that are harmful to national or international prosperity'. The meaning of 'measures destructive of national or international prosperity' has not been clarified in an authoritative interpretation by the Fund (*see infra*, paragraphs 112 ff.). From this general wording, it may be derived that 'destructive measures' refer to trade protectionism and exchange rate manipulation. Such measures were the ills of the Great Depression in the 1930s. Article V elaborates on conditional balance of payments support and other operations and transactions of the IMF.

31. '(vi) In accordance with the above, to shorten the duration and lessen the degree of disequilibrium in the international balances of payments of members.' This explains that the Fund contributes to the maintenance of equilibrium in the balance of payments positions of members and overall stability. Disequilibrium can be understood both as surplus and deficit in the balance of payments, but little attention has been paid to the need to address large surpluses.

32. Finally, the closing sentence stipulates that 'The Fund shall be guided in all its policies and decisions by the purposes set forth in this Article.' All activities should be conducted within the framework of Article I. This provision appears to support a preference for a teleological interpretation of the IMF Articles of Agreement.

33. The purposes of the IMF relate to the stability of the exchange rate system and the balance of payments of members. The Fund's primary concern and, correspondingly, the main obligations of its members, focus on how their national economies interact with one another – specifically through the balance of payments, exchange rates, and foreign exchange controls.

34. The Articles clearly assume that IMF members retain monetary sovereignty and have the authority to implement their own monetary policies. Throughout the Articles, member countries interact with the IMF primarily through actions related to their currencies and exchange rates. The key provisions of Articles IV and V support this argument. Under Article IV (as amended in 1978), each member undertakes 'to collaborate with the Fund and other members to assure orderly exchange arrangements and to promote a stable system of exchange rates'. Also, 'the Fund shall exercise firm surveillance over the exchange rate policies of members'. Accordingly, members are required to notify the Fund of their chosen 'exchange arrangement', which refers to the exchange rate policy they have adopted. Furthermore, Article V entitles a member to 'purchase the currencies of the Fund in exchange for an equivalent amount of its own currency … after the member declares that it has a need to make the purchase because of its balance of payments or its reserve position'. Clearly, 'own currency' and 'balance of payments' are matters over which members are expected to have control.

II. The Structure of the IMF Articles of Agreement

35. The structure of the IMF Articles of Agreement can be summarised as follows.

Introductory Article	Confirms the rule of law, determines the Fund's financial structure and principles for financial operations.
Article I	Defines the purposes of the Fund.
Article II	Explains conditions for membership.
Article III	Explains quotas and subscription; quotas determine the degree of participation in the Fund.
Article IV	Describes the essential purposes of the international monetary system and members' obligations and enables the Fund to oversee the international monetary system and exercise firm surveillance over exchange rate policies.

Article V	Describes the operations and transactions of the Fund; conditions governing the use of the Fund's general resources and their scope; and balance of payments support. Enables the IMF to adopt specific policies on the use of its general resources for a set of specific balance of payments problems and to provide technical services, including the administration of resources contributed by members through trust funds; such additional activities must be consistent with the purposes of the Fund.
Article VI	Explains that the Fund is not designed to support 'large or sustained outflow of capital' and allows members to introduce capital controls.
Article VII	Authorises the Fund to take measures to replenish the Fund's holding of scarce currencies and declarations on scarce currencies.
Article VIII	Determines members' obligations on current payments liberalisation, discriminatory currency practices, currency convertibility and furnishing of information.
Article IX	Establishes the Fund's legal personality, immunity and privileges.
Article X	Imposes a duty on the Fund to cooperate with other international organisations.
Article XI	Deals with relations with non-members.
Article XII	Determines the Fund's governance structure, the mandate of each institution, and the allocation and exercise of votes.
Article XIII	Determines the location of headquarters and designates central banks as depositories for the Fund holdings of currencies; members must guarantee assets.
Article XIV	Allows for restrictions on current payments through a 'transitional arrangement'; the time frame of the arrangement is not limited.
Articles XV to XXV	Contains extensive provisions on special drawing rights (SDRs) explaining their purposes, general conditions for allocations, valuation and many more facets.
Article XXVI	Explains voluntary and compulsory withdrawal of members from the Fund and settlement of accounts.
Article XXVII	Allows for suspension of provisions in emergencies or unforeseen circumstances.
Article XXVIII	Contains provisions on amendments to the Articles.
Article XXIX	Explains the procedure for authoritative interpretations.
Article XXX	Interprets key provisions and terms.

Article XXXI	Contains the final provisions on entry into force.
Schedules A–M	Contains further elaborations of provisions (e.g., on quotas and suspension of voting rights).

§2. MEMBERSHIP

I. Country-Based Membership

36. The IMF is a country-based organisation. Pursuant to Article II of the IMF Articles of Agreement, membership is open to 'countries' in accordance with the terms that may be prescribed by the Board of Governors. The IMF membership admission process requires the submission of a formal application to initiate the procedure. A country's application is initially considered by the IMF Executive Board, which then submits a recommendation to the Board of Governors. This recommendation includes the new member's quota amount (this is the most contentious issue, as the quota determines each member's relative voting power, on which *see infra*, paragraphs 59 ff.), the form of payment for the subscription, and other terms and conditions of membership. The final decision on membership – the Membership Resolution – is adopted by the Board of Governors through a simple majority of votes cast, provided that a quorum of two-thirds of the Governors, representing over 50% of the total voting power, is met. Governors have no obligation to provide reasons for their votes. The applicant country may become a member once it has completed the necessary legal steps under its domestic law to ratify the IMF Articles of Agreement and fulfil its membership obligations.

37. With the admission of Andorra in 2020 and of Liechtenstein in 2024, IMF membership has expanded to 191 countries. The only UN Member States that are not yet members of the Fund are Cuba, Monaco and North Korea. Cuba was an original member but withdrew from the Fund in 1964. IMF membership is a prerequisite for joining the IBRD and the other agencies of the World Bank Group.

38. Membership in the Fund is open to all countries, regardless of their economic systems. Therefore, there is no preclusion for centrally planned economies, which are eligible to join on equal terms with other countries. The Soviet Union was one of the principal negotiators at the Bretton Woods Conference, but eventually it did not ratify the treaty. After the dissolution of the USSR, the Russian Federation decided to join the IMF and in 1992 was admitted as a new member. China is one of the IMF's original members.

39. Notably, the IMF Articles do not define 'country', and the reasons for using this term instead of 'State' as a criterion for membership remain unclear. One possible explanation is that the term 'country' was preferred because of the characteristics of certain participants in the Bretton Woods Conference, such as the four British Dominions (Australia, Canada, New Zealand and South Africa). Another possible explanation is that the IMF Articles were negotiated when the exercise of monetary sovereignty was a key concern for many countries, especially in the context of post-war economic recovery. However, for colonies, the power to exercise such sovereignty was often limited, as their monetary policies were typically shaped or controlled by the colonial powers. While it was believed that the exercise of the sovereign right to issue a currency and formulate monetary policy was decisive for membership, at that time, statehood could not always be fully equated with monetary sovereignty.

40. The choice of the term 'country' instead of 'State' was probably adopted to allow an entity to apply for membership even if it could not yet be considered to have attained statehood under international law. This allowed, for instance, Kosovo to become a member of the IMF (and of the World Bank) in June 2009, when the request for an advisory opinion on the conformity with international law of the unilateral Declaration of Independence adopted by the Provisional Institutions of Self-Government of Kosovo was still pending before the International Court of Justice (ICJ). While some IMF members contended that only the United Nations had the authority to determine whether a given entity had acquired international legal personality, the IMF Legal Department asserted that the Fund, as an independent organisation, possessed the full power to make its own determination on the eligibility of countries for membership and, in particular, to decide whether a territory that had seceded from an existing Member State had actually achieved statehood, without being bound by the position of the United Nations. Following a recommendation from the IMF Executive Board, the decision to admit Kosovo was ultimately taken by the IMF Board of Governors. Since the IMF employs a weighted voting system (*see infra*, paragraph 59), it can be argued that Kosovo's Statehood was 'weighted' too: if the recognition of a newly formed State comes from advanced economies holding the largest voting power in the IMF, it matters little that a numerical majority of smaller countries expresses its opposition. Notably, to date, Kosovo has not acquired membership in the United Nations or in other UN specialised agencies.

II. Representation of the Euro Area

41. Even though monetary sovereignty may be surrendered to an international organisation or a currency union, these entities are not eligible for IMF membership. However, the European Union (EU) and its currency union deserve specific attention. Members of the European Economic and Monetary Union (EMU) share a single currency and have transferred control of monetary policy and foreign exchange operations to the European Central Bank (ECB), while retaining responsibility for economic policy decisions. The ECB is also entrusted with the task of holding and managing the common pool of reserves and of conducting all types of banking transactions with third countries and international organisations, including lending and borrowing operations. In addition, the EU enjoys the ability to conclude international monetary and exchange rate agreements, to decide upon the external representation of the euro area and, exceptionally, to restrict the flow of capital and payments.

42. The transfer of these competences to a supranational level is deemed to impair the ability of EMU members to fully discharge the duties and exercise the rights deriving from IMF membership. Nevertheless, participants in the EMU have thus far insisted on retaining their individual membership in the IMF. The key argument is that the IMF is a country-based organisation, and that the EMU is not a country. It is unclear, however, how EMU participants can contribute to the IMF objectives after having surrendered their monetary sovereignty. It seems reasonable to believe that the EMU, as the largest existing currency union, will eventually be accepted as a single IMF member. Many authors suggest that, should all EU members adopt the euro, the EU will deserve to become a member of the IMF, either by replacing its Member States or by becoming an additional member. This issue may be solved by amending Article II or by an authoritative interpretation under Article XXIX, clarifying that the term 'country' encompasses currency unions.

43. At present, within the IMF, each EU Member State holds its own seat, and euro area countries are not even grouped into a single IMF Executive Board constituency (*see infra*, paragraph 76). Instead, they are spread across geographically diverse constituencies, a situation that – somehow counterintuitively – enhances the political influence of the euro area within the organisation.

44. To minimise inconsistent positions and fragmented representation, coordination among euro area Member States within the IMF's decision-making bodies is facilitated through a multi-layered structure which includes the Subcommittee on the IMF (SCIMF) and the Eurogroup Working Group (EWG) in Brussels, as well as the meetings of the IMF Executive Directors from the EU (known as EURIMF) in Washington. Moreover, the ECB has held observer status since 2002 and is invited to send a representative to meetings of the IMF Executive Board on Article IV surveillance consultations on the euro-area or individual euro-area members, the use of Fund resources by euro-area Member States and other agenda items recognised by both the ECB and the Fund as being of mutual interest for the fulfilment of their respective mandates.

45. In 2015, the European Commission published a proposal for the gradual establishment of a unified representation of the euro area within the IMF by 2025. This initiative sought to consolidate the individual seats of euro-area Member States into a single constituency, thereby enhancing the EU's influence in IMF decision-making. However, the proposal was not adopted due to a lack of consensus among Member States, and the issue remains unresolved both within the EU and at the IMF.

III. Uniform and Preferential Treatment

46. The IMF Articles confer equal rights and obligations upon all Member States, thereby upholding the principle of uniformity – an expression of the broader doctrine of sovereign equality in international law. Accordingly, the Fund is expected to refrain from any form of discrimination, whether in favour of or against particular members, irrespective of their economic strength or weakness. The fundamental premise is that each member has a balance of payments, that the concept of balance of payments is uniformly applied to all members and that the differences in levels of economic development do not justify different treatment. Therefore, each member is entitled to draw upon the Fund's resources, irrespective of whether it is a low-income country, an emerging economy or an advanced economy.

47. Developing countries have consistently upheld the principle of uniformity to ensure that they would be treated without discrimination. In particular, they have criticised the discriminatory application of conditionality (*see infra*, paragraphs 174 ff.), claiming – especially in the 1970s – that industrialised countries were treated more favourably when requesting balance of payments support. Developing countries have also criticised the asymmetrical treatment reflected in the soft law of Article IV, which concerns IMF surveillance over all members but does not compel them to undergo such surveillance (*see infra*, paragraphs 235 ff.). They contrast this with the firm law of Article V, which governs the IMF's balance of payments support and is predominantly applied to developing countries (*see infra*, paragraphs 125 ff.). According to their claims, the non-binding nature of Article IV consultations stands in sharp contrast to the strict conditionality requirements imposed when the Fund provides balance of payments support.

48. Notably, developing countries have not always been satisfied with uniform treatment in all matters, demanding differentiated and preferential treatment in specific cases. For example, they have attempted to link SDRs allocations (on SDRs *see infra*, paragraphs 293 ff.) with the need for development assistance. However, proposals to incorporate this linkage into the 1978 Second Amendment were rejected because, if approved, it would have compromised the principle of uniformity. No mention of these issues is made in the Fourth Amendment on SDRs (*see infra*, paragraph 122).

49. Although the principle of uniformity still applies, it has been tempered by amendments and policies allowing for a more favourable treatment of certain categories of countries. Under Article V, section 2(b) and Article V, section 12(f), the IMF may establish trust funds and special facilities (*see infra*, paragraphs 144 ff.) to address the specific needs of certain categories of countries. These facilities operate with resources that are kept separate from the IMF's General Resources Account (GRA), to which the principle of uniformity continues to apply.

50. Certain political dynamics must also be acknowledged. The Fund's membership consists, on the one hand, of a small group of economically powerful countries and, on the other, of a large group of emerging, middle-income and low-income countries. As voting rights are based on economic strength, IMF policies are determined by wealthy countries, yet primarily affect developing countries.

IV. Withdrawal

51. Any member may withdraw from the Fund at any time by submitting a formal notice. Membership in the Fund may also be terminated by 'compulsory' withdrawal pursuant to Article XXVI, section 2. The latter measure may be taken if a member fails to fulfil any of its obligations under the IMF Articles. Before compulsory withdrawal is enforced, several measures may be implemented, including declaring the country ineligible to use the Fund's resources and suspending its voting rights. If, nonetheless, the member persists in its non-compliance, procedures for forced withdrawal may be initiated. During the withdrawal process, all operations and transactions with the Fund must cease, and any outstanding accounts between the Fund and the member must be settled.

§3. IMF Quotas

I. The Quota Formula

52. Given that the IMF is a monetary institution providing financial support to countries in financial distress, the economic size of its members cannot be ignored. Therefore, when a country joins the IMF, it is assigned a quota that reflects its size and position in the world economy on the basis of a specific formula.

53. The design of the quota formula has always been a contentious issue. It is enough to recall that, at the Bretton Woods Conference, the quotas of the United States, United Kingdom, China and the Soviet Union (which eventually decided not to ratify the IMF Articles) were determined at the highest political level, and that the formula adopted to distribute quotas among the remaining participants was not disclosed to country representatives. In his memoir, the economist Raymond Mikesell, who was a young advisor in the US delegation, recounts the origin of the first quota formula. He was asked by White to prepare a formula based on the members' gold and dollar holdings, national incomes, and foreign trade. However, White gave him no instructions on the weights to be used, only specifying that, in the final outcome, the United States was to have the largest quota, followed by the United Kingdom, the Soviet Union and China. White's main concern was, in fact, to ensure that allied countries had the largest quotas, with a ranking on which the US President and the Secretary of State had previously agreed. In practice, the quota formula devised at Bretton Woods was the result of a reverse-engineering exercise.

54. After Bretton Woods, to determine the quotas of new members, the Fund kept applying the original formula with minor changes in the weights and the definitions of the variables (i.e., Gross Domestic Product (GDP), average monthly reserves, annual average current payments, annual average current receipts and variability of current receipts). The quota formula remained largely unchanged for decades, failing to keep pace with developments in the world economy. Evidence of this is the fact that, at the end of the millennium, emerging economies were *de facto* under-represented, as their quotas did not reflect their actual weight in the global economy (for instance, during the 1990s, Belgium held a larger quota than Brazil or India).

55. This situation led to discussions on the need for a review of the quota formula. Two main arguments were raised in support. First, the distribution of quotas did not accurately reflect the relative economic importance of member countries in the global economy. Second, the distribution resulting from the application of the formula failed to correct this imbalance. Despite the soundness of these arguments, the main obstacle to any agreement was the distributional implications of a reform. This is because any change in the quota formula essentially consists of redistributing a fixed pool of resources (akin to slicing a pie), where any increase in one member's quota comes at the expense of others. Therefore, achieving the required 85% majority entails securing the agreement of those members who will lose voting power as a result of the reform.

56. After years of negotiations, a compromise on a new quota formula was finally reached in 2008. The current quota formula is calculated as a weighted combination of four key economic indicators: GDP (50% weight), openness (30% weight), economic variability (15% weight) and international reserves (5% weight), expressed in shares of global totals. However, discussions on a comprehensive review of the quota formula continue and are due for completion by 2028, as part of the 17th General Review of Quotas.

II. The Multiple Roles of Quotas

57. The quota is an amount, expressed in SDRs (on their nature and functions *see infra*, paragraphs 293 ff.), the extent of which determines, among other things, a member's relative economic position within the IMF. The quota serves four main functions and it determines: (a) each member's subscription (i.e., the maximum amount of financial contribution the member is obliged to provide to the Fund); (b) the number of voting rights allocated to each member; (c) the maximum amount of loans that each member can obtain from the Fund under normal circumstances; and (d) the share of SDR allocations that each member receives from the Fund.

58. First, quotas determine the amount of money a member is obliged to transfer to the IMF. A member's subscription to the IMF is equivalent to its quota: 75% must be paid in the country's own currency, while the remaining 25% is paid either in SDRs or in a widely accepted currency (usually the US dollar, the euro, the yen or the British pound). All subscriptions are held in the GRA and serve as a source of funding for the IMF balance of payments support and lending activities.

59. Second, the votes of each member are determined by the sum of 'quota-based votes' and 'basic votes'. Quota-based votes are proportional to a member's quota and amount to one vote for each fraction of the quota equal to one hundred thousand SDRs. Basic votes were intended as a counterbalance to the weighted voting system. They are equally distributed among members to reflect the principle of equality of States and to ensure that even the smallest members have a voice in the Fund's deliberations. Initially, the number of basic votes amounted to 250 per member, but to avoid erosion in voting shares of least-developed countries, the Fifth Amendment on Voice and Participation in the IMF (2011) established that they could not be less than 5.5% of all available votes. As a result, the ratio of total basic votes to total votes has become fixed, and basic votes are now automatically adjusted when quotas are increased.

60. Third, for any form of balance of payments support, the maximum amount of financial assistance is determined by the quota of the requesting member. For instance, since March 2023, under the Stand-By and Extended Arrangements, a member may borrow up to 200% of its quota annually and not more than 600% cumulatively. These are the so-called normal access limits, which may be exceeded only under exceptional circumstances. The amount of financing available also depends on the specific conditions of the member and the IMF facility under which resources are made available. An analysis of IMF lending is provided in Chapter 3.

61. Fourth, the IMF may allocate SDRs to members in proportion to their IMF quotas. The SDR is an international reserve asset created by the IMF that can be held by the central banks of member countries or other designated holders to supplement their official reserves. For more details on SDRs, *see infra*, paragraphs 293 ff.

III. The Review of Quotas

62. General quota reviews are usually conducted every five years by the IMF Board of Governors. They provide an opportunity to assess the adequacy of IMF resources to finance its activities and to reassess the size and allocation of quotas among members. Quota reviews may lead to both adjustments in the overall quota level and realignments of quota shares with each member's relative position in the world economy. If an overall increase in the IMF capital is needed, the Board of Governors establishes its size and decides on its allocation among members. In practice, quota reviews involve a three-step process that simultaneously: (a) assesses whether existing quotas are sufficient to meet the IMF members' financing needs; (b) determines the balance between quota increases and external borrowing, when additional resources are required (on IMF borrowing *see infra*, paragraphs 101 ff.); and (c) allocates any quota increases among members.

63. Any change in quotas must be approved by the Board of Governors with an 85% majority of the total voting power, and no member's quota may be changed without its consent. After the Board of Governors' approval, each member must approve its individual quota increase (or decrease), a process which often requires legislative authorisation. Members are expected to complete this process without delay and to pay the increase in their quotas to the Fund promptly.

64. Quota changes can be implemented in one of three ways: (a) proportional, where the overall quota increase is distributed to all members in proportion to their existing quotas; (b) selective, where quota adjustments focus on correcting disparities in allocations by redistributing shares, ensuring that countries whose economic position is not properly reflected in their current quotas receive fairer representation; and (c) ad hoc, where quota adjustments are made according to specific agreed-upon criteria, typically intended to correct underrepresentation of specific countries. Proportional quota increases are the most common, while ad hoc and selective quota adjustments have been seldom implemented.

65. (a) In December 2023, the IMF Board of Governors concluded the 16th General Review of Quotas and approved a 50% quota increase to be allocated to members in proportion to their current quotas, with no realignment of quotas. When the voting deadline ended on 15 December 2023, Governors representing 92.86% of the total voting power had cast votes in favour of the decision, exceeding the 85% majority required. However, the envisaged quota increase will only become effective once two conditions are satisfied: (1) that members having not less than 85% of total quotas consent in writing to the increases in their quotas; (2) that at least 90% of New Arrangements to Borrow (NAB) participants consent to a rollback of their credit arrangements (on NAB, *see infra*, paragraph 103).

66. (b) The most prominent example of an IMF selective quota adjustment occurred during the 14th General Review of Quotas, which was conducted in the aftermath of the 2008 global financial crisis. Alongside a general increase in quotas for all members (a doubling of quotas), a selective increase was approved to benefit under-represented countries, especially those with a large share of global GDP and trade. More than 6% of quotas were reallocated from over-represented to under-represented members, while safeguarding the voice and representation of the poorest countries. As a result, Brazil, China, India and Russia saw a significant quota increase that put them among the ten largest IMF shareholders, together with the United States, Japan and the four largest European countries (France, Germany, Italy and the United Kingdom). The 14th General Review of Quotas was completed in December 2010 but became effective only in January 2016, following approval by the required majority. As of October 2025, only two member countries, Eritrea and Syria, have not yet consented to their proposed quota increases under the 14th General Review of Quotas.

67. (c) *Ad hoc* quota adjustments involve targeted increases in quotas for specific member countries, typically triggered by exceptional circumstances or significant changes in their economic position in the world economy. For instance, in 2006, the quotas of four clearly under-represented countries (China, Korea, Mexico and Turkey) were increased.

68. It is worth noting that quota reviews directly impact voting rights in the IMF, as a member's voting power is determined by its quota share; thus, adjustments to quotas can alter the balance of influence among member countries.

IMF Top 10 Members' Quotas and Voting Power (as of October 2025)

Member	*Quota (as percentage of total)*	*Voting Power (as percentage of total)*
United States	17.42	16.49
Japan	6.47	6.14
China	6.40	6.08
Germany	5.59	5.31
France	4.23	4.03
United Kingdom	4.23	4.03
Italy	3.16	3.02
India	2.75	2.63
Russian Federation	2.71	2.59
Brazil	2.32	2.22
All other members	44.72	47.46

69. Since the last realignment of IMF quotas occurred over fifteen years ago – specifically, in 2010, with the 14th General Review of Quotas – critics argue that current quota allocations are out of step with the global economy and that this undermines the Fund's legitimacy. Emerging market and development economies (including China) account for 60% of global GDP but hold only 40% of IMF voting power.

§4. The IMF's Governance Structure

I. The Board of Governors and the Ministerial Committees

70. The Board of Governors is the IMF's plenary body and normally meets once a year in October during the IMF-World Bank Annual Meetings. It consists of one governor and one alternate for each Member State, usually the country's finance minister or central bank governor. The Board holds all the powers within the IMF's mandate, except those expressly assigned by the Articles to another organ. The Board of Governors may delegate to the Executive Board the authority to exercise its powers, except in certain reserved matters. While most of the powers have been delegated to the IMF's Executive Board, the Board of Governors retains those directly conferred upon it by the Articles. They concern: the admission of new members, the adjustment of quotas, the composition of the Executive Board, the allocation of SDRs, the suspension of members and the amendment of the Articles of Agreement. The quorum for any meeting requires a majority of Governors holding not less than two-thirds of the total voting power. Unless otherwise specified in the Articles, decisions are adopted by a majority of the votes cast by the Board members.

71. The Board of Governors is advised by two ministerial committees: the International Monetary and Financial Committee (IMFC) and the Development Committee. In 1999, the IMFC replaced the Interim Committee of the Board of Governors on the International Monetary System, which had been established in 1974 following the collapse of the par value system. The IMFC is mandated to report and advise the Board of Governors on matters pertaining to: 'the management and adaptation of the international monetary and financial system, including the continuing operation of the adjustment process, and in this connection reviewing developments in global liquidity and the transfer of real resources to developing countries'; 'proposals by the Executive directors to amend the Articles'; and 'sudden disturbances that might threaten the system' (Resolution No. 54-9 of the Board of Governors, 30 September 1999). The IMFC is composed of 25 members selected from the Board of Governors. The IMFC meets twice a year, during the IMF-World Bank Spring and Annual meetings. The Committee issues *communiqués* that provide guidance for the IMF work programme. It operates by consensus, and it is not authorised to adopt decisions.

72. The Board of Governors may decide, by an 85% majority of the total voting power, to establish a Council to take over the tasks of the IMFC. Such Council would comprise two categories of members: Councillors (governors, ministers or other government officials of equivalent rank) and Associates. The Council would supervise the administration and evolution of the international monetary system, including the adjustment process and global liquidity issues. In this context, it would also review developments in the transfer of real resources to developing countries. The Council's rules of procedure are detailed in Schedule D of the Articles of Agreement.

73. The other ministerial committee currently advising the Board of Governors is the Joint Ministerial Committee of the Boards of Governors of the Bank and the Fund on the Transfer of Real Resources to Developing Countries (the so-called Development Committee). It was established in 1974 by the IMF Board of Governors and the World Bank as a joint Committee. The Development Committee advises the Boards of Governors of both organisations 'on all aspects of the broad question of the transfer of real resources to developing countries' and 'shall give urgent attention to the problems of (i) the least developed countries and (ii) those developing countries most seriously affected by balance of payments difficulties' (Resolution No. 29-9 of the Board of Governors, as lastly amended in 2012). The Committee is composed of twenty-five members, typically ministers of finance or development, and it usually meets twice a year, after the IMFC meetings.

II. The Executive Board

74. Pursuant to Article XII, section 3(a), the Executive Board is responsible 'for conducting the business of the Fund' and exercises all the powers conferred upon it by the IMF Articles as well as those delegated to it by the Board of Governors. The

Executive Board usually meets several times per week and adopts decisions by consensus, except when a formal vote is required. The Managing Director serves as the Chairman of the Executive Board.

75. The Executive Board originally consisted of twelve Executive Directors, but the Board of Governors has used its power to gradually increase their number on multiple occasions, reflecting the evolving needs of the IMF and the changing global economic landscape. Each increase in the number of Executive Directors was intended to improve representation and ensure that the interests of a broader range of member countries were better reflected in the decision-making process. On 16 July 2024, the IMF Board of Governors passed a resolution to expand the number of Executive Directors from twenty-four to twenty-five, with the 25th chair designated for Sub-Saharan Africa. The resolution received overwhelming support from the Fund's membership, surpassing the required 85% majority of total voting power. The expansion took place during the 2024 Regular Election of Executive Directors and led to a reorganisation of the forty-five Sub-Saharan African member countries. Previously grouped into two constituencies (*see* below), they are now distributed across three newly formed constituencies for Central and Eastern Africa, Southern Africa, and West Africa. Each of such constituencies elected its own Executive Director in October 2024.

76. Not only has the number of Directors changed but the procedure for the formation of the Executive Board has also been revised. Under the system originally envisaged by the Articles, each of the five member countries holding the largest quotas had the right to *appoint* its own Director. At the beginning of the New Millennium, these members were: the United States, the United Kingdom, Germany, France and Japan. The remaining nineteen Directors were *elected* every two years by members who had formed a voting group (a so-called constituency). However, some member countries – such as China, Russia and Saudi Arabia – were able to obtain a special position, each forming a 'single constituency' and electing its own Director.

77. In 2016, the Board Reform Amendment (the Seventh Amendment) entered into force, thereby ending the category of *appointed* Executive Directors. As a consequence, members with the five largest quotas and voting powers are no longer entitled to appoint their own Executive Director. Directors are currently all elected by member countries or by constituencies. In practice, though, the United States, Japan, China, Germany, France, the United Kingdom, the Russian Federation (which more recently agreed to include the Syrian Arab Republic in its own constituency for political reasons) and Saudi Arabia have established a single-country constituency, with a view to electing their own Executive Director; the other seventeen Directors are elected by constituencies composed of multiple countries.

78. An Executive Director elected by a constituency is entitled to cast the number of votes that contributed towards his or her election, voting on behalf of the group as a whole: the votes of the constituency may not be split partly in favour and partly against a decision. Elections of Executive Directors are conducted every two years in accordance with regulations yet to be adopted by the Board of Governors. Once adopted, these regulations will establish 'a limit on the total number of votes than more than one member may cast for the same candidate', i.e., they will set a limit on the pooling of votes in a constituency, in order to avoid the formation of 'mega constituencies'.

79. The status of an Executive Director is somewhat ambivalent. The Executive Board should be regarded as a 'body consisting of officers of the Fund and not as the "representatives" of the bodies that appointed or elected them'. Nevertheless, Executive Directors are, in practice, held accountable by their own country, even though the salary is paid by the Fund. During Board meetings, an Executive Director may explain that he is communicating the views of members, but he is not required to clarify whether he is expressing their views. If he remains silent, it is likely that his views will align with those Member States that elected him. While this assumption may lend weight to an Executive Director's opinion, only the position formally taken when a decision is made holds legal significance. An Executive Director elected solely by his own country is generally expected to uphold that country's position, as deviating from it may affect future re-election prospects. By contrast, an Executive Director elected by a group of Member States has greater flexibility in shaping his stance, often needing to navigate and balance divergent views within the constituency. Should an individual member country challenge the Director's position, he may reasonably claim to represent the majority view of the constituency that elected him.

III. The Managing Director

80. The third main organ of the Fund is the Managing Director, who is the chairman of the Executive Board and the head of the IMF staff. Subject to the general control of the Executive Board, the Managing Director conducts the ordinary business of the Fund and is 'responsible for the organisation, appointment, and dismissal of the staff' (Article XII, section 4(b)). The Managing Director and the staff of the Fund 'shall owe their duty entirely to the Fund and to no other authority'. The Managing Director presides over Executive Board meetings, without being entitled to vote. The role as chair of Board meetings is important, as the Managing Director is required, if necessary, to summarise the 'sense of the meeting'. The summing-up may be made public and formally qualified as a decision of the Board. All contacts with member countries are maintained by the staff, acting under instruction from the Managing Director. Article IV consultations (*see infra*, paragraphs 235 ff.), as well as negotiations with member countries requesting balance of payments support (*see infra*, paragraphs 180 ff.), are conducted under the Managing Director's instructions. Proposals for decisions concerning balance of payments support are put to the Executive Board by the Managing Director.

81. The Managing Director is appointed by the Executive Board for a renewable five-year term. Historically, the practice was to select a European citizen as the

IMF's Managing Director and a US citizen as President of the World Bank. Currently, the Executive Board appoints the Managing Director according to an open, merit-based and transparent procedure first introduced in 2011. Nominations may be submitted both by Executive Directors and by Governors. Candidates are expected to have an outstanding professional background. At the end of the nomination period, the names of nominees who have confirmed their candidacy are announced. The Executive Board interviews the shortlisted candidates and decides either by consensus or by a majority of the votes cast. Christine Lagarde was appointed as the first female Managing Director in July 2011; she was reappointed for a second term in February 2016. Kristalina Georgieva has served as Managing Director since October 2019.

IV. Decision-Making

82. The basic principle is that IMF decisions – regardless of the organ adopting them – are taken by a simple majority of weighted votes. The IMF Articles require a qualified majority (70% or 85% of the total voting power, depending on the issue) only for certain selected decisions. However, formal votes within the Board of Governors and the Executive Board are typically avoided to bypass political differences and promote harmonious cooperation. Instead, there is a strong preference for reaching decisions by consensus, with the Managing Director establishing the 'sense of the meeting' rather than proceeding to a formal vote. In particular, the Managing Director plays a key role in the decision-making process of the Executive Board by seeking a compromise between the different standpoints of the Directors. The political reality is that, on important questions, the opinions of members with the highest quotas cannot be disregarded.

83. The flexibility that the members of the Executive Board enjoy in forming their opinions, together with the discretionary authority of the Managing Director, generally allows for a compromise to be reached. If the positions seem irreconcilable, the Managing Director may present the majority opinion of the Board, while also including the dissenting views of the minority in the summing-up. Accordingly, the Managing Director will summarise the discussions in the Executive Board, specifying the number of Directors who expressed particular views, as outlined in the box below.

Qualifier	*Number of Executive Directors*
A few Directors	2–4
Some Directors	5–6
A number of Directors	6–9
Many Directors	10–15
Most Directors	15 or more

Qualifier	*Number of Executive Directors*
A significant minority of the Board or, in exceptional cases, the required majority of the Board	Indication of the required voting strength, particularly useful in cases where a special majority is necessary

However, if a member insists on a formal vote, then decisions will be taken by a majority of 70% or 85%, depending on the subject. Decisions requiring special majorities are technical and based on provisions scattered throughout the Fund's Articles of Agreement; decisions that affect the financial position of members are more likely to require an 85% majority. The United States is the only member country able to block decisions that must be adopted by an 85% majority, since it has a voting power exceeding 15% and thus holds an effective veto over such decisions.

V. Corpus Juris

84. The Board of Governors and the Executive Board derive their powers to issue rules and regulations from the IMF Articles. To exercise their powers, they have at their disposal a number of instruments. The Board of Governors issues By-Laws and Resolutions. The Executive Board adopts Rules and Regulations, along with other decisions. The category 'other decisions' includes: interpretations, recommendations, guidelines, resolutions and decisions relating to balance of payments support. The hierarchical ordering of the above-mentioned sources is subject to the following: (1) The Articles of Agreement regulate all the activities of the Fund; (2) the By-Laws adopted by the Board of Governors are established under the authority of the Articles and are meant to complement them; they primarily concern procedural matters; (3) Resolutions of the Board of Governors are operational and include matters such as the admission of new members and quota reviews; (4) Rules and Regulations are adopted by the Executive Board to conduct the operations of the Fund and supplement the IMF Articles and By-Laws; they are subject to review by the Board of Governors; (5) the Executive Board has the authority to make decisions on a broad range of issues; however, no decision may conflict with the IMF Articles, nor may a decision of the Executive Board conflict with one of the Board of Governors.

85. The IMF Articles explicitly confer powers upon the institutions and upon 'the Fund'. It is particularly important to note that the Board of Governors has delegated nearly all of its powers to the Executive Board, except for those powers explicitly conferred upon it by the IMF Articles. This means that where the IMF Articles mention 'the Fund', the reference in practice is to the Executive Board. This reinforces the central role of the latter in most of the IMF's activities. Decisions concerning balance of payments support, Article IV consultations, the setting up of trust funds, the level of charges, the selling of gold and many other decisions are adopted by the Executive Board.

86. The regularly updated volume Selected Decisions and Selected Documents of the IMF includes decisions, interpretations and resolutions adopted by the Executive Board and the Board of Governors as well as other selected documents to which frequent reference is made in the activities of the Fund.

VI. Legal Status, Privileges and Immunities

87. The Fund enjoys 'full juridical personality' vis-à-vis its members. It has freedom to contract, to acquire and dispose of property and to institute legal proceedings. In addition, it enjoys immunity from judicial process, enforcement actions and taxation or customs duties. Its assets, archives and communication are protected against interference. The Fund has developed special procedures that are intended to ensure the physical safety of its employees, other officials and their families, thus discharging its 'duty of care' towards its staff.

88. The IMF has been granted the status of specialised agency within the meaning of Article 57 of the UN Charter. The Agreement between the United Nations and the IMF, as approved by the Board of Governors of the Fund and by the UN General Assembly, entered into force on 15 November 1947. The Fund also enjoys protection under the United Nations Convention on the Privileges and Immunities of the Specialised Agencies. Under Annex V of the Convention, the privileges and immunities conferred by the IMF Articles of Agreement are not to be diminished by those granted under the Convention.

§5. The IMF's Accountability

I. Membership and Constituency Accountability

89. The Fund considers itself accountable to its membership and subject to the scrutiny of multiple stakeholders, including the news media, civil society, academia, and its own internal watchdog, the Independent Evaluation Office (IEO) (*see infra*, paragraphs 95 ff.). A distinction may be drawn between membership accountability and constituency accountability.

90. Membership accountability means that the Fund is accountable for its actions as stipulated by the IMF Articles; any action (or inaction) must be explained to member countries. Accordingly, each member may ask the Fund to explain why a particular action was taken or not.

91. Constituency accountability refers to Directors in the Executive Board who take decisions based on the weighted voting system. The fact that decisions are adopted by a majority of weighted votes means that the Fund is, in practice, governed by a limited number of members and may only act (or refrain from acting) when the Executive Board approves (or disapproves) such action. In this accountability relationship, the major industrialised countries may even steer the Fund in directions not foreseen by the signatories of the IMF Articles. Practice has shown that compromises embedded in the IMF Articles may be overridden by subsequent interpretative decisions adopted by the Executive Board. In practice, constituency accountability tends to prevail over membership accountability.

92. The exchange of information and views with entities beyond its membership is considered a key aspect of IMF accountability. The Fund maintains that it actively seeks input from civil society and other stakeholders regarding its activities. Accordingly, it claims that it has developed a 'culture of listening and learning': in designing loan programmes, the Fund seeks 'constructive dialogue with civil society organisations' to establish 'mutual understanding and increase support for reform'. The IMF Articles allow for the publication of reports 'as it deems desirable for carrying out its purposes' (Article XII, section 7). The main goal of the IMF's transparency policy is to strengthen 'the Fund's effectiveness by providing the public with access to Fund views and deliberations, thus informing public debate and building traction for the Fund's advice, supporting the quality of surveillance and of programs, by subjecting the Fund to outside scrutiny, and enhancing the Fund's legitimacy by making the institution more accountable'.

93. A well-functioning international civil service is generally recognised as an important element of accountability. Civil servants should strive to uphold the highest standards of efficiency, competence and integrity. Meeting these standards also depends on the members' observance of their obligation to respect the principles of impartiality, loyalty to the Fund's aims and purposes, functional independence, and discretion.

94. There is no doubt about the necessity of hiring a highly qualified staff at the IMF. The staff serve as the primary contact for countries when discussing their economic and monetary policies. It reports to the Executive Board on the performance of individual members, provides technical assistance and forecasts developments in the global economy. Staff missions prepare decision documents when countries request balance of payments assistance. The Executive Board primarily relies on staff assessments and usually decides accordingly.

II. The Independent Evaluation Office

95. In 2001, the Executive Board established the IEO with a view to promoting transparency and accountability as well as strengthening the IMF's external credibility. The IEO operates at arm's length from the Fund and is expected to conduct critical reviews of the IMF's policies. The IEO is completely independent of the Fund's management and staff, and is entitled to access any internal information and documents (with limited exceptions). The terms of reference are broadly formulated and allow the IEO to put in its work programme any subject that is important for the IMF's membership and relevant to the Fund's mandate. For the selection of topics, the IEO may consult groups both inside and outside the Fund, including

Non-governmental Organisations (NGOs) and academic circles. Its work programme includes a variety of items ranging from evaluations of IMF activities in particular countries to assessments of the Fund's practice on structural conditionality and many other subject matters.

96. The IEO played an important role in reviewing the IMF performance in the aftermath of the global financial crisis, the European sovereign debt crisis and the COVID-19 pandemic. Four reports were particularly relevant: the 2011 'Report on the IMF Performance in the Run-Up to the Financial and Economic Crisis: IMF Surveillance in 2004-07', the 2014 'Report on the IMF Response to the Financial and Economic Crises' as well as the 2016 'Report on the IMF and the Crises in Greece, Ireland and Portugal'; and the 2023 'Report on the IMF's Emergency Response to the COVID-19 Pandemic'.

97. IEO evaluations are available on its website. Even if they do not have binding legal force, they have proven to be an important tool to enhance the learning culture within the Fund. Follow-up is critical, and to this end, the Executive Board usually approves a Management Implementation Plan, which outlines the actions planned to implement the recommendations from IEO evaluations that have been approved by the Board.

§6. The IMF's Financial Structure

98. As of mid-December 2024, the IMF's total resources amounted to approximately SDR 982 billion, with a lending capacity of around SDR 695 billion (equivalent to approximately USD 932 billion). These resources stem from three main sources: member quotas, multilateral borrowing agreements, and bilateral borrowing arrangements.

I. General Resources

99. Member quotas are the primary source of IMF funding. Quota payments are credited to the GRA. Of the total subscription, 25% is paid in SDRs or widely accepted foreign currency, while the remaining 75% is paid in the member's local currency, usually in the form of non-interest-bearing, non-negotiable promissory notes issued by either the member's central bank or its treasury. In 2025, IMF quotas totalled SDR 476 billion (about 627 USD billion).

100. IMF regular lending activities are financed from the fully paid-in capital subscribed by member countries. However, as national currencies from all members form a substantial part of quota payments, not all resources pooled in the GRA are usable resources, i.e., not all of them can be used to provide financial assistance to IMF members facing a balance of payments need. 'Non-usable resources' are the currencies of members with a weak balance of payments or reserve position (generally currencies of developing countries or countries under an IMF programme).

'Usable resources' are the currencies of members with strong external positions. Approximately half of the quota payments are made in usable resources. For this reason, the Fund needs to supplement its resources through multilateral and bilateral borrowing agreements and by selling its gold holdings.

II. Additional Borrowing: Multilateral and Bilateral Loan Agreements

101. Because resources in the GRA may prove to be inadequate, the Fund is authorised to borrow to supplement those resources. As financial emergencies will occasionally arise – as it has indeed happened in the past with the global financial crisis and, more recently, with the COVID-19 pandemic – the Fund might have to rely on additional borrowing to boost its lending capacity. Currently, the Fund relies on both multilateral and bilateral loan arrangements in order to be able to provide lending to its member countries. These standing borrowing arrangements create credit lines between the Fund and major industrialised countries. Therefore, they provide a temporary supplement to quota resources.

102. The first multilateral loan agreement, the General Arrangements to Borrow (GAB), was signed in 1962 by the G-10 industrialised countries and Switzerland. The objective was to assist the Fund in supporting the balance of payments needs of any member of the group or in addressing a threat to the stability of the international monetary system. The GAB was activated ten times, with the last activation occurring in 1998 for Russia, shortly before the NAB took effect. In 2017, participants unanimously agreed not to renew the GAB at the end of 2018, given its diminished usefulness as a backstop against potential systemic shocks.

103. In 1997, in the aftermath of the Mexican financial crisis, the IMF Executive Board adopted the decision to establish the NAB, which became effective in 1998. Today, the NAB is a standing set of credit lines under which forty member countries (Greece and Ireland being the last to join the group) have committed to provide supplementary resources to the IMF. In 2011, during the global financial crisis, the NAB was amended and expanded (resources available under the NAB increased from SDR 34 billion to SDR 370 billion). In the context of the 14th General Review of Quotas, however, NAB members agreed to transfer resources from the NAB to quotas in order to pay for their respective quota increases. As a result, the NAB was 'rolled back' to SDR 182 billion. In 2021, though, the size of the NAB was doubled and reached SDR 364 billion (approximately USD 489 billion). The NAB can be activated by a proposal of the Fund's Managing Director that is accepted by NAB participants representing 85% of total credit arrangements; approval of the Executive Board is also required. The NAB was activated the last time in 2016, but not in response to the COVID-19 crisis. The NAB was recently renewed until 2030, but once the 16th General Review of Quotas becomes effective, the Fund will reduce its reliance on borrowed resources by scaling down the size of the NAB and allowing bilateral borrowing arrangements to expire.

104. The IMF may also temporarily supplement its resources through bilateral borrowing agreements. They are the third line of defence after quota resources and the NAB. In 2012, the Fund had sixteen active bilateral loan agreements worth about USD 200 billion and two active bilateral note purchase agreements totalling approximately USD 60 billion. In 2013, the Executive Board approved the termination of any further drawings under these bilateral borrowing and note purchase agreements, which had been concluded prior to the activation of the new NAB. In 2016, taking into consideration the continued uncertainty in the global economy, the Executive Board approved a new temporary framework for bilateral borrowing and adopted the 'Guidelines for Borrowing by the Fund'. In 2020, the Executive Board approved a framework for a new round of bilateral borrowing to succeed the agreements previously in place. Under this framework, a new set of bilateral agreements was introduced to replace the 2016 bilateral agreements, which expired at the end of 2020. In this context, forty-two bilateral borrowing agreements were concluded by the Fund, for a total commitment of about 138 billion SDRs. The 2020 agreements were transitionally extended to maintain the Fund's lending capacity until the quota increases under the 16th General Review of Quotas take effect. Activation of bilateral agreements requires support from 85% of eligible lenders.

III. Gold in the IMF

105. Apart from currencies and SDRs, the Fund also holds substantial amounts of gold. This has historical reasons: in fact, until the breakdown of the par value system in the early 1970s, members could pay part of their quota subscription in gold. The Fund could also receive gold as a repayment for loans or through other channels such as payments of charges (e.g., interest on members' use of IMF credit). Until Nixon's declaration of inconvertibility of the US dollar into gold, the official price of gold was set at USD 35 per ounce. In 1975, though, the official price of gold was abolished and, as a consequence, its role in the international monetary system changed drastically. In 1978, the Second Amendment to the IMF Articles prohibited its use as the common denominator of the post-World War II par value system and ended the official role of gold in exchange rate arrangements. The Fund was also prohibited from managing or fixing its price when dealing in gold or buying it.

106. Today, the Fund remains one of the largest official holders of gold, with 90.5 million ounces held in its reserves. From time to time, members authorise the Fund to sell part of its gold reserves to replenish its holdings of currencies. In 2009, the Executive Board approved the sale of one-eighth of the Fund's total gold holdings to boost resources and, in particular, to provide additional financing for poor countries through trust funds. Gold sales were conducted with designated modalities to prevent market disruption. In 2012, the Executive Board decided to distribute to the membership, in proportion to their quota shares, the windfall profits earned from gold sales; simultaneously, members pledged to transfer at least 90% of the amount received to the Poverty Reduction and Growth Trust (PRGT, on which *see infra*, paragraph 154) so as to increase its annual lending capacity to LICs and its long-term sustainability. The Heavily Indebted Poor Countries Initiative (HIPC) (on which *see infra*, paragraphs 339 ff.) was partly financed by the sale of gold at market prices. At the end of 2024, many observers urged the IMF to sell 4% of its gold reserves to help offer debt relief to LICs through the Catastrophe Containment and Relief Trust (CCRT, on which *see infra*, paragraphs 344 ff.). With current gold prices exceeding USD 3,000 per ounce, selling a small fraction of gold could generate significant revenues and easily replenish the CCRT to support climate-vulnerable (and highly-indebted) countries.

IV. The Fund's New Income Model after the Fifth Amendment

107. In order to fund its activities, the IMF has also always relied on its lending income, which is derived from the charges levied on the use of credit from the GRA, as well as service charges and commitment fees. In 2006, following a deterioration of the IMF income position, various measures were taken to enable the Fund to diversify its sources of income. Among these, the Fifth Amendment to the IMF Articles of Agreement (which entered into force in February 2011) modified Article XII, section 6(f)(iii), broadening the Fund's investment mandate. The amendment was introduced to ensure the long-term sustainability of the Fund's finances and to make it less dependent on borrowing from Member States and on income generated from its lending activities. As a result, the IMF currently generates income not only from lending but also from investing. Under the new income model, the Fund is in fact allowed to invest part of its resources in fixed-income securities and short-term deposits with the aim of generating returns exceeding the SDR interest rate. More specifically, the Fund can purchase 'directly in the cash markets' obligations issued by member countries and other international financial institutions.

108. The IMF's Investment Account holds resources transferred from the GRA, profits from the sale of gold, and income from investments. Its resources are invested with the aim of broadening the IMF's income base. Due to the public nature of its funds, the IMF's investment policy includes safeguards to prevent actual or perceived conflicts of interest as well as risk control measures.

109. The Fund is authorised to invest resources held in its fixed-income subaccount in: (a) debt obligations issued by national governments of Member States or their central banks; (b) debt obligations issued by national agencies of members; (c) debt obligations issued by supranational institutions; and (d) obligations issued by the Bank for International Settlements (BIS). The Fund is enabled to invest resources held in its endowment subaccount in: global sovereign bonds, US Treasury securities, global corporate bonds, developed market equities, emerging market equities and other debentures.

110. The assets in the IMF Investment Account are managed by external operators with a clear separation of responsibilities from the IMF management. Credit risk is further minimised by restricting investments to financial instruments with a pre-established minimum credit rating, based on the Standard & Poor's rating scale;

if the rating threshold is breached, assets must be divested within three months of the rating downgrade. The consequence is that the Fund's external investment managers will be compelled to sell financial instruments in their portfolio as soon as these fall below the minimum rating threshold. In January 2022, the Executive Board also approved an updated investment strategy incorporating responsible-investing principles focused on environmental, social, and governance considerations. The earnings generated by the Fund's investments may be reinvested, retained in the account or transferred to the GRA to cover the costs of conducting the business of the IMF. The Rules and Regulations for the Investment Account were last revised in March 2022, with reviews scheduled every five years. Decisions on how to use the Investment Account income are taken by the Executive Board every financial year.

§7. Rules for Interpretation

111. Questions on the interpretation of the IMF Articles may first be addressed by the Fund's Executive Board. By adopting an authoritative interpretation, the Board may not only clarify the meaning of the Articles of Agreement but also, in fact, settle a dispute. First, a member may, for instance, challenge a Fund policy and insist on another interpretation of the provision underlying that policy. Second, an interpretation may also be sought from the ICJ through an advisory opinion. Third, the Fund's practice also allows for non-authoritative interpretations.

I. Authoritative Interpretation under Article XXIX

112. Article XXIX(a) provides that 'any question of interpretation of the provisions of this Agreement arising between any member and the Fund or between members of the Fund shall be submitted to the Executive Board for its decision'. The procedure set forth in Article XXIX(b) also provides for an appeal to the Board of Governors, which is assisted by a Committee on Interpretation of the Board of Governors. Each member of the Committee will have one vote, and the outcome will be final, unless the Board of Governors rules otherwise with an 85% majority of total voting power. The composition and equal division of voting rights of the Committee on Interpretation are noteworthy. The principle of one vote for each member of the Committee is in fact the only exception to the IMF's weighted voting system. Once an interpretation is adopted, the decision is binding and final.

113. In the first years, this procedure was used about ten times, and the decisions adopted explicitly referred to the interpretation clause. On one occasion, the legal channel under paragraph (b) was invoked, and the Board of Governors was involved in the interpretation. The last interpretation was given in 1959. It is puzzling why the conflicts between the Fund and developing members that surfaced in the 1960s and 1970s did not lead to requests for interpretations under Article XXIX.

It might as well be that, despite criticism, countries did not contest the interpretations that the Fund applied or maybe they believed that an authoritative interpretation would not lead to different outcomes.

II. Advisory Opinion from the ICJ

114. The second formal avenue for interpretation is provided by the Agreement between the United Nations and the IMF, according to which the Fund is authorised 'to request advisory opinions of the International Court of Justice on any legal question arising within the scope of the Fund's activities … '. However, to date, the IMF has refrained from seeking an advisory opinion from the Court. It is evident that the ICJ may also be called to interpret the Fund's Articles; this happened, for instance, in the case 'Certain Iranian Assets (Iran v. United States)' of 2023, where the Court dealt with exchange restrictions, which are prohibited by IMF Article VIII, section 2(a) (*see infra*, paragraphs 273 ff.). The Court may also discuss legal questions not directly relating to the IMF Articles but that, nevertheless, fall within the scope of the Fund's activities. The Court may also be requested to delineate the Fund's jurisdiction vis-à-vis other institutions within the UN system, through the application of the 'principle of speciality'.

III. Non-authoritative Interpretation

115. Article XXIX states that 'any question of interpretation' of the IMF Articles must be subject to the interpretation procedure. Nevertheless, the great majority of interpretative decisions are taken outside Article XXIX. Non-authoritative interpretations cover a broad range of the Fund's activities. Decisions and policies of the IMF's organs, as well as statements made by the Managing Director, qualify as interpretations. In a material sense, authoritative and non-authoritative interpretations are equivalent; differences are of a formal nature and concern the irreversibility of a 'final' decision by the Board of Governors under Article XXIX. Moreover, decisions that do not fall under Article XXIX can include interpretations of provisions other than those of the IMF Articles, such as By-Laws.

116. The avoidance of Article XXIX interpretations primarily reflects the Fund's and its members' preference for flexibility, as both seek to minimise the number of formal decisions, which can only be modified through the same procedure. Informal interpretations do not infringe members' rights in any way: a member may still request an explanation, with explicit reference to the interpretation clause under Article XXIX.

117. The Fund's neglect of the authoritative procedure for interpretations and its reliance on informal procedures are controversial. However, given that not a single member has contested the legality of interpretations rendered outside Article XXIX, it is unrealistic to insist that all interpretations should fall within its scope.

§8. AMENDMENTS

118. Article XXVIII provides for an amendment procedure requiring the approval by at least three-fifths of the members, representing 85% of the total voting power. Through this procedure, the IMF Articles of Agreement have been amended seven times since the organisation was established in 1944 to adapt to changing global conditions and achieve the desired degree of cooperation.

119. The First Amendment, adopted in 1969, gave the Fund the power to issue SDRs as a supplementary international reserve asset. In addition, it mandated the Fund to apply 'adequate safeguards' for the temporary use of its resources (Article I(v) and Article V, section 3(a)), thereby introducing stricter scrutiny of members' requests for balance of payments support and laying the foundation for the Fund's conditionality (*see infra*, paragraphs 174 ff.). Lastly, the First Amendment enhanced the authoritative interpretation procedure by introducing the Committee for Interpretation.

120. The Second Amendment, adopted in 1978, brought a fundamental change: the new Article IV, titled 'Obligations Regarding Exchange Arrangements', reflected the evolving practices of IMF members with respect to their exchange rate policies. The amendment officially ended the par value system, granting members the freedom to choose the exchange rate policy they deemed most appropriate. In addition, it introduced a system of surveillance over the economic and financial policies of member countries, supported by provisions that can be defined as soft law. The end of the par value system meant that the Fund no longer administered 'a system of stable exchange rates', assuming instead the responsibility 'to promote a stable system of exchange rates'. This shift reflected a change in the IMF's role: from custodian of the par value system to supervisor of members' exchange rate policies. Other changes concerned the declining role of gold and the promotion of the SDR as the principal reserve asset in the international monetary system. Moreover, under the new section 1 of Article IV, one of the Fund's primary objectives became 'the continuing development of the orderly underlying conditions that are necessary for *financial* and economic stability [emphasis added]'. This is the only reference to financial stability in the IMF Articles.

121. The Third Amendment, adopted in 1992, introduced new rules for the suspension of voting rights of members failing to repay the Fund (in response to the problem of growing arrears to the IMF which occurred in the 1980s and early 1990s).

122. The Fourth Amendment, adopted in 2009, introduced new rules providing for a special one-time allocation of SDRs to allow all participants in the SDRs Department to receive an equitable share of cumulative SDR allocations.

123. The Fifth and Sixth Amendments, both adopted in 2011, respectively introduced the following: new rules expanding the investment authority of the Fund and authorising the Fund to manage the proceeds of gold sales; and a reform of the

Executive Board regarding the appointment of Alternates and a tripling of basic votes (*see supra*, paragraph 59), accompanied by a realignment of member countries' quotas and voting shares (the so-called Voice and Participation Amendment).

124. The Seventh Amendment, adopted in 2010, established an Executive Board composed solely of elected Executive Directors (the so-called Board Reform Amendment). It entered into force in January 2016 after the US Congress eventually passed legislation to authorise the 2010 Quota and Governance Reforms.

Chapter 3. IMF Lending

§1. The IMF Primary Function

125. According to Article I(v), one of the main purposes of the IMF is 'to give confidence to members by making the general resources of the Fund temporarily available to them under adequate safeguards, thus providing them with opportunity to correct maladjustments in their balance of payments without resorting to measures destructive of national or international prosperity'.

126. In the practice of the Fund, balance of payments support has become its primary activity, virtually overshadowing its other functions. While all members are entitled to balance of payments support, until recently, the Fund's resources were predominantly borrowed by developing countries and economies in transition. Since the beginning of the New Millennium, however, global economic dynamics have affected both developing and advanced economies. During the 2008 global financial crisis, the financial position of several industrialised countries deteriorated considerably. In 2010, Greece became the first advanced economy and Euro area country to receive financial assistance from both the IMF and the EU since Italy and the United Kingdom received IMF support in the 1970s. Soon afterwards, Greece was followed by Ireland, Portugal and Cyprus. More recently, during the COVID-19 pandemic, the IMF provided an unprecedented volume of financial assistance to help countries mitigate the crisis. Through its emergency financing instruments (*see infra*, paragraphs 152 and 157), the Fund disbursed over USD 170 billion to more than ninety countries, including both low-income and emerging market economies.

§2. Balance of Payments Problems

I. The Balance of Payments

127. Each member country is required to regularly report balance of payments data to the IMF. To promote uniformity in accounting practices and facilitate the analysis of the figures, the Fund issues guidance to members on how transactions should be recorded. These guidelines are published in the 'IMF Balance of Payments and International Investment Position Manual'. The data on the balance of payments of member countries are published in the Annual Report of the IMF Committee on Balance of Payments Statistics.

128. The Fund defines the balance of payments as a statistical statement covering a given period that summarises transactions between residents and non-residents. It consists of the current account, the primary income account, the secondary income account, the capital account, and the financial account.

129. The current account includes: (a) the balance of trade in goods and services; (b) the primary income; and (c) the secondary income between residents and non-residents. In particular, the goods and services account covers transactions in items that are the result of production activities. The current account balance shows the difference between the sum of exports and income receivable, and the sum of imports and income payable.

130. The capital account records: (a) the acquisition and disposal of non-produced, non-financial assets (such as natural resources) between residents and non-residents; and (b) capital transfers receivable and payable between residents and non-residents.

131. The financial account records net acquisitions and disposals of financial assets and liabilities.

II. The Need for Support

132. A balance of payments problem arises when a country imports more goods and services than it exports. The capital account balance may also be negative due to capital flight or increased investments abroad. The causes of balance of payments problems can be domestic, external or a combination of both. Domestic factors include inappropriate fiscal and monetary policies, an unstable exchange rate, and political instability. External factors encompass natural disasters, geopolitical developments, epidemics or pandemics, commodity price shocks, and spillovers from other countries. Crises often arise from a combination of factors, such as sovereign debt vulnerabilities, deposit runs, and structural challenges, including those related to climate change. Balance of payments problems may emerge in either the country's current account or in its capital and financial accounts. If the resulting deficits are limited and temporary, official reserves can help stabilise the situation, and a subsequent surplus may restore reserves to the desired level. However, when the deficit is severe or persistent, countries may face financial distress as their reserves become depleted. In such cases, two responses are possible.

133. First, a country may seek external means to cover its deficit. One option is to issue sovereign bonds in a foreign currency to raise capital and finance the national budget. Countries can also attempt to secure loans from commercial banks operating in international financial markets. Additionally, a State may secure additional financial resources through bilateral loans from other countries. At the same time, a State can also rely on Official Development Assistance (ODA) which – according to the Organisation for Economic Co-operation and Development (OECD) – is defined as assistance 'provided by official agencies, including State and local government, or by their executive agencies, each transaction of which: (a) is administered with the promotion of the economic development and welfare of developing countries as its main objective; and (b) is concessional in character and conveys a grant element of at least 25 percent'. However, for developing countries, reliance on external financial sources has its limitations. When a country's balance of payments position fails to improve and its creditworthiness declines, creditors become increasingly reluctant to provide additional financial resources. Grants are the only form of funding that does not require repayment or incur interest obligations, but such resources are particularly scarce.

134. Second, a country can seek financial assistance from the IMF and implement an adjustment programme aimed at restoring the balance of payments equilibrium. Requesting IMF financial assistance signals a government's commitment to economic reform, typically through measures such as reducing public spending, adjusting exchange rates, curbing inflation and meeting targets for interest rates, exchange rates and other key economic and monetary policies. Adjustment becomes, in fact, unavoidable when confidence in the country concerned has declined to the point that new credit is no longer available. The IMF plays a crucial role in helping member countries design adjustment programs aimed at restoring macroeconomic stability. These programs are governed by a set of policies and procedures known as the 'IMF conditionality' (*see infra*, paragraphs 174 ff.).

135. The IMF may not lend to members with overdue financial obligations. 'Overdue financial obligations' (or 'protracted arrears') constitute a breach of a member's obligations under the IMF Articles of Agreement. Arrears undermine the financial integrity of the lending organisation, weaken its capacity to provide financial assistance, and erode the cooperative foundation of its membership. Recently, the number of overdue payments to the Fund has steadily declined. However, during the so-called arrears crisis, they reached significant levels: between 1983 and 1993, twenty-seven countries experienced protracted arrears to the Fund (i.e., of six months or more); by 1990, overdue obligations accounted for approximately 10% of all outstanding IMF credits. At the height of the crisis, the IMF faced substantial losses, prompting an increase in loan charges, effectively shifting the full cost of arrears to borrowing countries. As a result, the IMF gradually developed a framework to address members with overdue financial obligations. Initially, such countries only faced the risk of being declared ineligible for Fund assistance. However, this measure was a blunt instrument, as there was no formal rule preventing a country in arrears from accessing further resources under an existing (active) Stand-By Arrangement (SBA) or similar facilities (*see infra*, paragraphs 144 ff.). To deter arrears, the IMF introduced specific procedures for their clearance. The 1992 Third Amendment to the Articles of Agreement (*see supra*, paragraph 121) enabled the Fund to suspend the voting and representation rights of a member failing to meet its financial obligations. This sanction served as an intermediate step between the declaration of ineligibility to access the Fund's general resources and compulsory withdrawal from membership. Additionally, a new standard performance criterion was incorporated in all arrangements (*see infra*, paragraphs 200 ff.), prohibiting the disbursement of resources to countries until their arrears to the Fund were cleared. Since June 2021, when Sudan cleared its arrears to the IMF, there have been no remaining cases of protracted arrears with the Fund.

136. The Fund is also precluded from providing its financial assistance if a country's debt is assessed as unsustainable (i.e., when debt sustainability cannot be maintained through credible and sustainable policy adjustments), unless the member takes steps to address its debt issues and restore sustainability. The Fund assesses a country's debt situation through a Debt Sustainability Analysis (DSA), using a methodology that distinguishes between market-access countries (i.e., countries that retain access to the international capital markets) and low-income countries (*see infra*, paragraphs 330 ff.).

III. The Political Economy

137. Adjustment becomes necessary when various factors negatively affect the balance of payments, such as excessive imports driven by overconsumption, declining export revenues due to falling commodity prices, inappropriate exchange rate policies, ineffective tax incentives, capital flight, or an unfocused investment strategy. While some of these issues stem from domestic policy decisions, others – like falling raw material prices – are beyond a country's control. However, regardless of the cause or whether the country itself is at fault, adjustment becomes inevitable when facing a balance of payments deficit. Postponing adjustment is only possible when a country has unlimited access to international credit. Although the Fund cannot prevent adjustment, it can help mitigate its impact. IMF-supported adjustment is generally expected to be more gradual and somewhat less painful than a market-enforced adjustment.

138. The IMF insists on adjustment for several reasons. First, since its financial assistance is only temporary, the IMF must ensure that the borrowing member will be able to repay. In fact, one of the purposes of the Fund is to make its general resources *temporarily* available to member countries *under adequate safeguards* (Article I(v)). A country that fails to reform and continues to spend beyond its means will inevitably struggle to meet its repayment obligations. Second, the IMF aims to facilitate the expansion and balanced growth of international trade, and adjustment is necessary to ensure that countries remain active participants in the global trading system. A third reason is that countries depleting their foreign reserves risk default, which can create international financial instability.

139. During the formulation of an adjustment programme, fundamental differences of opinion may arise between the IMF and the borrowing country. While both parties agree that reforms should aim to restore equilibrium, they may disagree on the most appropriate approach to achieve it. In the end, they will reach an agreement in principle which is reflected in a memorandum of economic and financial policies attached to the country's Letter of Intent (*see infra*, paragraphs 135 ff.). This document outlines a set of reforms, but what truly matters will be their effective implementation. Such reforms usually include drastic budget cuts, tax reforms, price liberalisation, trade and foreign investment liberalisation, privatisations and deregulation of the private sector. In general, adjustment follows a familiar pattern: the public sector retreats while the private sector moves in. As a result, IMF reform programmes have faced criticism for frequently prioritising fiscal discipline at the expense of public services and poverty reduction, thereby leading to rising inequality and hindering the achievement of development goals.

140. Governments have not always been eager to seek IMF financial assistance, often preferring unconditional support that does not impose restrictions on their political priorities. Although the Fund encourages its members to take timely measures, in practice, countries usually turn to the Fund only when other creditors have withdrawn their support, and the ship is on the verge of sinking or has already sunk. Unintentionally, the Fund becomes a lender of last resort. As a result, adjustment under the Fund's guidance becomes more painful, frequently involving deep reforms. Social spending is reduced, negatively affecting health, education and pension systems. Government jobs are axed, and poor and vulnerable people often bear the brunt of austerity measures. Interest groups that have long enjoyed special benefits see their financial position undermined by the economic adjustments required by the Fund's conditionality. Governments must stand firm against pressure from lobbying groups and political opponents, and it is not uncommon for the Fund to be blamed for these painful measures. The IMF, however, has been prepared to bear such criticisms, as a tacit contribution to the adjustment process.

141. The Fund also plays a pivotal role in shaping the relationship between the programme country and its creditors. For creditors, such as bondholders who have invested in sovereign bonds issued by the country, the Fund serves as a key authority in assessing the country's creditworthiness. Practically all creditors trust the IMF's judgment and are only prepared to provide support (or debt relief) if the debtor country, in consultation with the Fund, implements an adjustment programme (on sovereign debt issues *see infra*, paragraphs 310 ff.). As long as the Fund continues to provide its support, creditors remain confident that the adjustment programme is on the right track and that the risk associated with providing their lending remains acceptable. Likewise, the debtor country also recognises that creditors will place their trust in an adjustment programme that has received the Fund's approval.

§3. IMF Financial Assistance

142. According to the principle of uniform treatment, access to the Fund's general resources is equally available to all members, irrespective of their level of economic development. A member country may request IMF financial assistance if it faces a balance of payments need (whether present, prospective or potential), meaning it is unable to obtain sufficient financing on affordable terms to meet its net international payment obligations (e.g., for imports or external debt repayments) while maintaining adequate reserve buffers.

143. Upon request from a member country, the IMF provides its resources through a lending arrangement. The loan is intended to facilitate the adjustment policies and reforms that a country must implement to correct its balance of payments problem and restore the conditions for strong economic growth. These reforms are typically guided by IMF conditionality (*see infra*, paragraphs 174 ff.), which sets specific policy measures that the country commits to implement in exchange for financial assistance. Fund's resources must be used in accordance with the provisions of the Articles of Agreement and relevant IMF policies. Financing can be provided through a variety of lending facilities.

I. IMF Facilities

144. IMF lending has evolved over the years. Originally, the IMF could only provide outright disbursement to requesting countries, contingent on an assertion of an actual or potential balance of payments need. The practice of lending in tranches through SBAs (*see infra*, paragraph 148) was introduced in 1952 and later formalised by the 1978 Second Amendment to the IMF Articles of Agreement. It was not until the 1960s that the Fund began introducing 'special' facilities (or lending windows) to address specific balance of payments problems that ordinary SBAs could not adequately address. Beginning in the mid-1970s, the IMF began to provide concessional lending to LICs through trust funds separate from its general resources (*see supra*, paragraphs 99 ff.).

145. It is important to recall that, according to the principle of uniformity, the IMF does not differentiate between member countries based on their stage of development when providing financial assistance from its general resources (on the GRA, *see supra*, paragraphs 99 ff.). However, to overcome this limitation and better accommodate the specific circumstances of its members, lending activities have also been organised under various 'facilities' designed to address the diverse balance of payments needs of countries. Additionally, the Fund may establish administered accounts, financed through voluntary member contributions, to provide financial and technical assistance to its members.

146. IMF facilities can be divided into two broad categories: (a) *non-concessional* facilities, designed for countries with sound fundamentals experiencing a balance of payments problem; and (b) *concessional* facilities, tailored to address the specific circumstances of LICs. Each facility defines: the maximum amount a member may borrow; disbursement schedules (phasing), maturities and charges; the type of conditionality attached to the loan; as well as procedures for assessing the borrowing country's performance. LICs typically borrow on more favourable terms, such as lower charges, and may be granted a grace period.

147. The legal basis for the adoption of *non-concessional facilities* is Article V, section 3(a), which empowers the Fund to formulate specific policies on the use of its general resources to address various balance of payments problems. The establishment or modification of special facilities requires the approval of Executive Directors representing at least 85% of the total voting power. Currently, IMF members have access to the GRA on non-concessional terms through the following facilities: the SBA, the Flexible Credit Line (FCL), the Precautionary and Liquidity Line (PLL), the Extended Fund Facility (EFF), and the Rapid Financing Instrument (RFI). All non-concessional facilities are subject to the payment of the IMF's market-based interest rate, known as the 'rate of charge' which is based on the SDR interest rate. Financial assistance provided under non-concessional facilities is always disbursed through the GRA.

148. The SBA is the main lending instrument of the IMF. It provides short-term financial assistance to countries facing present, prospective or potential balance of payments needs. Programs are designed to support adjustment policies aimed at addressing the underlying issues that led the country to seek IMF lending. Disbursements are conditional on meeting performance criteria (*ex post* conditionality), while prior actions are required only when necessary (*see infra*, paragraph 203). The length of an SBA is typically twelve to eighteen months (with a maximum duration of three years), and repayment is due within 3¼–5 years of disbursement. SBAs may be provided on a precautionary basis, allowing countries to forgo drawing on approved amounts while retaining the option to do so if conditions worsen. The SBA provides for flexibility with respect to phasing, with front-loaded access where appropriate.

149. The FCL is designed to help States with strong fundamentals and track records of policy implementation to meet actual or potential balance of payments needs and boost market confidence during a period of heightened risks. FCL arrangements are approved at the member country's request for a period of one or two years. Under the FCL, a single upfront disbursement is usually made available to the requesting country, without further conditionality to apply. *Ex ante* qualification criteria and annual reviews for the two-year arrangements under the FCL ensure that only countries with very strong economic fundamentals and institutional policy frameworks can access this financing instrument.

150. The PLL is designed to assist countries with sound fundamentals that do not fully meet the FCL qualification criteria due to some remaining vulnerabilities. The PLL combines *ex ante* conditionality in the form of qualification criteria and *ex post* conditionality.

151. The EFF was established in 1974 to assist members with serious medium-term balance of payments problems due to structural weaknesses that require time to be addressed. Its use has increased substantially in crisis periods, reflecting the structural nature of some members' balance of payments problems. Arrangements under the EFF have a maximum duration of four years. This longer duration reflects the prolonged nature of the adjustment required to restore macroeconomic stability and the country's commitment to implement deep and sustained structural reforms to address institutional and economic weaknesses. Repayment is due within 4½–10 years from the date of disbursement.

152. The RFI provides rapid financial assistance to member countries facing urgent balance of payments needs that, if not addressed, may lead to severe economic disruption. These needs may arise from large natural disasters (where damage is assessed to be equivalent to, or exceeds, 20% of the country's GDP), acute food insecurity or other food shocks, and domestic instability, exogenous shocks and fragility. In such situations, even if a fully-fledged programme is not necessary or feasible, countries may sometimes be asked to adopt prior actions.

153. The IMF began providing *concessional* financing to developing countries in 1976 through its Trust Fund (which was terminated in 1981), funded by the proceeds from IMF gold sales. The establishment of the Trust Fund marked a departure from the principle that general resources should be made available to all member countries on an equitable basis. This principle aimed to prevent discrimination among members based on their stage of development and to ensure uniformity in accessing IMF resources and in the definition of loan conditions. With the 1978 Second Amendment to the IMF Articles of Agreement, special provisions were introduced to allow the allocation of surplus proceeds from IMF sales of gold to concessional lending. As a result, balance of payments assistance could be made available on special terms to developing countries facing difficult circumstances, and for this purpose, the Fund could take into account factors such as the level of per-capita income.

154. In 2009, in order to provide financial assistance to LICs in a more effective way, the IMF reformed its concessional lending framework and transformed the Poverty Reduction and Growth Facility into the PRGT. The trust is mainly funded through bilateral loan agreements (which are provided at market rates), donations from advanced economies, and income from the 2009–2010 IMF gold sales. Additionally, the IMF contributes to the PRGT from its general resources, which helps to supplement the funding for concessional lending to LICs. These various funding sources allow the PRGT to provide financial assistance to countries facing balance of payments problems at favourable terms, such as low or zero interest rates and longer repayment periods. A country can receive concessional lending from the PRGT if it is unable to access international financial markets on a substantial basis and it is eligible for IDA support. The PRGT covers three facilities: the Standby Credit Facility (SCF), the Extended Credit Facility (ECF), and the Rapid Credit Facility (RCF). Access to PRGT facilities is capped at 145% of quota per year and 435% of quota cumulatively.

155. The SCF provides financial assistance to LICs that have achieved broadly sustainable macroeconomic positions, but may face occasional, short-term financing and adjustment needs, including those caused by shocks. IMF programme conditionality focuses on achieving short-term macroeconomic stability while aligning with poverty reduction and growth goals. For arrangements lasting more than two years, a Poverty Reduction and Growth Strategy (PRGS, *see* below paragraph 158) must be submitted to the IMF's Executive Board, outlining policies that support growth, poverty reduction, and financing needs. The programme duration ranges between twelve to thirty-six months. Borrowing countries are not required to pay interest rates but only a small fee. They also benefit from a grace period of four years.

156. The ECF provides medium-term support to LICs with protracted balance of payments problems. Borrowing countries agree to implement economic programs that make significant progress towards achieving a stable and sustainable macroeconomic position, in line with long-term poverty reduction and growth objectives. The programme duration ranges between three to five years. Borrowing countries are not required to pay interest rates. They also benefit from a grace period of five and a half years.

157. The RCF provides prompt financial assistance to LICs facing an urgent balance of payments need. Similarly to the RFI, it covers a wide variety of situations, including external shocks, natural disasters, and emergencies connected to fragility. Countries receive financial assistance in a single disbursement and are not required to pay interest rates and benefit from a grace period of five and a half years.

158. Currently, a PRGS is mandatory for PRGT arrangements that have an initial duration exceeding two years. PRGSs were first introduced by the IMF and the World Bank in 1999, in the context of the HIPC initiative (on which *see infra*, paragraphs 339 ff.). A PRGS describes the macroeconomic, structural and social policies and programs that a country will pursue over several years to promote growth and reduce poverty. It identifies external financing needs and key funding sources, serving as a foundation for a comprehensive, country-driven strategy for poverty reduction. Given the interconnected nature of challenges in developing countries, PRGSs emphasise coordinated interventions involving multiple stakeholders rather than isolated measures. Beyond guiding IMF and World Bank programmes, PRGSs can also inform the strategies of other international organisations contributing to the country's development. Unlike Letters of Intent (on which *see infra*, paragraphs 180 ff.), PRGSs emphasise national 'ownership', promoting the broad-based participation of the civil society. They are adopted through a participatory process involving domestic stakeholders, external donors and development partners, including the IMF and the World Bank. Since 2018, though, the World Bank no longer requires a PRGS for its IDA financing, relying instead on Country Partnership Frameworks. Moreover, given the Fund's expanding engagement in new areas closely linked to poverty reduction and growth – such as governance, social spending, climate, fragility, and gender – a comprehensive review of the Poverty Reduction Strategy policy seems justified.

159. As a complement to the PRGT, in 2022, the IMF established the Resilience and Sustainability Trust (RST) to support LICs and vulnerable middle-income countries (including small States) in increasing their resilience to external shocks and promoting sustainable growth. The Resilience and Sustainability Facility (RSF) complements the IMF's existing lending framework by offering affordable, long-term financing to help countries undertaking reforms to reduce macro-critical risks associated with climate change and pandemic preparedness. Borrowing countries should be under a concurrent IMF-supported programme, maintain a sustainable debt position and an adequate capacity to repay, and demonstrate a credible reform agenda aligned with climate or health-related objectives. The RST offers financing with a 20-year maturity and a 10½-year grace period during which no principal repayments are required.

II. The Reserve Tranche Position and the Upper Credit Tranche Policy

160. Before requesting IMF financial assistance, a member can draw on its 'reserve tranche', a portion of its quota that is in many aspects similar to a demand deposit in a commercial bank. The reserve tranche is considered part of the member's external reserves and represents a liquid claim on the Fund. A country can, in fact, draw up to the full amount of its reserve tranche position at its own discretion and at any time, subject only to the member's representation of a balance of payments need. A reserve tranche drawing does not constitute a use of IMF credit and is not subject to charges or to an expectation or obligation to repay (repurchase) those funds to the IMF. Moreover, purchases in the reserve tranche are unconditional, meaning a member can access these funds immediately and replenish its reserves without being subject to the IMF's conditionality requirements (on which *see infra*, paragraphs 174 ff.).

161. A country's reserve tranche is calculated as the difference between its quota and the Fund's holdings of its national currency, excluding any amounts resulting from the use of IMF credit. Initially, this tranche typically corresponds to the portion of the quota paid in widely accepted foreign currency (25% of the quota). However, the exact amount of the reserve tranche also depends on the members' use of IMF resources. In fact, reserve tranche positions increase not only through quota payments but also when the IMF sells the currency of members with strong external positions to help other countries facing balance of payments difficulties.

162. If the country needs foreign currencies in an amount which exceeds its 'reserve tranche position in the IMF', it should seek financial assistance under the 'tranche policy'. However, it is not obliged to draw on its reserve tranche before requesting a loan.

163. Under the tranche policy, IMF lending is subject to phasing and increased conditionality. Drawings in the 'upper credit tranches' (any amount above 25% of a member's quota) are disbursed in instalments, referred to as 'the first, second, third credit tranche', and so on. Conditionality becomes stricter for financing in the higher tranches, with performance criteria and periodic reviews used to assess programme implementation (*see infra*, paragraphs 200 ff.). Such drawings are typically associated with a Stand-By or Extended Arrangement.

III. Purchasing Currencies from the Fund

164. According to Article V, section 2(a), the IMF provides financing in the upper credit tranches through a specific 'purchase-repurchase mechanism', which is the functional equivalent of a loan. In practice, the IMF lends resources from the GRA by selling its holdings of widely accepted foreign currencies to borrowing countries in exchange for their domestic currency. In other words, member countries 'purchase' foreign currencies from the IMF using an equivalent amount of their own currency (or by depositing promissory notes). The borrowing country is then under the obligation to 'repurchase' (buy back) its own currency using a currency selected by the Fund within a specified timeframe. The loan is considered repaid when the borrower completes this repurchase with its foreign reserve assets. The 'purchase/repurchase approach' to IMF lending affects only the composition of the IMF's resources held in the GRA, but not their overall value. For drawings in the upper credit tranches, a charge must be paid, which usually corresponds to market interest rates.

165. Under Article V, section 3(b), the member 'shall be entitled to purchase currencies of other members from the Fund in exchange for an equivalent amount of its own currency'. It is important to note that members are 'entitled' to receive IMF financial assistance, meaning that membership already creates an initial right. The IMF merely determines the conditions under which the purchase may be made.

166. According to Article V, section 3(a), the Fund must adopt policies governing the use of its general resources. These policies must ensure that balance of payments problems are addressed in accordance with the IMF Articles of Agreement and that 'adequate safeguards for the temporary use' of the Fund's general resources are established. The temporary nature of the IMF's assistance is ensured through IMF conditionality (*see infra*, paragraphs 174 ff.) and repurchase obligations, which require a member to buy back its own currency from the Fund after 'temporarily' exchanging it for foreign currency.

167. Once a member submits a request, the Fund determines its consistency with the IMF Articles and IMF policies. Under Article V, section 3(d), (e) and (f), decisions are adopted on the selection of currencies to be sold and the exchange rate to be applied. The resources provided by the Fund must be SDRs or 'freely usable currencies', i.e., currencies that are widely used to make payments for international transactions and actively traded in major exchange markets.

168. In practice, member countries with a sufficiently strong balance of payments and reserve position provide the Fund with 'usable currencies', which constitute the 'operational budget' of the Fund. These 'usable currencies' are then converted into 'freely usable currencies' (the US dollar, euro, renminbi, yen and pound sterling). Members in a position to provide usable currencies receive a remuneration based on the SDR interest rate. This remuneration is part of the Fund's mechanism to compensate members for providing liquidity that is available for the IMF's operations.

IV. The Access Policy

169. The access policy defines the maximum financing a member can obtain from the Fund based on its quota. The access limit, or the maximum amount a country can borrow from the IMF, varies depending on the type of loan but is typically a multiple of a member's quota. Access limits under the different lending facilities are reviewed by the Executive Board every two years, taking into account potential demand for IMF resources and developments in the Fund's liquidity position.

170. In 2016, the access limits to the Fund's general resources (GRA) were set at 145% of a member's quota annually and 435% cumulatively. This means that, in a given year, a member could make conditional purchases of the requested currency up to 145% of its quota, without exceeding the upper cumulative limit of 435%. During the COVID-19 pandemic, the access limits were temporarily increased to 200% annually and 600% cumulatively. At the end of 2024, following a Comprehensive Review of GRA Access Limits, the IMF Executive Board decided to maintain such higher access limits unchanged due to continued uncertainty in the global economic environment.

171. In exceptional circumstances, when members' financing needs exceed normal limits, the Fund may grant access above those limits. In 2002, the Fund decided to formalise conditions for the use of exceptional access, building on its long-standing principle that higher access must be accompanied by higher safeguards, primarily achieved through programme design. The 2002 Exceptional Access Policy set forth both procedural and substantive requirements. One of the four substantive criteria was 'the high probability that the member's public debt is sustainable in the medium term'.

172. During the European sovereign debt crisis, however, the Executive Board decided to revise the exceptional access policy criterion on debt sustainability to make it possible to lend to Greece. In fact, in May 2010, Greece needed financing amounting to 3200% of its quota, well above the access limits. On top of that, the IMF seriously doubted that the Greek debt was sustainable without a restructuring that was, however, strongly opposed by European institutions. In order to grant exceptional access to Greece without seeking pre-emptive debt restructuring, a major revision of the exceptional access policy was adopted, introducing the option of granting an exemption to the debt sustainability criterion. According to the new policy, exceptional access could be granted if it were determined that a debt restructuring, necessary to ensure a high probability of debt sustainability, would have 'adverse international spillover effects'. This significant policy change was not thoroughly discussed, and the modification process was not at all transparent (as pointed out by the IEO in its 2016 Report on the IMF and the Crises in Greece, Ireland and Portugal). The new criteria were later applied also to Ireland and Portugal, creating the impression of a preferential treatment for Europe. The exceptional access policy was only reviewed in 2016, when an Executive Board decision removed the systemic spillover waiver and introduced the option to provide access in situations where debt is considered sustainable but not with a high probability, provided that certain additional requirements are met.

173. A new 2024 IEO evaluation report covering thirty-eight exceptional access arrangements from 2002 to 2023 found that, despite the expectation that higher access should be accompanied by stronger safeguards and additional scrutiny, these were often lacking. The report thus recommended that the IMF Executive Board review the exceptional access policy decision in 2026 to address these issues and other identified shortcomings.

§4. IMF Conditionality

I. Definition and Main Issues

174. The IMF's 'conditionality policy' refers to the body of policies and procedures adopted by the Fund to govern the use of its resources in a manner that fulfils the purposes of the Articles. Conditionality is essential to ensure that the borrowing country will be able to repay the loan and that IMF resources remain available to other member countries. Conditionality thus embodies the *adequate safeguards* clause under which, according to Article I(v) and Article V, section 3(a), the Fund can make its general resources *temporarily available* to members. At the same time, it helps countries solve their balance of payments problems 'without resorting to measures destructive of national or international prosperity'.

175. In addition, the term 'conditionality' refers to the policies a member is required to follow in order to access the Fund's resources. When a country borrows from the Fund, it agrees to implement macroeconomic and structural reforms to overcome the crisis and restore growth and stability. Policy adjustment and conditionality make the IMF a 'co-author' of the country's economic policies and co-responsible for the outcomes of the adjustment.

176. Just as a government makes policy choices based on political, moral and legal values, the IMF must also take these into account. Given the IMF's practice of insisting on firm adjustment efforts, important questions arise about the scope of conditionality. Can the IMF request the closure of State-subsidised hospitals and schools? Can it demand a policy that requires parents to pay a user fee for their children's primary education? Does the IMF consider itself bound by human rights? What are the ethical implications of the Fund's actions?

177. Searching for values and human rights in the IMF Articles does not yield clear answers. According to the Articles, the IMF must avoid measures that are harmful to national or international prosperity, but this obligation carries little practical meaning for the protection of non-economic values without a proper interpretation. Significant is the 2002 opinion of the IMF's General Counsel on the relationship between the Fund and the UN Covenant on Economic, Social and Cultural Rights. The opinion suggests that, by supporting policies that aim to stabilise economies in the long term, the IMF is factually contributing to the promotion of socio-economic standards. The opinion also maintains, though, that the IMF is not legally bound by the Covenant because it is not a party to the treaty. Some authors, assuming that human rights are part of a broader framework of international law, argue instead that both the IMF and the World Bank are bound to respect customary human rights obligations in their activities (on the IMF and human rights, *see also infra*, paragraphs 377 ff.).

178. Sovereignty and political independence are also relevant legal notions. In negotiations with country officials, it may be tempting for the IMF to disregard such concepts. Critics contend that the IMF undermines national sovereignty, acts as a tool of the wealthiest countries, and exacerbates economic problems, worsening the living standards of the poor and vulnerable through its emphasis on privatisation, market deregulation and austerity measures. In July 2017, for instance, the UN Independent Expert on the Promotion of a Democratic and Equitable Economic Order affirmed that the IMF imposes conditions 'which discourage social spending and therefore hinder States' fulfilment of their human rights obligations. Often these conditions increase unemployment, lower standards governing labour, health and the environment, and reduce access to free quality education'. He concluded that the IMF's lending policies undermine human rights, hinder development policies and interfere with the work of other international organisations.

179. Besides, it is worth noting that the IMF provides financial assistance to countries facing a balance of payments problem even when they have very poor human rights records. The IMF justifies its non-interference in the internal political affairs of its members by invoking the so-called political prohibition of Article IV, section 3(b), which states that, 'in helping members to devise economic and financial programs, the Fund shall respect the domestic social and political policies of members' (on the IMF and human rights *see also infra*, paragraphs 377 ff.).

II. Procedure and Modalities

180. Only member countries are eligible to request balance of payments support from the IMF. Upon receiving a request, the Fund dispatches a mission to the country concerned. An IMF mission is typically composed of a team of economic, financial and legal experts drawn from the Fund staff. In cooperation with the IMF mission, the country's authorities outline a series of adjustment measures that are then detailed in a Letter of Intent and in a Memorandum on Economic and Financial Policies (MEFP), which are sometimes accompanied also by a Technical Memorandum of Understanding (TMU). The country's policy intentions documents, prepared in close consultation with the Fund's staff, contain a declaration of aims and describe the policies and reforms that the borrowing country intends to implement. They are submitted to the IMF Managing Director for circulation to the Executive Board which has the power to approve loans. These documents are made available on the IMF website, subject to the requesting country's consent. The release of financial resources is then formalised in a SBA or another loan arrangement, such as an Extended Arrangement (*see supra*, paragraphs 144 ff.). A Fund arrangement is an Executive Board decision that outlines the terms under which a member may make purchases or receive disbursements from the Fund, within a specified period, and up to a specified amount. All Fund arrangements include consultation clauses.

181. The Letter of Intent and the IMF loan arrangement do not give rise to any obligation under international law, not even when read together. They do not constitute an international agreement from the perspective of public international law, nor do they amount to unilateral legal acts, as there is no consent to be bound. The absence of such consent also entails further consequences: treaty law does not apply, and national procedures required for the ratification of international agreements do not need to be followed.

182. An important consequence of the absence of a binding relationship between the IMF and the borrowing country is that, from a combined reading of the Letter of Intent and the loan arrangement, it cannot be inferred that the execution of the adjustment programme is mandatory. The programme merely outlines the conditions under which IMF tranche disbursements are possible (*see* below); if these conditions are not met, the disbursements will not take place. Furthermore, the IMF seeks to avoid the perception that adjustment programmes impose a set of obligations. Presenting the results of the negotiations as a bilateral agreement would be inconsistent with the principle of national ownership which emphasises the country's responsibility and control over the design and implementation of the programme.

183. Financing under Fund arrangements is typically phased, with members receiving additional tranches as their balance of payments needs evolve and as they meet additional or incremental conditions. Phasing mitigates risks to the Fund by aligning its financial exposure with the member's progress in addressing its balance of payments difficulties, thereby enhancing its capacity to repay the Fund. Programme reviews allow the IMF Executive Board to assess whether the programme is on track and if modifications are needed (*see infra*, paragraph 202). While phasing is linked to adjustment and reform, frontloading may also be granted under certain circumstances.

184. The adoption of a Fund decision in the form of a SBA (or another loan arrangement) offers a number of advantages for both the IMF and the borrowing country. *Speed is essential*: the procedure for drafting a Letter of Intent and a SBA can be completed quickly; the procedure is simple, and since the requesting country is under no obligation, there is less need for legal detail. *Confidentiality*: the procedure can be conducted with complete confidentiality, since there is no requirement for an agreement to be submitted to a legislative assembly. Confidentiality is particularly important, for instance, when currency devaluation is part of the adjustment programme, as public disclosure of the programme could trigger capital flight or speculation against the currency undergoing devaluation. An objection to confidentiality is that radical austerity measures are adopted without the democratic scrutiny of a parliament or other stakeholders. *Exercise of economic sovereignty*: the member may, at any time, halt the adjustment programme without breaching any international law obligation or facing formal sanctions from the IMF (such as the suspension of voting rights, on which *see supra*, paragraph 121). However, invoking economic sovereignty does have practical consequences, as the continuation of the programme is a condition for continuing to receive IMF financial assistance. If balance of payments support is indispensable, the country, in practice, has no choice but to complete the adjustment programme. Should a member nevertheless decide to terminate the adjustment programme prematurely, the relationship of trust will be seriously compromised. If a new request for support is made, the IMF will require additional assurances before proceeding with a new loan arrangement.

III. Guidelines on Conditionality

185. In the past, countries have criticised the IMF for intruding on their national sovereignty, while developing countries have also alleged unequal treatment. In 1979, this led the Fund to adopt its Guidelines on Conditionality, which establish the principles that should guide the Fund in designing and setting conditionality. The Guidelines were revised in 2002 and later supplemented by Operational Guidance Notes to assist the staff in discussions with member countries. In 2006 and 2014, the IMF further modernised its conditionality framework. After the 2018 comprehensive review of conditionality (conducted to assess programme design since the global financial crisis) and the 2021 IEO report on Growth and Adjustment in IMF-Supported Programs, a new Operational Guidance Note on Program Design and Conditionality was adopted in January 2024. Two key findings stand out in the IEO evaluation report: first, it found no evidence of a consistent bias towards excessive austerity in IMF-supported programs during the 2008–2019 period, even if growth outcomes fell short of projections in programme countries; second, among other recommendations, the IEO urged the Fund to pay adequate attention to the social and distributional consequences of reform programs.

186. The Guidelines on Conditionality – lastly amended in 2006 – are still relevant today as they set the principles and modalities of IMF conditionality. They should be read together with the 2024 Operational Guidance Notes.

187. The first guideline concerns the basis and purpose of conditionality. It makes it clear that 'Conditionality – that is, program-related conditions – is intended to ensure that Fund resources are provided to members to assist them in resolving their balance of payments problems in a manner that is consistent with the Fund's Articles and that establishes adequate safeguards for the temporary use of the Fund's resources.' Fund resources are provided solely to address balance of payments problems; being a least developed country or a fragile State (*see infra*, paragraphs 212 ff.) does not, in itself, constitute a sufficient basis for financial assistance.

188. Guideline 2 on early warning and prevention explains that conditional balance of payments support is one of the ways in which the IMF helps members to strengthen their economic and financial policies. Bilateral consultations conducted under IMF Article IV and multilateral surveillance exercises (*see infra*, paragraphs 235 ff.) may also highlight developments of concern that require policy adjustments or corrective measures by the member country. The IMF advises members against postponing difficult decisions and encourages them to take corrective measures at an early stage.

189. In Guideline 3 on ownership and capacity to implement programs, the Fund acknowledges that programs cannot be imposed on countries. In the past, the IMF too often prescribed policies it deemed necessary or appropriate for governments. Governments were asked to sign documents on policy reforms that had been prearranged by IMF missions with limited input from national authorities. The Guidelines therefore explain that 'the member has primary responsibility for the selection, design and implementation of its economic and financial policies' and stress that 'national ownership of sound economic and financial policies and an adequate administrative capacity are crucial for successful implementation of Fund-supported programs'. This is an important warning sign to all IMF missions to listen carefully to government officials. The country must also have an appropriate institutional framework and adequate administrative capacity for the implementation of programme reforms.

190. The 2024 Operational Guidance Note further clarifies that 'in helping the authorities design a Fund-supported program, objectives should be formulated in discussion with them, and their preferences and policy choices should be accommodated, subject to consistency with resolving balance of payments problems, macroeconomic stability and all other program goals'. Moreover, 'To the extent possible, program objectives should be aligned with the authorities' own reform plans (e.g., national reform plans and poverty reduction and growth strategies) including on growth, labour market, and distributional targets.' By stressing that the programme is country-owned, the IMF seeks to avoid being made a scapegoat, as it has often happened. Many governments conveniently blame the IMF for painful measures to evade political responsibility for necessary but unpopular economic reforms.

191. Guideline 4 on circumstances of members explains that: 'in helping members to devise economic and financial programs, the Fund will pay due regard to the domestic social and political objectives, the economic priorities, and the circumstances of members, including the causes of their balance of payments problems and their administrative capacity to implement reforms'. The language of this principle suggests a degree of flexibility in preserving domestic policies when an adjustment programme is being implemented. In reality, however, this latitude is limited. First, 'due regard' does not equate 'to respect' and does not oblige the IMF to give overriding priority to domestic policies. If the economic consequences of domestic choices conflict with IMF policies, the latter will take precedence. Second, the Fund's influence over sovereign decision-making has been expanding since the

1990s. Noteworthy is the IMF Standards and Codes Initiative (*see infra*, paragraph 271), through which the Fund has endorsed twelve internationally recognised standards and adopted a set of guidelines and codes to strengthen the international financial system, thereby increasingly influencing decision-making in member countries. Guideline 4 also highlights 'past performance' as a relevant circumstance. This refers to the behaviour of members in previous periods. In the past, some countries misled the IMF by providing false economic data to demonstrate that programs were on track.

192. Guideline 5 concerns the approval of access to Fund resources. It provides for the 'consistent application of policies' related to the use of resources to ensure the uniform treatment of members. However, proving that uniform treatment has not occurred is challenging, as the economic circumstances of countries are always different. Besides, the capacity and commitment of the requesting country are important criteria for granting credit.

193. Guideline 6 on programme goals provides that the Fund's financial assistance should be directed primarily towards solving the member's balance of payments problem 'without recourse to measures destructive of national or international prosperity' (as provided also by Article I(v)). The provision is softly phrased, and it is unclear what is meant by 'prosperity' and whose prosperity should be preserved. Does prosperity refer to GDP or socio-economic standards? Clearly, it is difficult to ensure that all parties involved remain prosperous when an adjustment programme is being implemented. Moreover, a programme must aim to achieve 'medium-term external viability while fostering sustainable economic growth'. The term 'fostering' is significant, as it suggests that the IMF does not directly promote 'sustainable' economic growth but principally facilitates conditions for 'growth', focusing on macroeconomic policy issues rather than on broader development priorities.

194. Guideline 7 on the scope of conditions explains that programme-related conditions to access the Fund's resources will be applied 'parsimoniously', which actually means cautiously. This approach seeks to avoid the proliferation of conditions that in the past burdened many countries under IMF programs. Conditions should be of 'critical importance' for the achievement of programme goals. A condition is deemed of critical importance when its non-implementation would jeopardise the achievement of programme goals or make effective monitoring impossible. All critical measures must be subject to conditionality, as the Fund needs to be able to suspend purchases or disbursements if the programme goes off track or if adequate information for monitoring is not provided. According to the 2024 Operational Guidance Note, criticality 'should be established on the basis of those variables or measures that are generally, either (i) of critical importance for achieving the goals of the member's program or to monitor its implementation; or (ii) necessary for the implementation of specific provisions of the Articles of Agreement or policies adopted under them'.

195. Specific attention should be given to the policies clause. As explained above, the IMF has not been particularly 'parsimonious' in developing new policies. In practice, more policies mean more conditions. Furthermore, the IMF will impose conditions that 'normally consist of macroeconomic variables and structural measures' within the Fund's core areas of responsibility. Inclusion of non-macroeconomic variables must be explicitly justified. Macroeconomic variables have not been formally defined, but likely they refer to aggregate data. Accordingly, the IMF may request a reduction in overall government spending, but it should not systematically impose conditions detailing the specific schemes for such reductions. Structural measures, first introduced in the 1980s, have also been a major source of controversy because the attached conditionality was considered to go beyond the Fund's mandate. In fact, structural adjustment programs saw the IMF involved in politically sensitive reforms, such as the privatisation of State-owned enterprises, trade and financial liberalisation, labour market restructuring, and reforms to social policies. In 2009, the Fund decided that structural performance criteria would no longer be part of the conditionality framework. Since then, however, the use of structural measures has declined only marginally and, during the global financial crisis, they once again became a prominent feature of IMF programs. Today, structural conditions typically focus on reforms aimed at addressing governance vulnerabilities and combating corruption, along with measures regarding insolvency frameworks, creditor rights, and the energy and social sectors.

196. Guideline 8 addresses the IMF's responsibility for conditionality, emphasising that it falls under the Fund's sole responsibility. In addition, the IMF commits to avoiding any form of cross-conditionality, under which the use of the Fund's resources would be directly subjected to the rules or decisions of other organisations. Borrowing countries, in fact, fear the domino effect of conditionalities imposed by multiple international financial institutions and creditors, whereby failing to meet one creditor's conditions could prompt others to cut off their credit lines. On the other hand, though, the IMF also acknowledges the need for cooperation with other organisations, particularly the World Bank. In their cooperation agreement (the Concordat, on which *see infra*, paragraphs 392 ff.), the IMF and the World Bank have accepted the concept of a 'lead agency'. Depending on the reforms required, one institution would take primary responsibility, with the other expected to follow its lead.

197. The Guidelines do not address the problem of socio-economic consequences that may follow from adjustment. However, adjustment must take into account the plight of the poor, and the 'national prosperity' clause of Article I(v) should be applied: adjustment should be carried out 'without resorting to measures destructive of national or international prosperity'. Accordingly, the Guidelines could have clarified that international human rights standards should be upheld during adjustment. For that purpose, they could have indicated that the Fund ought to cooperate with UN bodies, such as the treaty-based Committee on Economic, Social and Cultural Rights. To address some of these concerns (but always without adopting a human rights law approach), the 2014 Revised Operational Guidance included a reference to conditionality related to macro-social (jobs and growth) issues, affirming that 'where feasible and appropriate, policy measures to mitigate adverse impacts on the most vulnerable should be included in program design'. Following this path, the 2024 Operational Guidance Note placed greater emphasis on fiscal policy conditionality and, in particular, on its social implications, stating that IMF-supported programmes 'should seek to protect social spending and mitigate the adverse effects of program measures on the poor and vulnerable'. Social spending includes expenditures on social protection programmes – such as social insurance and social assistance – as well as spending on education and healthcare. Objectives for social spending within IMF-supported programmes can be defined in various ways, such as a percentage of public expenditure, a share of GDP, or in real per-capita terms. Conditionality targets can also be more narrowly tailored to prioritise social protection programmes for the most vulnerable groups. Where relevant, structural measures can be introduced to strengthen social safety nets, such as introducing new social assistance schemes or reforming existing ones. The Fund is also expected to engage with civil society organisations, labour unions, business and experts to ensure effective policy design.

198. Another inherent flaw is the absence of even a basic accountability mechanism related to the IMF conditionality framework, which makes it difficult to assess the impact of the conditions imposed on member countries and to hold the Fund accountable for the outcomes of its programmes. States may disagree with the Fund on programme reforms, and they may be wrong or right. The point is that the Fund's view will always prevail. The Fund might take the World Bank as an example. The Bank has established an independent Inspection Panel for the purpose of providing people directly affected by a World Bank project with an independent forum through which they can request the Bank to act in accordance with its own policies and procedures. Accordingly, the IMF should establish a procedure enabling member countries to contest instances where the Fund is believed to be failing to observe its Articles of Agreement or implementing its own policy decisions, including the Guidelines. A member country should be afforded the opportunity to request that the IMF refrain from imposing conditionality that would lead to a breach of the country's international obligations. An example of such controversial policy was the IMF's insistence on the introduction of a 'user fee' for basic health and education services. Imposing a user fee for primary education would not only contradict the Guidelines – according to which conditions should primarily be 'macroeconomic' – but it would also violate international human rights instruments that require free and compulsory elementary education.

IV. Monitoring and Measuring Performance

199. Once an arrangement is approved by the Executive Board, resources (either in the form of purchases of international reserve currencies or disbursements from the Fund) are usually made available to the requesting country in phased instalments. Disbursements made in instalments are linked to demonstrable policy actions, with quantitative performance criteria (QPCs), structural benchmarks, indicative targets and/or prior actions established to assess the member's compliance with the programme and progress in its implementation.

200. QPCs constitute the core of IMF conditionality. The 2002 Guidelines on Conditionality defines QPCs as a set of variables or measures 'whose observance or implementation is established as a formal condition for the making of purchases or disbursement under a Fund arrangement'. They are specific and measurable conditions related to macroeconomic variables, or to those variables through which special clauses of the IMF Articles, or derived policies, are implemented. QPCs are 'normally' related to the Fund's core areas of responsibility (e.g., macroeconomic stabilisation; monetary, fiscal, and exchange rate policies, including the underlying institutional arrangements and closely related structural measures; financial sector stability). They are typically established as ceilings or floors on macroeconomic variables deemed essential for achieving programme goals or monitoring implementation. Criteria cannot prescribe the method by which public expenditure is reduced when setting a maximum public expenditure deficit, nor can they involve redistribution issues or mandate specific reductions in areas such as defence, education, or food subsidies. In addition, QPCs should relate to macroeconomic variables under the control of the country's authorities such as monetary and credit aggregates, international reserves, fiscal balances and external borrowing. They must be as few as possible in number as well as explicit, objective and objectively verifiable. Differences of interpretation about whether the criteria have been adequately met should, ideally, not occur: a member country should always be able to determine at any given moment whether it has met the criteria and is therefore eligible to receive the next instalment. QPCs may only be included in lending arrangements and subsequent programme reviews: criteria in 'secret side letters' are not permitted. If a QPC is not met, the Executive Board may, however, approve a formal *waiver*, but only if it is satisfied that 'the program will nevertheless be successfully implemented' – i.e., it will achieve its goals – either because of the minor or temporary nature of the non-observance or because of corrective actions taken by the country's authorities (2024 Operational Guidance Note on Conditionality).

201. In addition to QPCs, indicative targets and structural benchmarks may also be established. Indicative targets are indicators used to assess the country's progress in meeting the objectives of the programme when there is substantial uncertainty about economic trends. Structural benchmarks refer to other non-quantifiable variables and can be established only when essential to achieve programme goals. The rationale for limiting the use of structural benchmarks is that the IMF's objectives should normally be adequately achieved by influencing macroeconomic variables. Therefore, structural benchmarks, which involve adjustments to one or more microeconomic variables, should only be applied if expected to have a critical macroeconomic impact. These benchmarks usually concern areas such as public financial management, tax policy and revenue administration, natural resource governance, and reforms related to energy subsidies, pensions, gender equality, and public healthcare. Notably, in 2022, the Fund adopted a new Strategy Towards Mainstreaming Gender, acknowledging that narrowing gender disparities contributes to stronger economic growth, greater stability and resilience, and lower income inequality. Unlike QPCs, indicative targets and structural benchmarks do not require a formal waiver if they are not met; however, deviations serve as an indicator that the programme may be off-track.

202. Before new purchases or disbursements, the Fund checks if the programme is on track. Through periodical programme reviews, the Executive Board assesses if conditions are being met according to the agreed timetable and establishes if the programme needs to be modified in light of new developments. A programme review will be completed only if the Executive Board is satisfied, based on the member's past performance and policy understandings for the future, that the programme remains on track to achieve its objectives. Reviews are typically conducted every six months, but significant uncertainties about economic trends or policy implementation may require more frequent monitoring.

203. A member may also be required to take 'prior actions' and to implement certain measures before the IMF's Executive Board approves financing, completes a review, or grants a waiver, particularly when upfront implementation is essential to achieve programme goals. Prior actions ensure that the programme has a solid foundation for its successful implementation, or that it gets back on track if needed. Following the global financial crisis, the Fund developed a new framework that incorporates a more systematic use of this type of *ex ante* conditionality.

204. The Monitoring of Fund Arrangements (MONA) database contains comprehensive data on the economic objectives and outcomes of Fund-supported programs, providing a history of these programs from their Executive Board approval to completion. Data are available for most arrangements since 2002.

V. Conditions on Governance

205. In 1997, the IMF adopted a policy on addressing economic governance issues. The origin of this policy can be traced to a growing recognition in the 1990s – especially after the Asian financial crisis – that poor governance and corruption could undermine macroeconomic stability and the effectiveness of Fund-supported programmes. The 1997 Guidance Note on 'The Role of the IMF in Governance Issues' remains relevant today and recognises the Fund's role in promoting good governance and combating corruption in its surveillance, lending and technical assistance activities.

206. The concept of 'governance' is generally understood as a framework that encompasses various institutions, mechanisms and practices through which a country exercises governmental authority, fulfils its responsibilities and manages its public resources. While 'governance' is a neutral term, 'good governance' is a more qualitative concept, defined as a crucial factor in eradicating poverty and promoting development. It is acknowledged that poor governance creates opportunities for corruption and undermines social and economic development as well as confidence in the government and in market integrity. The definition of 'corruption' adopted by the IMF – 'the abuse of public office for private gain' – is consistent with the 2003 UN Convention Against Corruption and the OECD 1997 Convention on Combating Bribery of Foreign Public Officials in International Business Transactions. The Convention stipulates that contracting parties have to adopt any legislative and non-legislative measure necessary to class as criminal offences the following acts, when committed intentionally: (a) promising, offering or giving to a public official – either directly or indirectly – an undue advantage, for the benefit of that official or another person or entity, with the intent of inducing the official to act or refrain from acting in the exercise of his or her official duties; and (b) soliciting or accepting, by a public official – either directly or indirectly – an undue advantage, for the benefit of that official or another person or entity, with the intent of inducing the official to act or refrain from acting in the exercise of his or her official duties.

207. The Guidance Note stipulates that the Fund's involvement is limited to the economic aspects of governance and that the IMF staff may address issues of poor governance whenever these have 'significant current or potential impact on macroeconomic performance in the short and medium-term, and on the ability of the government's credibility to pursue policies aimed at external viability'. Widespread corruption harms the culture of compliance and encourages tax evasion. In resource-rich countries, corruption exacerbates the mismanagement of natural resources, leading to the diversion of public funds that could otherwise be used for development projects, infrastructure and poverty reduction. High levels of corruption significantly hinder a State's ability to perform basic functions and maintain a sustainable debt level.

208. There are six core government functions that are most relevant to the IMF's governance diagnostics: fiscal governance, financial sector oversight, central bank governance and operations, market regulation, rule of law, and anti-money laundering and combating the financing of terrorism. The accumulation of instances that could trigger the Fund's involvement suggests that any major governance issue may fall within the Fund's remit. Key decisions on taxation or public expenditure, which have a significant macroeconomic impact, can bring governments' policies within the scope of the Fund's jurisdiction. However, the 1997 Guidance Note further clarifies that: 'IMF judgment should not be influenced by the nature of a political regime of a country, nor should it interfere in domestic or foreign politics of any member.'

209. The IMF's ambition to assess multiple key administrative functions of governance before approving balance of payments support requires expertise in various areas. The Guidance Note specifies that conditionality may even extend to policies that are outside the Fund's core areas of expertise. Therefore, when deciding on financial support, the Fund may apply principles and rules that go beyond its corpus juris, i.e., the Articles of Agreement and subordinate rules and regulations. Notably, the IMF staff are expected: 'to keep abreast of changes in the policies of partner organisations and specific efforts in member countries on governance issues'. This should include the activities of other international organisations (particularly the World Bank) aimed at addressing governance issues in areas beyond the IMF's competence but nonetheless important for the achievement of the economic policies advocated by the IMF. Rules on governance applied by the World Bank, WTO, United Nations and by any other 'partner organisations' are therefore also monitored by the IMF. Such rules may include procurement procedures, public enterprise reforms, and those promoting good governance in general. The Fund may rely on various frameworks, such as the WTO's Agreement on Government Procurement, the World Bank's Operational Directives, UN Development Program (UNDP) policy statements on democratic governance and the G-20 Anti-Corruption Working Group principles.

210. In 2017, following a request from the IMFC, the Fund carried out a review of the IMF engagement on governance issues. It was assessed that the Fund had undertaken various initiatives to promote good governance and combat corruption, and that considerable progress had been made. However, in cases where corruption was systemic, the IMF's failure to address these issues was also considered capable of giving rise to reputational risks and could undermine the safeguarding of IMF resources. The review therefore recommended strengthening the Fund's engagement by adopting a broader perspective on corruption, establishing improved methods to assess its extent and macroeconomic impact, while continuing cooperation with other international organisations.

211. In 2018, the IMF Executive Board approved the new Framework for Enhanced Fund Engagement on Governance to supplement the 1997 Guidance Note. The new Framework consists of four key elements designed to promote more systematic, effective, candid and impartial engagement with member countries on governance vulnerabilities, including corruption, which are deemed macroeconomically significant. The first element enables the Fund to assess the nature and severity of governance vulnerabilities. The second element outlines how the Fund will evaluate their macroeconomic impact, in particular by taking into account the applicable standards for surveillance (under the Integrated Surveillance Decision, on which *see infra*, paragraphs 244 ff.) and the use of Fund resources (under the Guidelines on Conditionality, on which *see supra*, paragraphs 185 ff.). The third element establishes a framework to provide policy advice and capacity development support to countries where Fund engagement is necessary. Lastly, the fourth element focuses on measures to prevent private actors from offering bribes or facilitating the concealment of the proceeds of corruption.

§5. The IMF and Fragile and Conflict-Affected States

I. Fragile and Conflict- Affected Countries

212. The challenges posed by Fragile and Conflict-Affected States (FCSs) are complex. Their economic performance and ability to deliver basic social services are weak. They face institutional and policy implementation weaknesses that make them more prone to fall into a vicious cycle of conflict and instability (the so-called fragility trap). Low income levels and sluggish growth heighten the risks of conflict. FCSs are likely to generate negative spillovers into neighbouring countries (e.g., because of refugee flows or humanitarian crises). They are usually burdened by high levels of debt and protracted payment arrears and are unable to attract external assistance or investments. Moreover, even when rich in natural resources, these countries may suffer from violence, corruption, and mismanagement, resulting in the enrichment of an élite (the so-called resource curse). Economic development is therefore critical to preventing both the onset of conflict and relapse into it. However, FCSs tend to receive considerably less external assistance than other LICs. Overcoming their deep-seated capacity constraints and achieving sustained stability and growth requires long-term support as well as the coherent, coordinated and complementary engagement from the international community.

213. As there is no universally agreed definition of FCSs, the IMF currently adopts the methodology, thresholds, and criteria established by the World Bank, which reflect the typology and severity of challenges faced by FCSs and divide them into two main groups. The first group comprises countries suffering from high levels of institutional and social fragility due to: (i) weak economic management, limited institutional capacity and inadequate social inclusion policies, as measured by the World Bank's Country Policy and Institutional Assessment score (CPIA); (ii) significant refugee flows; (iii) the deployment of a UN peacekeeping or peacebuilding operation. The second group includes countries experiencing a conflict, which are identified on the basis of the number of conflict-related casualties, both in absolute terms and relative to their population. Although the World Bank's FCS list is publicly available and updated annually, the IMF publishes a separate list each year, retaining the autonomy to update its methodology when necessary.

II. The IMF Strategy for Fragile and Conflict- Affected Countries

214. In 2018, the IEO published a report entitled 'The IMF and Fragile States'. While acknowledging the important contributions made by the IMF in FCSs – such as helping to restore macroeconomic stability, build core macroeconomic policy institutions, and catalyse donor support – the IEO also highlighted numerous shortcomings. It found that the IMF's financial toolkit, with its relatively short-term focus, was not well suited to the needs and circumstances of fragile countries. Initiatives to adapt IMF policies and practices to the specific needs of FCSs fell short of expectations, 'leaving questions about the credibility of the Fund's commitment in this area'. Moreover, the IEO report noted that strategic coordination with development partners proved difficult, due to their different institutional mandates, priorities and budget cycles.

215. In 2022, in response to the IEO report, the Fund adopted a new Strategy for FCSs, which was complemented in 2023 by a Staff Guidance Note. As part of this revised framework to enhance the Fund's engagement with FCSs, a new tool was introduced: Country Engagement Strategies (CES). Developed with inputs from all relevant IMF departments, CES will identify a country's main drivers of fragility and/or conflict, as well as obstacles to the implementation of reforms, outlining long-term macroeconomic policies necessary to exit fragility, strategic priorities for capacity development support and scope for strategic partnerships. Notably, CES aim to: integrate surveillance, capacity development and lending; inform programme design and conditionality; and facilitate dialogue with national authorities as well as humanitarian, development and peace actors. According to the new framework, IMF conditionality must be calibrated to reflect the country's political and social context when determining the pace and sequencing of reforms; it should also take into account the distributional impacts of macroeconomic adjustments, support the strengthening of good governance, and promote country ownership of key reforms. The new strategy also emphasises opportunities for leveraging cooperation not only with the World Bank, the United Nations, and Multilateral Development Banks, but also with civil society.

216. During periods of active conflict or political instability, the Fund must make efforts to maintain its engagement with the country concerned. In accordance with its obligations under Article IV, the Fund should keep conducting surveillance whenever feasible. However, if there is a full-scale conflict, widespread civil unrest or strong security concerns that make missions impracticable, Article IV consultations may be delayed until authorities are ready to engage. Moreover, as outlined in the FCS Strategy, the Fund may also provide capacity development if the authorities are able to absorb such support and may extend lending, provided that adequate safeguards and other policy requirements are met.

217. When a government loses control over parts of its territory due to conflict, the Fund must adapt its engagement accordingly, tailoring access to its financial resources, surveillance activities and technical assistance to the country's specific circumstances. In these cases, an irregular change of government, such as a military coup, may occur. Staff may communicate with competing factions only with the authorisation of the government recognised by the Fund.

218. The IMF's approach to government recognition applies to all member countries regardless of their FCS status. It is based on two key elements: (a) a general principle of engaging with the authorities that exercise effective control over the country; and (b) an exception, whereby engagement is suspended if there is clear evidence that the international community – as represented by a majority of the IMF's total voting power – refuses to recognise or to interact with the member's regime. Therefore, if the international community declines to engage with the regime in question (such as in the case of the Taliban regime in Afghanistan), the Fund suspends its activities: the country loses access to Fund resources and SDRs, and the Fund is precluded from conducting surveillance or providing capacity development.

219. Despite the specific needs and challenges of FCSs, the Fund has maintained its long-standing practice of not distinguishing them from low- or middle-income members, nor has it established a lending facility dedicated to FCSs. Therefore, the Fund makes use of all existing financing instruments and facilities for which FCSs are eligible. Lending is usually provided either through the SCF (*see supra*, paragraph 155) or – in the case of PRGT-eligible countries – via the ECF (*see supra*, paragraph 156). Conditionality should reflect the specific circumstances of FCSs, striking a balance between essential reform measures and the country's unique challenges, without compromising its ownership. If the local authorities are deemed unable to implement an IMF-supported programme, the Fund's staff should discuss options for staff-monitored programs (*see* below), which can be combined with emergency financing (as was the case for South Sudan).

III. Staff-Monitored Programs

220. Staff Monitored Programs (SMPs) became an important instrument in the IMF's toolkit at the end of the 1990s (when an internal guidance note on their use was adopted), but they are still employed today. An SMP is an informal and non-financial arrangement between the IMF and a member country designed to help the country establish a track record of sound economic policies, often as a step towards a future IMF-supported programme involving financial assistance.

221. SMPs are in fact typically used when a loan arrangement is not feasible and serve as a tool for the Fund to monitor a member's economic situation and offer policy advice outside the context of an IMF-supported programme or Article IV consultations. A country can resort to SMPs when facing limited institutional capacity and domestic instability, when lacking recent Fund-supported programme experience or when a previously negotiated IMF-supported programme has derailed. The purpose of an SMP is to help the country establish a track record that could pave the way for the provision of emergency assistance, the conclusion of a formal loan arrangement or the resumption of a suspended one. SMPs are approved by IMF management, without requiring formal approval by the Executive Board.

222. SMPs are not subject to conditionality requirements but are based on a macroeconomic policy framework that includes quarterly performance benchmarks. The key features of the country's economic programme are usually outlined in a Letter of Intent. However, they do not entail an endorsement of the country's policies by the IMF Executive Board, nor do they involve any commitment of resources by the Fund. IMF staff closely monitor the implementation of the country's economic programme and meet regularly with national authorities to review progress against predefined benchmarks. The typical duration of SMPs is between six and eighteen months, but they may be extended in exceptional circumstances if performance is not satisfactory. In many cases, to keep the momentum of policy reform, recourse to SMPs can be reiterated for subsequent periods of time.

223. After completing an SMP, most countries move to a regular IMF-supported programme. For instance, Liberia – a country torn apart by prolonged periods of civil war – was able to initiate an SMP only in 2006, after democratic elections. The key objectives of Liberia's SMP were to rebuild public institutions, restore credible financial management and accelerate structural reforms. Thanks to the successful implementation of the SMP, Liberia moved to a Poverty Reduction and Growth Facility arrangement in 2008 and received debt relief under the HIPC initiative in 2010 (on the HIPC, *see infra*, paragraphs 339 ff.), after clearing its arrears with the Fund. More recently, a similar path was followed by Somalia, which established a strong track record of reform implementation through four SMPs, subsequently obtaining debt relief under the HIPC initiative and the approval of an ECF loan in 2020.

224. In October 2022, the IMF Executive Board decided to introduce a new tool: Staff-Monitored Program with Board Involvement (PMB). Like SMPs, the PMB aims to help countries build or restore a track record of sound policy implementation towards an upper-credit-tranche-quality IMF-supported arrangement. Use of the PMB is narrowly defined, being limited to member countries that are either (1) engaged in a concerted international effort by creditors or donors to deliver substantial new financing or debt relief in support of the country's policy programme, or (2) holding significant outstanding credit under emergency financing instruments at the time of a new financing request. The PMB permits the Executive Board to assess the strength of the member's policies in achieving programme objectives at the time of programme approval and to determine whether the country is on track to meet those goals during programme reviews. In February 2024, the IMF Executive Board concluded its review of the policy on PMBs, endorsing its continued inclusion in the IMF's toolkit, with another review scheduled in three years. To date, only Malawi, Ukraine and South Sudan have made use of PMBs.

Chapter 4. Other IMF Activities

§1. The IMF and the International Monetary System

225. The international monetary system has been described as the economic, institutional and political framework that aims to deliver international monetary stability. In particular, it consists of a set of rules, conventions, policies and institutional agreements governing official actions and policies affecting the following: exchange rate regimes and exchange rates; arrangements related to reserve assets and global liquidity; the convertibility of currencies and the making of payments and transfers for current international transactions; international capital movements; global, regional and bilateral surveillance arrangements.

226. The current international monetary system is radically different from the post-war one. In fact, the post-war system was the result of the international negotiations of the Bretton Woods Conference and had a strong institutional architecture. It was centred around the gold exchange standard and the obligation of IMF members to establish a par value for their currencies, either directly in terms of gold or indirectly in terms of US dollars (*see supra*, paragraphs 12 ff.). Due to changes in the world economy and in US policies, the par value system collapsed in the early 1970s. It was replaced by a more flexible system of exchange rate arrangements that allowed countries to choose their own exchange rate regimes, including floating, pegged or managed exchange rates. The new provisions for 'a stable system of exchange rates' were codified in the 1978 Second Amendment to the Articles of Agreement (*see supra*, paragraphs 15 ff.).

227. A major characteristic of the current international monetary system is the freedom of IMF members to choose the exchange rate policy they deem appropriate. The current system has also been described as a 'non-system', characterised by decentralisation and involving multiple currencies linked through a complex matrix of floating and fixed exchange rates regimes. In contrast to the uniformity of the Bretton Woods system, the international monetary system has evolved into a patchwork of different approaches to exchange rate policy. Many advanced economies with open capital markets now let their exchange rates float freely, while medium- and low-income countries tend to peg or heavily manage their exchange rates. Moreover, while the post-war economic order was characterised by restricted capital flows, today's global economy is largely built on their liberalisation. Capital flows – given their scale and economic impact – have become a central feature of the international monetary system. Nevertheless, some emerging and developing economies still combine managed exchange rate regimes with the use of capital controls (*see infra*, paragraphs 282 ff.).

228. Currently, the international monetary system is managed first and foremost by the IMF, national monetary authorities (central banks) and treasuries. Attempts to promote international monetary policy coordination are also made outside the IMF, notably through intergovernmental groups of leading economies (such as the Group of 7 and the Group of 20, on which *see infra*, paragraphs 355 ff.). Following the global financial crisis, meetings of the Group of 20 Finance Ministers and Central Bank Governors began to play a greater role in promoting international cooperation to strengthen and stabilise the global monetary system. However, international monetary cooperation remains extremely difficult to achieve and sustain, given that the system is built upon globally competing national monetary monopolies and sovereign rights. Moreover, it is important to remember that the international monetary system is closely interconnected with the international financial system, which is largely dominated by private rather than public actors.

§2. The IMF and Exchange Rate Stability

229. After the collapse of the par value system, IMF members regained the freedom to choose the exchange rate regime they considered most suitable for their economic needs. In line with this, the 2023 IMF Annual Report on Exchange Arrangements and Exchange Restrictions (AREAER) classifies exchange rate regimes into several categories, reflecting the diverse approaches adopted by countries in managing their currencies. These include: hard pegs (currency boards and exchange arrangements with no separate legal tender, i.e., currency unions); soft pegs (conventional pegged arrangements, pegged exchange rates within horizontal bands, stabilised arrangements, crawling pegs and crawl-like arrangements); floating regimes with market-determined rates (floating and free floating); and other residual managed arrangements.

230. The growing diversity of exchange rate regimes has altered the patterns of international monetary collaboration. The IMF, though, has struggled to respond effectively to these developments, constrained by institutional limitations and political inertia. In the new context, some regimes (such as currency or monetary unions) have emerged as potential alternatives to the traditional concept of monetary sovereignty, which refers to a State maintaining its own currency and conducting an independent monetary policy under the IMF's framework of soft surveillance.

231. A major development in the international monetary system was the creation of the Economic and Monetary Union (EMU) within the EU. One of the key motivations for introducing a single European currency was the desire to create a single market free from exchange rate fluctuations that might hinder the free flow of trade. Under the EMU framework, Euro area Member States have surrendered their sovereign right to issue national currencies and conduct independent monetary policies to the ECB. Their currencies were replaced by the euro, which is managed by the ECB, the first supranational central bank. Since the introduction of the euro, monetary policy has been determined by the ECB (whose primary objective is price stability), while exchange rate policy is defined by the EU Council of Finance Ministers. As the EU and the EMU are not – nor are they entitled to become – IMF members (*see supra*, paragraphs 36 ff.), the ECB has only been granted observer status at selected Executive Board meetings. The EMU and its central bank, as key players in international monetary relations, are subject to IMF surveillance conducted through annual Article IV consultations on euro area policies (*see infra*, paragraphs 256 ff. and 416 ff.).

232. Few other regional monetary unions are currently in place: the Central African Economic and Monetary Community, the West African Economic and Monetary Union and the Eastern Caribbean Currency Union. Notably, a country joins a multilateral currency union expecting economic benefits to outweigh the costs, despite losing control over monetary policy and exchange rates, which may limit its ability to respond to country-specific shocks. For a more detailed discussion of the IMF's relationship with currency unions, *see infra*, paragraphs 256 ff.

233. A second important development in exchange arrangements has been the emergence of currency boards. A primary reason for adopting a currency board is to control inflation and restore international confidence in the domestic currency. Under this regime, a country's monetary authority is required to maintain a fixed exchange rate between the domestic currency and a foreign currency. A defining feature of currency boards is that they operate under a hard peg, backed by foreign currency reserves equivalent to the entire domestic money supply. This strict reserve backing requirement prevents the central bank from creating money at will or providing loans to the government or the banking system, as doing so would undermine the fixed exchange rate and jeopardise the stability of the monetary regime. In a currency board arrangement, conventional monetary policy objectives are therefore subordinated to the exchange rate target. The monetary authority's priority is to maintain sufficient foreign currency reserves to guarantee that all holders of domestic banknotes and coins can convert them into the reserve currency at the fixed rate. The right to exchange domestic currency is typically guaranteed as long as the board holds adequate foreign reserves. However, in extreme circumstances – such as during a financial crisis, when reserves are depleted or the currency peg comes under severe pressure and becomes unsustainable – convertibility may be suspended or abolished. For example, Argentina was forced to abandon its currency board regime in 2002, following a severe recession and a sovereign debt default. In some cases, if the domestic economy becomes sufficiently strong and stable, a country may transition away from the currency board, adopting a more flexible exchange rate system. Notably, Hong Kong operates a currency board arrangement, with its currency pegged to the US dollar.

234. A third development is the (*de facto* or *de jure*) dollarisation or euroisation of countries, meaning that the domestic currency is replaced by the US dollar, the euro or another key currency. *De facto* (or unofficial) dollarisation is a phenomenon of currency substitution, which can be defined as the holding of cash, assets or liabilities denominated in a foreign currency by residents, primarily to preserve the store-of-value function of money. Countries may even forgo their own national currency through *de jure* (official) dollarisation or euroisation, recognising legal tender status to the dominant foreign currency and thus becoming entirely dependent on the monetary policies set by foreign monetary authorities. While the advantages are evident – such as moderate inflation and a fully convertible currency – the disadvantages may be considerable. A dollarised or euroised economy loses its ability to control liquidity and interest rates and thus its capacity to respond to economic cycles. For instance, it is not expected that the US monetary authorities will take economic developments in dollarised economies into account when monetary policy objectives are formulated. Examples include Ecuador, El Salvador and Timor-Leste, which have adopted the US dollar as legal tender, while Montenegro uses the euro despite not being a member of the EU.

§3. The IMF Surveillance Activities

I. Article IV: 'Obligations Regarding Exchange Arrangements'

235. A core responsibility of the IMF is to oversee the international monetary system and monitor developments in the economic and financial policies of its members with a view to identifying potential risks to stability. This process, known as 'surveillance', takes place at bilateral, regional and global (or multilateral) levels and is grounded in Article IV of the IMF Articles of Agreement. This provision, as revised by the 1978 Second Amendment, outlines, on the one hand, the obligations of member countries regarding exchange rate stability; on the other hand, it requires the Fund to conduct consultations with each member and exercise 'firm surveillance' over their exchange rate policies, with a view to ensuring stability within the system. Notably, the Second Amendment also expanded the Fund's mandate beyond exchange rate policies to encompass monetary, fiscal, and financial policies, reflecting the recognition that in the post-Bretton Woods system, such policies had an impact on both domestic and external stability.

236. Article IV, section 1 of the IMF Articles of Agreement sets out the general obligations of member countries regarding their exchange arrangements. It requires member countries to cooperate with the IMF and with one another to ensure orderly exchange arrangements and to promote a 'stable system of exchange rates'. Such cooperation should be conducted within 'a framework that facilitates the exchange of goods, services and capital among countries, and that sustains sound economic growth'. Cooperation is in fact essential for maintaining the orderly conditions necessary for financial and economic stability. The obligation to cooperate applies equally to all IMF members, regardless of whether they are experiencing a balance of payments surplus or deficit. Cooperation also includes a commitment to share relevant information with the Fund and consider its policy advice.

237. Section 1 of Article IV contains four key provisions. The first two are framed in a soft law language and pertain to domestic policies that may influence the exchange rate. States are asked: '(i) to endeavour to direct [their] economic and financial policies toward the objective of fostering orderly economic growth with reasonable price stability'; and '(ii) to seek to promote stability by fostering orderly underlying economic and financial conditions and a monetary system that does not tend to produce erratic disruptions'. In contrast, the other two provisions set legally binding obligations aimed at preserving the operation and stability of the international monetary system. Member countries have to: '(iii) avoid manipulating exchange rates or the international monetary system in order to prevent effective balance of payments adjustment or to gain an unfair competitive advantage over other members'; and (iv) 'follow exchange policies compatible with the undertakings [mentioned above]'.

238. Whereas section 1 of Article IV generally requires the IMF and its members to collaborate, diverging views persist, both within and outside the Fund, on the appropriate policies needed to promote monetary stability. Depending on prevailing economic conditions, the IMF may advise a member to revalue, devalue or float its currency, or may support the maintenance of a fixed exchange rate by providing financial assistance. Economists argue however that any exchange rate regime can be viable, provided it is underpinned by sound economic fundamentals.

239. Section 2(a) of Article IV refers to 'exchange arrangements', meaning the decisions of national monetary authorities regarding the exchange rate regime and policy of their domestic currency. Section 2(b) clarifies that a country may, for example, peg its currency to another currency or to a basket of currencies, such as the SDRs. This provision anticipated, for instance, the creation of arrangements like the so-called European snake in the tunnel and the European Monetary System (EMS). In the EMS, established in 1979, the currencies of most of the members of the European Economic Community were linked to the European Currency Unit (ECU) to prevent large exchange rate fluctuations between them. Beyond these examples, all other categories of exchange arrangements are available to IMF members (*see supra*, paragraphs 229 ff.).

240. Section 3 of Article IV empowers the Fund to exercise firm surveillance over the exchange rate policies of its members and to oversee the international monetary system to ensure its effective operation. This includes monitoring members' compliance with their obligations under Article IV – particularly the duty to foster orderly economic growth and financial stability, and to avoid exchange rate manipulation – through both bilateral and multilateral surveillance. Under *bilateral* surveillance, the Fund exercises firm oversight over each member's exchange rate policies and establishes specific principles that members are required to follow. Through *multilateral* surveillance, the Fund monitors developments in the international monetary system as a whole and assesses global and regional economic trends as well as their implications for systemic stability. However, unlike bilateral surveillance, the Articles of Agreement do not impose specific policy obligations on members in relation to the Fund's multilateral surveillance activities. Bilateral and multilateral surveillance are described in details below.

II. Bilateral Surveillance: The 1977 and 2007 Executive Board Decisions

241. The first decision on *bilateral* surveillance was adopted in 1977, but it was implemented only when the Second Amendment entered into force in 1978.

According to the 'Surveillance over Exchange Rate Policies Decision' (IMF Executive Board Decision No. 5392-(77/63), 29 April 1977), 'surveillance of exchange rate policies shall be adapted to the needs of international adjustment as they develop' and the 'Fund's appraisal of a member's exchange rate shall be based on an evaluation of the developments in the member's balance of payments, including the size and sustainability of capital flows, against the background of its reserve position and its external indebtedness.' Developments in the capital account could, in fact, indicate the need for bilateral consultations between the IMF and a member country. Such consultations were specifically prescribed following: 'the introduction or substantial modification for balance of payments purposes of restrictions on, or incentives for, the inflow or outflow of capital; or the pursuit, for balance of payments purposes, of monetary and other financial policies that provide abnormal encouragement or discouragement to capital flows'. In principle, the 1977 Decision neither favoured nor encouraged capital account liberalisation (*see infra*, paragraphs 282 ff.); however, since then, issues related to capital flows have been systematically incorporated into Article IV bilateral consultations.

242. The 1977 Surveillance Decision was periodically revised to reflect changes in the world economic and financial system. In 2007, the Executive Board decided to replace the 1977 Decision to update guidance to both the Fund and its members regarding their obligations under Article IV. The new 2007 'Decision on Bilateral Surveillance over Members' Policies' (IMF Executive Board Decision No. 13919-(07/51), 15 June 2007) introduced the concept of 'external stability' and clarified that country surveillance should focus on assessing whether national policies promote both domestic and external stability. External stability was, in fact, considered critical to achieve systemic stability and was defined as 'a balance of payments position that does not, and is not likely to, give rise to disruptive exchange rate movements', therefore encompassing developments in both the current account and the capital account. As a result, discussions increasingly focused on monetary, fiscal, financial and exchange rate policies, with an emphasis on assessing potential risks and vulnerabilities.

III. Strengthening Surveillance: From the 2012 Integrated Surveillance Decision to the 2021 Comprehensive Surveillance Review

243. In July 2012, following the completion of a Triennial Surveillance Review, the IMF Executive Board adopted a new decision on 'Bilateral and Multilateral Surveillance', and the 2007 Surveillance Decision was repealed. The so-called Integrated Surveillance Decision (IMF Executive Board Decision No. 15203-(12/72), 18 July 2012) further strengthened IMF monitoring activities.

244. The 2012 Integrated Surveillance Decision provides guidance to members with respect to the conduct of their exchange rate policies. Under Principle A, a member shall avoid manipulating exchange rates or the international monetary system in order to prevent effective balance of payments adjustment or to gain an unfair competitive advantage over other members. Under Principle B, a member should intervene in the exchange market if necessary to counter disorderly conditions, which may be characterized, *inter alia*, by disruptive short-term movements in the exchange rate of its currency. Under Principle C, members should take into account in their intervention policies the interests of other members, including those of the countries in whose currencies they intervene. Under Principle D, a member should avoid exchange rate policies that result in balance of payments instability. In addition, filling an important gap, the Decision recognises that systemic stability is most effectively achieved when a member promotes not only its own balance of payments stability but also its domestic stability. According to these premises, the Decision adds a new Principle E pursuant to which a member should seek to avoid domestic economic and financial policies that give rise to domestic instability. For greater clarity, the term 'external stability' used in the 2007 Decision was replaced with 'balance of payments stability'.

245. By integrating bilateral and multilateral aspects in Article IV consultations, the new surveillance framework enables the Fund to better assess spillovers as well as global and country-level risks to economic and financial stability. However, policies not specified in the Decision can be covered only if they are macro-critical (e.g., social spending can become macro-critical when it significantly affects fiscal sustainability). When the Fund does not have expertise on the issue, staff will analyse the issue in collaboration with external partners but will not be required to offer specific policy advice.

246. More recently, the 2021 Comprehensive Surveillance Review (an exercise that is conducted every five years) identified four surveillance priorities: (i) confronting risks and uncertainties; (ii) pre-empting and mitigating spillovers; (iii) ensuring economic sustainability; and (iv) adopting a more unified approach to policy advice. In addition, the Fund acknowledged that the causes for economic instability are not only linked to poor economic or financial policies and political deficiencies; rather, they are increasingly associated with: trends in demographics, such as aging and declining population growth; technological change, such as digitalisation and automation; inequality in income and opportunities, including gender; socio-political and geopolitical developments, including declining social capital and trust on the government, political polarisation and fragmentation, and cross-country tensions; and, most notably, climate change. While continuing to cover fiscal, monetary, exchange rate and financial issues, IMF bilateral surveillance has evolved to give greater attention to issues of economic sustainability, which are deemed relevant to the extent that the policies designed to address them influence members' balance of payments or domestic stability.

247. The 2022 'Guidance Note for Surveillance under Article IV Consultations' further directs IMF country teams in their consultations with members. It identifies the formal requirements for Article IV reports, which in particular must include: recent developments in the country's economic and financial issues and political and social factors that may impact stability; a clear and candid assessment of the outlook and risks, vulnerabilities and spillovers; a substantive and candid discussion on policies that affect the country's balance of payments and domestic stability as well as those that may significantly impact global stability; policy recommendations; and the national authorities' views. Article IV reports should integrate the DSA (on which *see infra*, paragraphs 330 ff.) and Financial System Stability Assessment (FSSA) (on which *see infra*, paragraph 266). Article IV reports should also discuss governance vulnerabilities and corruption issues when these are deemed macro-critical (on the IMF framework for engagement on governance issues, *see supra*, paragraphs 205 ff.).

248. From a more practical point of view, the 2022 Guidance Note sets forward a list of best practices for Article IV consultations that should permeate all aspects of surveillance work. Consultations should be conducted on the following bases. *Collaboration:* surveillance is based on dialogue with country authorities and other stakeholders as well as on the use of persuasion; while this dialogue should be continuous, it is particularly important to seek country authorities' opinion on issues of their interest before an Article IV consultation; staff can also draw on the expertise of other international institutions. *Candour*: effective dialogue requires candour, both in discussions with country authorities and in staff reports, including about risks. *Even-handedness*: surveillance should be even-handed, whether economies are large or small, advanced or developing, and pay due regard to country circumstances; countries in similar circumstances should be treated in a similar way (LICs, advanced economies, emerging market economies, FCSs, members with Fund-supported programs, members of currency unions). *Data and analysis integrity*: Fund analysis informs policy decisions of members and other stakeholders, making it essential to safeguard staff's expert, independent and technical analysis. *Practicality*: staff advice should take into account country-specific circumstances and implementation capacity. *Consistency of forecasts and risk analysis*: staff reports and discussions should be based on realistic projections and discuss short- and medium-term objectives and policies, and possible policy responses to the most relevant contingencies. *Cross-country experiences and multilateral perspective*: where relevant, Article IV consultations should draw from experiences in other countries and discuss potential or actual spillovers as required by the Integrated Surveillance Decision. *Selectivity and focus*: while the Guidance Note presents the issues in a comprehensive manner, staff should not view it as a prescriptive list; reports should be focused and selective, except for certain issues that must routinely be covered; country teams should exercise judgment in selecting issues for in-depth coverage, and take a risk-based approach, leveraging the expertise of functional departments and other institutions. *Timeliness*: to ensure that Article IV staff reports are up to date when discussed at the Board and published, staff should minimise the time between the end of discussions with authorities and the Board meeting.

249. Today, while surveillance continues to focus on fiscal, monetary, exchange rate, and financial issues – the core areas of the IMF's mandate – it has progressively broadened to include macro-critical issues that influence economic sustainability and stability, such as governance, climate change, and inequality. Progress in understanding the complex and interrelated drivers of economic instability has led the Fund to gradually expand the scope of its surveillance under Article IV. Moreover, the IMF's surveillance framework remains under continuous review, with several policy updates over time aimed at enhancing its relevance, effectiveness, and adaptability to the evolving nature of the global economy.

IV. The Modalities of Bilateral Surveillance

250. According to the 2012 Integrated Surveillance Decision and the 2022 Guidance Note, bilateral and multilateral surveillance are mutually supportive and reinforcing, and should be operationally integrated. These two documents establish modalities that broadly apply to policy discussions in both surveillance contexts, with the aim of ensuring coherence and consistency across the Fund's monitoring activities.

251. In this context, *bilateral* surveillance refers to the IMF's regular and structured engagement with each member country through comprehensive consultations. These are known as 'Article IV consultations', as they are conducted under Article IV of the IMF Articles of Agreement. This provision mandates the IMF to assess members' economic policies and performance on a regular basis, with the aim of evaluating their implications for both domestic stability and the broader international monetary system.

252. Article IV consultations are generally expected to take place annually, and excessive delays should be avoided. The process starts with the preparation of a Policy Note, an internal IMF document that outlines all the key issues and policy advice staff intend to discuss during the mission. An IMF mission is then sent to the member country to meet with government and central bank officials, as well as representatives of the private sector, civil society organisations and other stakeholders, and to collect economic and financial data. Discussions are intended to assist the country in making policy choices through an open dialogue built on mutual trust. Assessment and advice are formulated paying due regard to the country's specific circumstances and its implementation capacity. The Fund is obliged to respect the country's 'domestic social and political policies' (Article IV, section 3(b)). Spillovers, key linkages among members, and the broader multilateral framework are duly taken into account. At the end of the mission, a staff report is prepared and submitted to the Executive Board for discussion. During the Board meeting, Executive Directors review the member's policies, while IMF staff answer questions and provide clarifications. The meeting serves as a formal surveillance exercise (peer review) and concludes the Article IV consultation process. The Executive Directors' assessment is summarised in the Chairman's Summing Up, which is subsequently transmitted to the country's government. The assessments, which are non-binding, may range from favourable to neutral, critical or strongly critical. If the member country agrees, a press release providing background and a summary of the Board discussion is published, either with or without the full Article IV Report.

253. Today, bilateral surveillance consultations often have limited impact on member countries (especially on the larger ones) for the simple reason that Article IV recommendations have a soft law nature and that non-compliance carries no far-reaching consequences. During consultations, only the weight of arguments and, to a certain extent, peer pressure play a role in persuading a country to bring its economic policy more in line with the IMF's conclusions. Effective surveillance by the IMF thus depends crucially on the willingness of its members to follow the Fund's advice. To make surveillance more effective, members could be asked to respond within a specific timeframe to Article IV assessments. In cases where a member's policies appear to diverge from the Fund's advice, the member should receive progressively stronger warnings to align its policies with the recommended course. However, under the current interpretation of Article IV, it is not possible for the Fund to give legally binding directives or to impose sanctions.

V. Multilateral Surveillance: Overseeing Global and Regional Economic Trends

254. The scope of *multilateral* surveillance over the international monetary system is defined by Article IV, section 3(a). In conducting multilateral surveillance, the Fund is called to focus on issues that could hinder the effective operation of the international monetary system. According to the 2012 Integrated Surveillance Decision, members are encouraged to adopt policies that promote their own domestic and external stability, while also considering the potential spillover effects of their policies on the global economy. In addition, member countries have a procedural obligation to consult with the Fund and to provide relevant data for multilateral surveillance.

255. The key instruments of multilateral surveillance are the World Economic Outlook (WEO), the Global Financial Stability Report (GFSR), the Fiscal Monitor, the External Sector Report, the Regional Economic Reports and the Global Policy Agenda. These periodic reports analyse regional and global economic trends as well as the impact of members' policies on neighbouring countries and the global economy. The WEO is a semi-annual IMF publication that discusses the economic and monetary developments within the global framework; members are expected to tailor their policies in accordance with its findings. The GFSR addresses the global financial system and financial markets; it analyses market conditions and highlights systemic issues that could pose a risk to financial stability. The Fiscal Monitor surveys and analyses the latest public finance developments, updates medium-term fiscal projections and assesses policies to put public finances on a sustainable footing. The External Sector Report assesses the external position of twenty-nine systemically large economies plus the Euro area. The Regional Economic Reports provide an analysis of the economic trends across the five major regions of the world. The Global Policy Agenda, informed by the other multilateral surveillance reports, outlines the IMF's future policy priorities and recommendations to its members.

VI. Surveillance over Currency Unions

256. The IMF also exercises surveillance over currency unions, which – while unable to join the IMF due to its country-based membership structure (*see supra*, paragraphs 36 ff.) – influence the international monetary system through their policies. In particular, the introduction of the euro in 1999 prompted the Executive Board to establish new protocols to conduct surveillance over Euro area members within the framework of Article IV bilateral consultations. In 2002, the Executive Board clarified that discussions with EMU institutions were to be held separately from those with individual Euro area countries. For further details on IMF surveillance over the Euro area, *see infra*, paragraphs 416 ff. The most recent document on the topic is the 2022 Guidance Note for Surveillance Under Article IV Consultations, which includes an annex on consultations with members of currency unions.

257. The IMF has also established a framework for policy discussions with the other existing currency unions: the Eastern Caribbean Currency Union, the Central African Economic and Monetary Community and the West African Economic and Monetary Union. Effective surveillance in these contexts involves engaging with regional institutions responsible for the exchange rate and other union-level policies, providing essential context for bilateral discussions with individual members. An annual staff report summarising discussions with regional institutions is prepared and subsequently reviewed in an Executive Board discussion. These discussions are considered a key part of the Article IV consultations with individual Member States, as they incorporate both country-level and union-wide surveillance. IMF staff should evaluate policies at both the currency union and individual member levels, considering how developments at these levels interact with one another and with the global economy.

258. According to the 2012 Integrated Surveillance Decision (*see supra*, paragraphs 244 ff.) 'members of currency unions remain subject to all of their obligations under Article IV, Section 1 and, accordingly, each member is accountable for those policies that are conducted by union-level institutions on its behalf'. This provision means that members of currency unions are held accountable for monetary policies – such as decisions on interest rates and liquidity management – even when these policies are formulated at the supranational level. However, the decision also contains a caveat: 'Because, in a currency union, exchange rate policies are implemented at the level of the union, the principles for the guidance of members' exchange rate policies and the associated indicators set out [in the paragraphs of this Decision concerning exchange rates management policies] only apply at the level of the currency union.'

VII. The Prohibition of Exchange Rate Manipulation

259. An exception to the soft law nature of IMF Article IV is the obligation to avoid exchange rate manipulation. Such manipulation was one of the economic distortions that characterised the Great Depression during the interwar period. At the conclusion of the Bretton Woods conference in 1944, Henry Morgenthau, then US Secretary of the Treasury and president of the conference, opened his closing address by stating that the conference had successfully developed 'methods which would do away with the economic evils – the competitive currency devaluations and destructive impediments to trade – which preceded the present war'. In underlining the role such actions might have played in the lead-up to World War II, Morgenthau advocated for the inclusion of specific provisions on the issue. As a result, Article I of the IMF Articles lists among the Fund's purposes the objective of avoiding competitive exchange rate depreciation. Additionally, the original text of Article IV stipulated that members 'undertake to collaborate with the Fund … to avoid competitive exchange alterations'. Over time, amendments have refined this language into a more definitive, albeit conditional, binding provision: each member 'shall avoid manipulating exchange rates or the international monetary system in order to prevent effective balance of payments adjustment or to gain an unfair competitive advantage over other members' (Article IV, section 1 (iii)). However, subsequent interpretations by the Executive Board have progressively softened the scope of this obligation.

260. In fact, according to the 2012 Integrated Surveillance Decision and its Annex, 'a member will only be considered to be manipulating exchange rates in order to gain an unfair competitive advantage over other members if the Fund determines both that: (A) the member is engaged in these policies for the purpose of securing fundamental exchange rate misalignment in the form of an undervalued exchange rate and (B) the purpose of securing such misalignment is to increase net exports'. The Fund's legal department clarified that the phrase 'in order to' implies the determination of intent. Two elements must therefore be demonstrated: there must be both an intention to manipulate exchange rates to boost exports and a causal link between the relevant policies and the level of the exchange rate. The Fund may request an explanation of the member's policies, but denial of manipulation appears to be enough to avoid a negative finding: 'Any representation made by the member regarding the purpose of its policies will be given the benefit of any reasonable doubt.' In the final analysis, intent is virtually impossible to prove unless statements or documents clearly show that the manipulation was deliberate.

261. The Fund's reluctance to address exchange rate manipulation stands in stark contrast to repeated demands from Member States to address this issue. In 2013, the matter featured on the G-20 agenda but was downplayed by the IMF Managing Director. In 2014, the US administration acknowledged that 'recent developments in the Renminbi exchange rate would raise particularly serious concern', yet the Treasury concluded that no major US trading partner could be considered a currency manipulator under US law. The following year, in 2015, the IMF Executive Board determined that the renminbi met the criteria for inclusion in the SDR basket (*see infra*, paragraph 294). In the United States, currency manipulation continues to feature on the agenda of Congress, but no proposed legislation has been enacted. Attempts to classify manipulation as a trade-distorting practice such as dumping or subsidies have consistently run up against practical and legal obstacles.

VIII. The Financial Sector Assessment Programme

262. Since the 1978 Second Amendment, one of the principal objectives of the Fund has become 'the continuing development of the orderly underlying conditions that are necessary for *financial* and economic stability' [emphasis added] (Article IV, section 1). The IMF justifies its mandate over financial stability on the grounds that it is a key determining factor of members' domestic and external stability. However, it was not until 1999 that the IMF established the Financial Sector Assessment Program (FSAP) to assess the stability and soundness of members' financial sectors, identify vulnerabilities, and promote financial sector development and reforms.

263. From 1999 until the global financial crisis, FSAPs were conducted regularly as part of the IMF's efforts to assess the stability and resilience of the financial systems in its member countries. However, they were an instrument of technical assistance, covered by IMF Article V, section 2(b) and were therefore of a 'voluntary' nature. Despite the valuable insights provided by these assessments, the global financial crisis of 2007–2008 revealed the limitations of the FSAP framework. In particular, the 2008 US sub-prime mortgage crisis raised concerns about the Fund's capacity to identify and predict systemic risks in financial markets, and to issue timely warnings of the impending global financial and economic crisis. The Fund's role prior to the crisis was subject to close scrutiny by various commentators and by the IEO (*see supra*, paragraphs 95 ff.), which, in its 2011 evaluation report on 'IMF Performance in the Run-Up to the Financial and Economic Crisis' assessed the performance of the staff that had analysed market developments and conducted surveillance tasks in the period 2004–2007. Although the report was prepared when the crisis was not over yet, it describes how the staff failed to provide 'clear warnings about the risks and vulnerabilities associated with the impending crisis before its outbreak'. The IEO explicitly referenced Article IV reports on the United States, the jurisdiction where the financial crisis originated. The IEO underlined that, in these Article IV reports, the staff praised sophisticated financial innovations in the housing market, downplayed the risks associated with sub-prime securitisation, and considered default risks in financial markets as negligible. In a response to the IEO, staff complained that important impediments had obstructed its work, pointing to the fact that the United States had refused to provide data to the IMF staff in the context of FSAP. To address these concerns, the Fund undertook a review of the effectiveness of its surveillance process. The exercise highlighted that surveillance was overly fragmented and that it suffered from weaknesses and loopholes requiring prompt attention.

264. In 2010, the IMF Executive Board made FSAPs a mandatory component of surveillance under Article IV for jurisdictions with financial sectors deemed by the Fund to be systemically important. Shortly after, the 2012 Integrated Surveillance Decision formally incorporated macro-financial analysis into Article IV surveillance (*see supra*, paragraphs 235 ff.). In 2021, the Executive Board concluded the quinquennial Review of the FSAP, reaffirming that assessments are mandatory for countries with a systemically important financial sector, while remaining voluntary for all other members.

265. FSAPs provide a comprehensive evaluation of a country's financial sector stability and soundness, assess its contribution to economic growth and development, and offer policy advice on how to reduce financial vulnerabilities. In developing and emerging market economies, FSAPs are jointly conducted by the Fund and the World Bank, and include two elements: a financial stability assessment (under the IMF's responsibility) and a financial development assessment (under the World Bank's responsibility). In advanced economies, FSAPs are conducted by the IMF alone.

266. Financial sector assessments are expected to occur every five or ten years, depending on a jurisdiction's systemic relevance in transmitting shocks across borders. Among the forty-seven mandated to undergo FSAP assessments, the Euro area, the United States, China and thirty other countries are reviewed every five years, while emerging market economies are assessed every ten years. FSAPs conclude with the preparation of a FSSA, which is discussed at the IMF Executive Board together with the country's Article IV report. FSSAs comprise an evaluation of three key components of a country's financial sector: the source, probability, and potential impact of the main risks to macro-financial stability in the near-term (and, by extension, the risk of contagion); the country's financial stability policy framework; and the authorities' capacity to manage and resolve a financial crisis should the risks materialise. Notably, though, overseeing the stability of financial markets remains a primary responsibility of national supervisory authorities. The publication of FSSAs is presumed but voluntary, with many being made public and highly regarded by national authorities. Despite the IMF FSSAs providing valuable insights into financial system vulnerabilities, their impact is often limited by the non-binding nature of their recommendations and by the voluntary nature of follow-up actions for most members. According to many, the absence of an international financial authority with binding oversight of cross-border financial markets remains a significant gap in the global financial architecture.

§4. Transparency at the IMF

267. Transparency of economic and fiscal data is critical for informed and sound decision-making and for strengthening accountability of policymakers. The IMF promotes greater transparency among its member countries by encouraging the publication of documents, especially those related to surveillance activities and IMF-supported programmes.

268. As for the IMF's surveillance, at the conclusion of Article IV consultations the vast majority of Member States consent to the publication of the country report and a press release. Press releases summarise the Executive Board's discussions with a member country on its macroeconomic and financial situation and present the Board's overall assessment. In attracting foreign capital and investment, countries may benefit from a widely disclosed favourable conclusion of Article IV consultations, as it signals to investors that the country's economic and financial policies are in alignment with the IMF's recommendations and international standards (*see* below).

269. As for IMF-supported programmes, members may decide to release to the public Letters of Intent and similar documents (on which *see supra*, paragraphs 180 ff.). These documents, issued by a government requesting balance of payments support, describe policy intentions. While publication is voluntary, it is generally expected and typically proceeds on a non-objection basis from the member. Country documents are available on the Fund's website.

270. The IMF has further promoted country data transparency by establishing standards for the voluntary dissemination of economic and financial data. Since its launch in 1996, the IMF Data Standards Initiatives have achieved near-universal participation among member countries. The framework is structured into three tiers – the Enhanced General Data Dissemination System, the Special Data Dissemination Standard (SDDS) and the SDDS Plus – each with progressively stricter requirements for data dissemination based on countries' capacity.

271. Another salient development in the Fund's contribution to transparency is the Standards and Codes Initiative. In this context, the IMF – in collaboration with the World Bank – assesses members' compliance with international transparency standards across twelve policy areas deemed essential for the operational work of the Bretton Woods institutions. These standards cover: accounting; auditing; anti-money laundering and combating the financing of terrorism; banking supervision; corporate governance; data dissemination; fiscal transparency; insolvency and creditor rights; insurance supervision; monetary and financial policy transparency; payments systems; and securities regulation. In a number of these areas, the IMF assesses the implementation of standards developed by other institutions such as the Basel Committee on Banking Supervision, the International Organization of Securities Commissions, the International Association of Insurance Supervisors, or the OECD. Reports on the Observance of Standards and Codes (ROSCs) summarise the extent to which countries observe internationally recognised standards and codes. They are prepared and published at the request of the member country and are published on the IMF's website. Compliance with international transparency standards may be considered during Article IV consultations.

272. For its part, the Fund has taken significant steps to improve transparency on its policies, decision-making processes and the advice it offers to member countries. In November 2024, the IMF's Executive Board concluded a comprehensive review of its Transparency and Open Archives Policies, introducing reforms aimed at expediting the publication of Board documents and communications. This notwithstanding, concerns persist among NGOs and civil society organisations about the IMF's lack of transparency.

§5. CURRENCY CONVERTIBILITY

I. Current Account Convertibility and Exchange Restrictions

273. Currency convertibility refers to the ability to convert domestic currency into foreign currencies at a given exchange rate, allowing their use for foreign commercial transactions. A distinction is made between current account convertibility, which entails unrestricted payments and transfers for current transactions, and capital account convertibility, which entails unrestricted inflows and outflows of capital.

274. Under the IMF legal framework, there is a clear asymmetry in the regulation of current international payments and capital movements. In fact, the convertibility obligation under Article VIII only applies to current international transactions. Article XXX(d) defines the scope of 'current transactions': payments for current transactions are not intended for the transfer of capital and include, *inter alia*, all payments due in connection with foreign trade, other current business (including services), and normal short-term banking and credit facilities.

275. Under Article I, the IMF is authorised to facilitate the expansion and balanced growth of international trade and to assist in the elimination of foreign exchange restrictions that may hamper its growth. To this end, members are expected to uphold – after a transitional period – the obligations set forth in IMF Article VIII, sections 2, 3 and 4. By doing so, members commit not to impose restrictions on the making of payments and transfers for current international transactions and not to engage in discriminatory currency arrangements or multiple currency practices without the IMF's approval. For instance, the IMF has considered the following types of measures as constituting prohibited exchange restrictions: quantitative limits on the availability of foreign exchange for certain current international transactions (such as the imposition of annual allowances on cross-border education and medical expenses); the creation of a foreign exchange budget to set a limit on the amount of foreign exchange available for specific categories of authorised imports; and restrictions on the repatriation of investment income by non-residents.

276. The IMF's founding fathers recognised, however, that – subject to adequate safeguards to protect what was believed to be the general interest of the international community – exchange restrictions could be a useful tool to temporarily address balance of payments problems. Therefore, even though current account convertibility lies at the heart of the IMF Articles of Agreement, the Fund has maintained an approach of limited tolerance towards exchange restrictions. Consequently, the following exceptions to the liberalisation of current international payments and transfers apply.

277. First, under IMF Article XIV, member countries are allowed a transitional period before accepting the obligations on currency convertibility. During this period, they are permitted to 'maintain and adapt to changing circumstances' those currency restrictions that were already in force at the time they joined the IMF.

IMF's members must expressly renounce Article XIV status for IMF Article VIII to apply. Currently, only very few countries have yet to accept the obligations arising from Article VIII (at the beginning of 2025: Afghanistan, Albania, Angola, Bhutan, Bosnia and Herzegovina, Burundi, Eritrea, Ethiopia, Iraq, Liberia, Maldives, Mozambique, Myanmar, Nigeria, Sao Tomé and Principe, Somalia, South Sudan, Syria, Turkmenistan and Tuvalu).

278. Second, under specific circumstances, the Fund may approve the introduction of exchange restrictions, which as a general principle remain prohibited. IMF Article VIII, section 2(a) allows member countries to introduce such restrictions in derogation of the current account convertibility rule, but only with the Fund's approval. The provision, however, does not specify the exact circumstances that would justify the introduction of such restrictions, nor does it establish exhaustive criteria for approval. Instead, the determination of these circumstances is left to the discretion of the Executive Board, which already in the 1950–1960s adopted a series of decisions on the matter that continue to apply today. Notably, Executive Board Decision No. 1034-(60/27) states that: 'if members, for balance of payments reasons, propose to maintain or introduce measures which require approval under Article VIII, the Fund will grant approval only where it is satisfied that the measures are necessary and that their use will be temporary while the member is seeking to eliminate the need for them'. A member country must obtain the Fund's approval prior to introducing exchange restrictions. The request must be made in writing and properly justified. If the criteria mentioned above are met, the Executive Board grants its approval for a limited period (usually until the completion of the next Article IV consultation or, if the country has a loan arrangement in place, until the next programme review). Importantly, the Decision clarifies that the use of exchange restrictions for reasons other than balance of payments issues 'should be avoided to the greatest possible extent'. Nonetheless, the IMF has always tolerated the introduction of exchange restrictions on national and international security grounds.

279. The third exception concerns the introduction of exchange restrictions for essential national or international security reasons. Under the original IMF Articles, no relevance was given to the circumstances in which restrictions were imposed: Article VIII did not even make explicit reference to balance of payments problems. However, the issue of *security restrictions* assumed centre stage already during the early years of the Fund, particularly with the onset of the Cold War. In 1952, supported by the United States, the IMF Executive Board adopted Decision No. 144-(52/51), which allows the introduction of exchange restrictions for national or international security reasons. This Decision, which has never been updated since its adoption, outlines the following procedure. A Member State must notify the Fund in advance of its intention to impose security restrictions. Once the notification is received, it is immediately forwarded to the IMF Executive Board. If the Board does not reply within thirty days, the Member State 'may assume that the Fund has no objection to the imposition of the restrictions', which will take effect retroactively from the date of the notification. However, in the unlikely case that the Executive Board is called to a vote, an ordinary majority would be sufficient to block the approval of security restrictions.

280. The IMF has consistently tolerated security-related restrictions, refraining from challenging any justification provided by the notifying State. This inherently passive stance – the Fund's (expected) tacit approval – has been understood as reflecting 'a general policy of the Fund not to object to the imposition of exchange restrictions'. Members of the Fund can rely on Decision No. 144-(52/51), especially when required to impose economic sanctions by a UN Security Council resolution adopted pursuant to Chapter VII of the Charter of San Francisco. Security restrictions typically entail the freezing of assets and local bank accounts opened by natural and legal persons of the targeted country, in either domestic or foreign currency. In such cases, deposits are made inconvertible, and their transfer abroad is prohibited, including for the purpose of making payments or transfers for current international transactions. More recently, IMF members have invoked the security exception to introduce restrictions targeting individuals or entities linked to terrorism (for instance, not only to implement UN Security Council resolution 1373 (2001) on the Prevention and Suppression of Terrorism Financing but also in the context of their unilateral sanctions policies). Notably, the Fund has never formally distinguished between these two types of restrictions: (a) those imposed by its members to comply with the obligations arising from resolutions adopted by the UN Security Council under Chapter VII of the UN Charter ('multilateral security restrictions'); and (b) those imposed by a State on its own initiative as part of its economic sanctions policy ('unilateral security restrictions'). More precisely, the Fund has refrained from establishing specific criteria to assess the legitimacy of unilateral restrictions, shielding itself behind the fact that it is not the proper forum for the discussion of members' foreign policy and national security strategies (thus relying on the so-called inappropriate forum theory).

281. Adopting or maintaining exchange restrictions and multiple currency practices in conflict with the IMF Articles may result in three distinct sets of consequences. (a) One important consequence, particularly for private contracts, derives from Article VIII, section 2(b) which stipulates the unenforceability of 'exchange contracts which involve the currency of any member and which are contrary to the exchange control regulations of that member maintained or imposed consistently with this Agreement'. This provision requires that members refrain from enforcing exchange contracts that violate exchange restrictions authorised by the Fund, through judicial or administrative authorities. The interpretation of 'exchange contract' can be controversial. A broad interpretation might include all contracts involving international payments or transfers, as well as domestic contracts payable in foreign exchange – such as sales, loans, and deposits. The Fund may offer guidance on the consistency of exchange control regulations with the Articles of Agreement. (b) Another consequence arises for countries under a Fund-supported programme, as these typically include a standard performance criterion stipulating that tranche disbursements may be withheld if a member country imposes or intensifies exchange restrictions, unless a waiver is granted (for more on performance criteria and waivers, *see supra*, paragraphs 200 ff). (c) Lastly, according to Article XXVI, section 2(a), a member that breaches its obligations to the IMF may be declared ineligible to use the Fund's general resources, and its voting rights may be suspended (*see supra*, paragraph 121).

II. Capital Account Liberalisation and Capital Flow Management Measures

282. Capital account liberalisation should be clearly distinguished from current account liberalisation. Notably, while current account liberalisation is one of the core objectives of the IMF, as reflected in IMF Article I, capital account liberalisation is not listed among the purposes of the Fund.

283. At the Bretton Woods Conference, negotiators held differing views on the desirability of capital account liberalisation. John Maynard Keynes argued that, while the liberalisation of current account transactions should be pursued once international conditions had sufficiently stabilised, countries should retain the ability to protect themselves from destabilising short-term capital flows, given the extent to which these flows had contributed to the instability of the pre-war monetary system. On the contrary, Harry Dexter White believed that capital controls were generally unnecessary under normal circumstances. A compromise was ultimately reached recognising that countries could be allowed to impose and enforce controls to prevent speculative capital movements from disrupting normal trade relations. This position is reflected in Article VI, section 3 which recognises the right of member countries to determine, at their own discretion, whether controls are 'necessary' to regulate international capital flows: 'Members may exercise such controls as are necessary to regulate international capital movements, but no member may exercise these controls in a manner which will restrict payments for current transactions or which will unduly delay transfers of funds in settlement of commitments.' At the same time, pursuant to Article VI, section 1(a), the Fund is entitled to request that a country introduce controls to prevent capital flight. Moreover, when receiving financial assistance, members are not entitled to use the Fund's general resources to meet large or sustained outflows of capital.

284. In its practice, though, the Fund has never insisted that its members introduce capital controls. On the contrary, it has gradually embraced capital account liberalisation, exerting pressure through conditionality, technical assistance and surveillance. The same approach was adopted by other international organisations. For instance, in 1961, the OECD adopted its 'Code of Liberalisation of Capital Movements' aimed at progressively removing barriers to capital movements while providing flexibility to address situations of economic and financial instability. During the 1960s, many industrialised countries implemented policies ensuring the free movement of capital.

285. However, since capital account liberalisation is not within the Fund's mandate, introducing a general obligation to gradually liberalise capital movements – subject to appropriate safeguard provisions – would require an amendment to the

IMF Articles. In 1997 and 1998, proposals were made to amend the IMF Articles to include provisions on liberalisation of capital movements, but they were ultimately set aside. While many observers regard the unimpeded flow of private capital as a crucial element of an efficient international monetary system, the amendment proposal was never put to a vote, largely due to opposition from developing countries.

286. Currency crises in the 1990s and the global financial crisis of 2007–2008 made many IMF members increasingly reluctant to further pursue capital account liberalisation. A broad consensus emerged on the fact that liberalising capital movements can only succeed when certain prerequisites are in place. It should be pursued gradually and accompanied by appropriate macroeconomic, exchange rate and financial sector policies. In 2010, the Fund began to reconsider its longstanding pro-capital liberalisation stance, acknowledging that capital controls can help mitigate the harmful effects of large and volatile capital inflows. In 2011, the Fund went further, recognising that controls on capital outflows may also be justified in times of crisis or in near-crisis conditions, but only as a temporary complement to more fundamental policy adjustments.

287. In 2012, the IMF adopted a new 'Institutional View on the Liberalisation and Management of Capital Flows', without altering members' rights and obligations under the Articles. The Fund's approach seeks to manage capital flows in a way that allows recipient countries to benefit from financial globalisation while also minimising the risks associated with surges of inflows or sudden outflows. The Institutional View recognises that, while capital flows can bring substantial benefits for countries, they also carry risks. Therefore, the liberalisation of capital flows should be carefully planned, timed and sequenced. Moreover, when countries face rapid surges of capital inflows or disruptive outflows, they may resort to capital flow management measures (CFMs). These measures, however, should not be used as a substitute for warranted macroeconomic adjustments.

288. In 2013, the Fund adopted a Guidance Note on the liberalisation and management of capital flows providing guidance to staff on how to apply the Fund's Institutional View. For instance, staff advice should not assume that full liberalisation is an appropriate goal for all countries at all times. Instead, the appropriate degree of liberalisation should be tailored to the country's specific circumstances and overall economic objectives. Additionally, staff may consider a temporary reintroduction of CFMs under certain circumstances, provided that these measures are consistent with a broader strategy of capital flow liberalisation.

289. In 2016, the Executive Board acknowledged that the capital flow environment had changed significantly since the adoption of the Institutional View and that the challenge had shifted from managing capital inflow surges to dealing with capital flow reversals. To manage these reversals, since 2012, countries have primarily relied on macroeconomic policies, reserving CFMs for crisis or near-crisis situations, consistently with the Institutional View. A few countries also employed macroprudential measures to mitigate financial risks associated with capital outflows.

Overall, the trend towards greater capital account openness had persisted. Based on a review of countries' experiences, the Executive Board concluded that the Institutional View remained relevant.

290. In 2022, the Executive Board concluded a second review of the Institutional View, drawing on the findings of the 2020 IEO report on 'IMF Advice on Capital Flows' as well as on developments in theoretical and empirical research. The review reaffirmed the core principles of the Institutional View: namely, that capital flows can bring substantial benefits for countries, and that CFMs — while potentially useful in certain situations — should not replace necessary macroeconomic adjustments. At the same time, the review introduced two notable changes to existing policies. First, the 2022 review broadened the range of policy options available to authorities by allowing the pre-emptive use of CFMs, which also serve as macroprudential tools, to manage capital inflows. This can be done when existing vulnerabilities in the financial system pose risks to economic and financial stability, even if there is no immediate surge in inflows. Second, Directors agreed to grant special treatment to certain categories of CFMs. While staff must assess the appropriateness of macro-critical CFMs against the Institutional View criteria, four specific categories will now be exempt from this test due to their particular nature: measures introduced solely for national or international security reasons; certain measures adopted pursuant to internationally agreed prudential frameworks (including reciprocity agreements); anti-money laundering and counter-financing of terrorism measures, implemented consistently with international standards; and measures arising from certain international cooperation standards aimed at preventing tax avoidance or evasion. Directors agreed, in fact, that the Institutional View is not the appropriate framework to assess the suitability of these measures, while noting that they should nonetheless be categorised as CFMs. These revisions are primarily designed to prevent unintended conflicts from arising between the Institutional View and these types of measures.

III. Convertibility of Foreign-Held Balances or 'Official Convertibility'

291. Article VIII, section 4 establishes certain obligations with respect to the convertibility of officially held balances of currencies: an IMF member is required to buy back the holding of its currency detained by another member if so requested and if the balances have been recently acquired as a result of current international transactions, or if conversion is needed for making payments related to current international transactions. 'Official convertibility' refers to transactions between central banks or monetary authorities.

292. Developments in monetary practice have rendered Article VIII, section 4 largely obsolete. This is mainly due to the provision's close connection to the par value system that collapsed in the early 1970s. Nevertheless, section 4 remains part of the IMF Articles of Agreement, and if a member were formally requested to convert balances of its currency, it would in principle breach its obligations by refusing conversion. In practice, however, excess holdings of foreign currencies are sold on the currency market. The Report on the Second Amendment suggests that no obligation to convert should be enforced so long as exchange markets normally serve this function. The development of interbank foreign exchange markets has in effect deprived section 4 of any operational relevance.

§6. Special Drawing Rights

I. The Origins of SDRs

293. The 1969 Amendment to the IMF Articles introduced the possibility of supplementing member countries' monetary reserves with SDRs to keep pace with the growth of international trade under the par value system. The economic rationale behind the creation of the SDRs was that, as the volume of global trade increased, countries would need a larger stock of international reserves to settle external transactions and maintain exchange rate stability. Relying solely on an increase in the speed at which existing reserves circulate through the system – that is, on higher money velocity – was considered insufficient and potentially destabilising. Additional reserves could be created in two ways: by borrowing (e.g., from official bilateral creditors or issuing sovereign bonds) or by expanding the money supply (in this case, without incurring debt). SDRs fall within this latter option as they are supplementary international reserve assets that can be issued by the IMF whenever a long-term global need so requires. SDRs can also be considered a form of 'fiat money' allocated to IMF members and backed by members' obligations under the IMF Articles of Agreement. Moreover, the SDR is the IMF unit of account.

294. Originally, the value of the SDR was pegged to gold. However, after the collapse of the par value system, it was decided to define the SDR's value on the basis of a basket of major international currencies. The composition of this basket is reviewed by the IMF Executive Board every five years to reflect changes in the relative importance of currencies in the international trade and financial system. After the introduction of the euro on 1 January 1999, and until September 2016, the SDR basket consisted of four currencies: the US dollar, the Japanese yen, the pound sterling and the euro. In October 2016, the Chinese renminbi was added to the SDR basket. Each currency in the SDR basket carries a specific weighted, determined by its relative importance in international trade and financial markets. The value of the SDR is determined daily, based on market exchange rates. The SDR value in terms of the US dollar is published on the IMF's website.

295. Pursuant to Article XVIII, section 1 of the IMF Articles, the issuance of SDRs should meet a 'long-term global need to supplement existing reserve assets in a manner that will promote the attainment of the IMF's purposes and avoid economic stagnation and deflation, as well as excess demand and inflation in the world'. The decision to create SDRs is taken by the IMF Board of Governors with a majority of 85% of the total voting power. The same majority is required to cancel SDRs, although this has never occurred.

II. General and Equity SDRs Allocations to IMF Members

296. Once created, SDRs are allocated to members participating in the SDR Department (currently, all 191 IMF members) in proportion to their respective quotas (as established by Article XV, section 1 and Article XVIII). Only members participating in the SDRs Department are entitled to receive SDRs allocations and engage in SDR-related transactions. An allocation provides each member with a costless and unconditional international reserve asset that, at the outset, neither generates nor incurs interest. However, an interest mechanism applies once SDRs are distributed among members: members holding SDR balances in excess of their cumulative allocations earn interest on the surplus, while those whose holdings fall below their allocation are required to pay interest on the deficit.

297. The IMF can also empower 'official' organisations to hold SDRs (like multilateral development banks), including institutions performing the functions of a central bank for more than one IMF member (like the ECB and the Eastern Caribbean Central Bank). 'Prescribed holders' can acquire and use SDRs in exchange for an equivalent amount of a monetary asset (other than gold) in transactions and operations with other prescribed holders or with an IMF member. Prescribed holders, though, cannot receive direct allocations from the IMF.

298. Despite their prominent features, the IMF has seldom exercised the power to issue SDRs, and their role to date has been limited. SDRs have been distributed to IMF members only four times before 2021. The first two allocations were respectively made in the 1970–1972 period (while the par value system was still in operation) and in the 1979–1981 period (after the entry into force of the 1978 Second Amendment to the IMF Articles). The third (special) and fourth (general) SDR allocations were eventually approved in 2009, after having been under consideration since the mid-1990s.

299. At the 1994 IMF-WB annual meeting, the IMF Managing Director Michel Camdessus proposed a new general allocation of 36 billion SDRs to be approved together with a special allocation targeted at the forty developing countries and economies in transition that had joined the Fund after 1981. Since the SDR allocation in the early 1980s, the Fund's membership had in fact expanded by more than one-fifth, also to include countries from the former Soviet Union. However, the IMF Articles did not – and continue not to – permit selective allocations, not even for countries that acquired membership at a later stage and thus did not benefit from earlier allocations. The sole permissible reason for a new SDR allocation is to support the smooth operation of the international monetary system. Neither the needs of individual members and groups of members, nor considerations of equitable distribution between existing and new members, may be taken into account. The only way to overcome the legal requirement that SDRs be distributed in proportion to quotas would be through an amendment of the IMF Articles of Agreement. A proposal to this effect was indeed put forward in 1997, but it failed to secure the required majority of three-fifths of IMF members representing at least 85% of the total voting power.

300. In 2008, in the aftermath of the global financial crisis, the Fund reconsidered the case for a new SDR allocation. It was argued that, since membership in the Fund had further expanded, a simultaneous selective and corrective allocation in favour of those members that had never received SDRs was necessary. At long last, the 1997 Amendment proposal obtained the required qualified majority and was adopted. The Fourth Amendment to the IMF Articles entered into force in August 2009, allowing a 'Special One-Time Allocation' of 21.5 billion SDRs (about USD 33 billion), which benefited particularly the thirty-eight IMF members that had never received any SDR allocation. The amendment was considered not to undermine the principle that allocations are only permitted when there is a long-term global need that justifies them. Soon afterwards, the IMF Board of Governors approved a new issuance of 161.2 billion SDRs, equivalent to USD 250 billion. Together, the 2009 general and special allocations raised the total of cumulative SDRs to 204.1 billion.

301. In March 2020, at the onset of the COVID-19 pandemic, civil society organisations began advocating for a new SDR allocation equivalent to USD 3 trillion, to help developing countries withstand the crisis. In April 2021, however, the IMFC recommended a general SDR allocation of only 456.5 billion SDRs, equivalent to USD 650 billion. This amount was mainly determined by political considerations. Notably, according to the 1968 Special Drawing Right Act, the US government is authorised to vote in favour of SDR allocations up to a certain ceiling, which was set at USD 680 billion (at the SDR/USD exchange rate of the time). Any allocation beyond this threshold requires explicit approval from the US Congress to authorise by law the Chair of the US Federal Reserve to vote in favour of the SDR allocation at the IMF Board of Governors. Eventually, in August 2021, after securing US support, the IMF Board of Governors approved the new SDRs issuance. The fourth SDR allocation is the largest in history, yet it was strongly criticised for being too late, too little, and too unequal (high-income countries received 67% of the allocation, while low-income countries received only 3.2% of the allocation).

302. In IMF history, some countries have been barred from accessing or using their SDR allocations: in 2009, Madagascar and Honduras; in 2021, Afghanistan and Venezuela. This treatment does not constitute an IMF sanction, nor is it linked to multilateral sanctions imposed by the UN Security Council. Rather, it stems from the IMF's longstanding practice concerning government recognition. Only recognition enables a new government to exercise the country's membership rights within the Fund. On this issue, the IMF asserts that it is guided by the views of the 'international community' (i.e., the perspective of its members representing a majority of the total voting power). Therefore, 'in the event of a lack of recognition, or a lack of clarity regarding the recognition of a member's government', said government 'would continue to be unable to use SDRs (including newly allocated SDRs) until the recognition issue is resolved'. However, the application of this practice remains subject to a degree of subjectivity and can lead to outcomes that are clearly contentious.

III. Operations and Transactions in SDRs

303. Upon receiving their allocation, IMF Member States may: (a) hold SDRs to strengthen their international reserves and improve market access; (b) exchange SDRs for 'freely usable currencies' (*see supra*, paragraphs 167 ff.) to diversify the composition of their international reserves, ease liquidity constraints or create fiscal space for additional spending; (c) use them in a set of authorised transactions with other IMF members (such as to extend bilateral loans or settle financial obligations); or (d) use them to discharge financial obligations to the IMF, including loan repayments and quota increases (the Fund may therefore hold SDRs in the GRA). Additional uses may be authorised by the Executive Board with a 70% qualified majority (Article XIX, section 2(c)).

304. Notably, IMF members do not have to meet specific requirements to initially receive from the Fund their share of a general SDR allocation; they can exchange SDRs on the voluntary market (on which *see* below) even in the absence of a balance of payments need and without entering an IMF macroeconomic adjustment programme; moreover, they are decoupled from any kind of conditionality or repayment obligation. In fact, SDRs do not have to be repurchased, do not have a maturity date and do not have a scheduled amortisation plan. SDR allocations thus provide each member with a supplementary, unconditional and almost costless reserve asset.

305. Actually, the only cost that receiving countries may incur relates to their use. When an IMF member exchanges part of its SDR allocation for hard currency, it will have to pay interest to the IMF on the balance between its cumulative SDR allocation and its SDR holdings (i.e., on the shortfall). Conversely, when a member's SDR holdings rise above the amount allocated, it will receive from the IMF interest income on the excess. As a result, SDRs do not add to a country's sovereign debt if not in a negligible way.

306. The IMF Executive Board can also grant prescribed holders the power to hold SDRs. Pursuant to IMF Article XVII, section 3, this decision requires an 85% majority of the total voting power. Designated prescribed holders may acquire and receive SDRs (e.g., as loan repayments), but they are not entitled to receive direct allocations from the Fund. Currently, there are fifteen prescribed holders: four central banks, three intergovernmental monetary institutions and eight development organisations. Needless to say, SDRs are not a form of currency as they may not be used as a means of payment by private entities or individuals.

307. All operations and transactions involving SDRs are conducted through the SDRs Department. IMF members can convert SDRs into hard currency in two different ways: (a) on the so-called voluntary market; or (b) through the 'designation mechanism'.

308. In the first case, exchanges are the result of bilateral agreements between members and/or prescribed holders. Nowadays, the exchange of SDRs is either directly arranged between members and/or prescribed holders or facilitated by the Fund through Voluntary Trading Agreements (VTAs). VTAs are bilateral arrangements between the Fund and a member country (or prescribed holder) under which the latter volunteers to buy or sell a capped amount of SDRs in exchange for specific currencies. In this case, the IMF acts as an intermediary, assigning purchase and sale requests among VTAs with a view to ensuring their equitable distribution. At present, thirty-three countries and only one prescribed holder – the ECB – have a VTA in place. This group includes most of the G-20 countries, and, among BRICS, only China. Notably, States participating in a VTA retain the right to refuse any request to exchange SDRs. This reflects the position of the United States, which refrains from swapping SDRs for dollars to the benefit of countries 'whose policies run counter to US interests', including those targeted by US unilateral sanctions.

309. In the second case, the IMF acts as an intermediary. The designation mechanism provided for by IMF Article XIX, section 5 ensures that countries unable to find a counterparty on the voluntary market still have the possibility to exchange their SDRs. In this case, contrary to what happens when SDRs are voluntarily traded, the requesting country will have to demonstrate that it has a balance of payments need. The Fund will then designate the member with a strong external position that will be obliged to provide freely usable currencies to the requesting country in exchange for SDRs up to a specified amount. Since September 1987, no transactions have taken place under the designation mechanism. Nevertheless, even though the voluntary market has effectively replaced the designation mechanism since the late 1980s, the mechanism remains central to safeguarding SDR liquidity and preserving its character as a reserve asset.

§7. The IMF and Sovereign Debt Management

I. Bretton Woods and the IMF's Early Approach to Sovereign Debt

310. The founding fathers of the IMF had opposing views on the involvement of the organisation in sovereign debt issues. Harry Dexter White of the US Treasury envisioned a central role for the IMF. His Plan for a Stabilisation Fund of April 1942 (the so-called White Plan) provided the following: 'III. Eligibility for membership [in the IMF]. Any member of the United or Associated Nations is eligible for membership provided it agrees: […] 7. Not to permit any defaults on foreign obligations of the governments, Central Bank or government agency without approval of the Fund.' Harry Dexter White explained the rationale behind the inclusion of this provision in the following terms: 'It can hardly be expected that objective decisions on defaults can be made by the defaulting country or by the country gaining most by continued servicing of a debt. To make what takes on the character of compulsory arbitration in debt adjustment an acceptable and workable instrument, the proposed judgment must be that of a large group of nations, the majority of whom are not directly and immediately affected by the decision. Consideration of the pros and cons of a contemplated default by the Fund would seem to promise that kind of objectivity, and therefore not be a requirement that would stand in the way of acceptance by any government.'

311. According to François Gianviti, a former IMF Legal Counsel, 'one consequence of this power would have been that the defaulting State, if it did not obtain the Fund's approval, would have been in breach of its obligations not only under the contract with its creditor but also under the Fund's Articles of Agreement. Even if the debt had been to a private party, a default would have been a violation of international law, as a sanction of which the defaulting State could have been declared ineligible to use the Fund's resources and possibly expelled from the Fund'.

312. No trace of this part of White's proposal can be found in the Joint Statement by Experts on the Establishment of an International Monetary Fund of April 1944, which formed the basis for the negotiations on the IMF Articles of Agreement. The reason lies in the opposition of John Maynard Keynes, the delegate for the British government, who knew that the United Kingdom would emerge from World War II bearing a huge war debt. During the negotiations, Keynes made it clear that he believed that 'the settlement of these debts must be, in our clear and settled judgment, a matter between those directly concerned [...] The Fund is not intended to deal directly with war indebtedness'. The United States and France supported his position, and the conference ultimately rejected the idea of the IMF facilitating the settlement of war (and other) sovereign debts. As a result, the 1944 wording of the IMF Articles only contained the following provision: 'The Fund is not intended to provide facilities for relief or reconstruction or to deal with international indebtedness arising out of the war' (Article XIV, section 1). This provision was deleted by the Second Amendment to the IMF Articles in 1978 as it was no longer considered relevant.

II. Sovereign Debt Governance and the Role of the IMF

313. 'Sovereign debt', whether external or domestic, refers to the debt issued or guaranteed by a country's central government. States can borrow from a variety of sources. They can receive loans from international financial institutions (the IMF, World Bank and multilateral development banks), foreign governments, and commercial banks (either individually or as part of a syndicate). Additionally, they may issue sovereign bonds in international capital markets.

314. 'Sovereign debt restructuring' refers to a set of operations through which debtor countries seek debt relief from their creditors by modifying the original terms of their debt obligations – typically through extensions of maturity dates, reductions in face value, and/or lower interest rates. There are two main ways to change a debtor country's original payment terms to provide relief and fiscal space in times of distress: (a) debt rescheduling (or reprofiling), which involves a relatively short-term extension of maturity dates and interest payments deadlines, possibly including grace periods, but without altering the interest rate or the principal amount; and

(b) debt reduction (or cancellation), which entails considerable 'haircuts' to the principal and/or interest rates (referred to as 'coupon adjustments' in the case of bond debt). These restructuring techniques can be applied either pre-emptively – to avoid default – or post-default, as part of the resolution process. Additionally, private commercial bank creditors may contribute to debt relief by rolling over their short-term claims.

315. The features of sovereign debt restructuring have been shaped by both the type of creditors involved and the nature of the debt. Accordingly, debt restructuring mechanisms vary based on the category of creditors: (a) official bilateral debt is typically renegotiated under the auspices of the Paris Club; (b) commercial bank debt is restructured through the London Club process or via Bank Advisory Committees; and (c) bond debt is restructured through exchange offers or collective action clauses (CACs), with the applicable procedures depending on the governing law of the bond contract – most commonly the laws of England or the State of New York.

316. In the nineteenth century and the early years of the twentieth century, most sovereign debt took the form of bonds or loans extended by private banks, primarily for short-term trade financing or interbank credit lines. In cases of sovereign defaults, bondholders' committees were often established and, occasionally, Western powers even resorted to 'gunboat diplomacy' to enforce repayment of debts owed to their nationals.

317. After World War II, government-to-government loans became the predominant form of sovereign borrowing, and sovereign debt restructurings were primarily handled through the Paris Club. Today, the Paris Club remains the leading intergovernmental forum for restructuring official bilateral debt – that is, debt owed by or guaranteed by a national government to other countries. The Paris Club is composed of twenty-two permanent members, all of whom hold large claims on other sovereign debtors. Representatives of the IMF and the IBRD are invited to attend Club meetings as observers, to provide economic assessments and technical advice. The Club engages in negotiations with a debtor country only at the country's request and only if the country is implementing – or has formally committed to implement – an IMF-supported programme and its attached conditionality (on which *see supra*, paragraphs 174 ff.).

318. It was only in the 1970s that States began to borrow from international commercial banks through long-term syndicated loan agreements. In the 1980s, however, a majority of emerging market countries defaulted on these loans, which had to be restructured by small creditor banks' committees. This process came to be known as the London Club. The term refers to meetings held between commercial bank creditors and a debtor State, typically organised through an *ad hoc* Bank Advisory Committee, composed of around ten to twenty senior representatives from the banks with the largest exposures to the debtor country. Although used less frequently today, the London Club mechanism remains a recognised forum for restructuring commercial bank debt when needed. While the IMF does not participate directly in the negotiations, the debtor country is usually required to enter into an IMF-supported programme – demonstrating commitment to economic adjustment – before the restructuring is finalised.

319. During the 1990s, bank lending to emerging economies declined as compared to sovereign bond financing, and nowadays, sovereign external debt is mainly held in the form of bonds. Sovereign bonds are actively traded on secondary markets and purchased by a diverse community of investors. Current bondholders include many categories of creditors, both domestic and foreign, ranging from retail to institutional investors (such as banks, investment funds, hedge funds, pension funds, and insurance companies), also encompassing sovereign wealth funds, central banks, international financial institutions like the IMF, and supranational institutions like the ECB. Bond debt is restructured through exchange offers or CACs (on which *see* below). In a voluntary exchange offer, the sovereign proposes to bondholders to swap existing bonds for new ones with modified terms – such as extended maturities, lower interest rates, or reduced principal – often incentivised by financial sweeteners or the threat of default. Alternatively, if the bond contracts include CACs, a qualified majority of bondholders (usually 75%) can agree to amend the terms of the bonds, and the decision becomes binding on all holders, including dissenting minorities.

320. CACs are contractual provisions designed to streamline the sovereign debt restructuring process by limiting the ability of individual bondholders to initiate litigation. They specify in advance what will occur in the event of a default, allowing a supermajority of bondholders to agree on modifications to the terms of a bond – including its payment schedules or interest rates – with such changes becoming binding on all holders, including dissenting minorities (the so-called holdouts).

321. In 2002, the IMF explored the feasibility of establishing a universal legal framework for sovereign debt restructuring. The Fund argued that the contractual approach – i.e., relying on the inclusion of CACs in sovereign bonds contracts – would not, on its own, provide a comprehensive solution to sovereign debt restructuring challenges. As a result, the IMF proposed a complementary statutory approach envisioning the creation of a Sovereign Debt Restructuring Mechanism (SDRM), which would offer a formal, rules-based process for restructuring sovereign debt.

322. Under the proposed SDRM framework, a 75% majority of creditors would have had the power to bind all creditors to accept or reject a restructuring offer. Moreover, an arbitration body – the Debt Resolution Forum – would have been empowered to approve a government's restructuring plan and facilitate the smooth resolution of debt disputes. The IMF would have provided interim financing to the distressed debtor country. However, the implementation of the SDRM required an amendment to the IMF Articles, which was never agreed upon due to the opposition of the US Treasury. The proposal raised many concerns: on the one side, creditors feared that a more predictable and orderly restructuring framework would reduce the costs of default and thus incentivise sovereigns to restructure more readily; on the other side, debtors worried that creditors' concerns would lead to higher borrowing costs. When, in 2003, the IMFC (*see supra*, paragraphs 71ff.) discussed the proposal, its members expressed a clear preference for the contractual approach and chose to promote a broader use of CACs, thereby definitively setting aside the SDRM initiative.

323. At the time of the SDRM proposal, however, CACs had not yet been adopted under New York law, and many observers were sceptical that they would be included in future sovereign bonds issuances. Today, CACs have become boilerplate provisions in standard market practice and represent the cornerstone of the contractual approach to debt restructuring, as opposed to the statutory approach. In fact, they are now routinely included in sovereign bonds governed by both New York and English law, following coordinated initiatives by the IMF and the International Capital Market Association (ICMA) to promote their adoption.

324. The 2012 European sovereign debt crisis revived the debate over sovereign debt restructuring. In April 2013, the Fund advocated for a new approach to debtor countries in a policy paper titled 'Sovereign Debt Restructuring – Recent Developments and Implications for the Fund's Legal and Policy Framework'. In that paper, the Fund argued that if a country faced a high and potentially unsustainable debt burden, financial assistance should be contingent upon debt restructuring (typically involving a rescheduling of payments rather than a reduction in the nominal debt stock). In essence, the IMF signalled its willingness to impose upfront losses on bondholders as a condition for granting the country bailout support. The message was couched in opaque language: 'There may be a case for exploring additional ways to limit the risk that Fund resources will simply be used to bail out private creditors. For example, a presumption could be established that some form of a creditor bail-in measure would be implemented as a condition for Fund lending in cases where, although no clear-cut determination has been made that the debt is unsustainable, the member has lost market access and prospects for regaining market access are uncertain.' Providing the member with a more manageable debt profile helps prevent creditor flight during periods of IMF financial assistance, while also strengthening market confidence in the country's adjustment efforts. This approach aims to avoid the typical situation in which the Fund is asked to lend money to a country which has already accumulated an unsustainable debt, resulting in the immediate outflow of IMF resources as coupon payments to foreign bondholders. It aligns with the 'private sector involvement' principle, which seeks to ensure that private creditors contribute to crisis resolution, rather than benefiting from IMF support without sharing in the associated risks.

325. In October 2014, the Executive Board discussed the paper 'Strengthening the Contractual Framework to Address Collective Action Problems in Sovereign Debt Restructuring'. The paper evaluated the effectiveness of the market-based contractual approach to debt restructuring and, in particular, proposed the inclusion of CACs with aggregation features in international sovereign bond contracts. Until then, CACs had operated within a single bond issue, therefore binding only the holders of that specific issue but not affecting the bondholders of other bond issuances. Aggregated CACs enable instead restructuring terms to be applied collectively across multiple bond series. Executive Directors endorsed the promotion of enhanced contractual provisions in new international sovereign bond issuances. Following the IMF's recommendation, the ICMA updated its standard model clauses in 2014. These enhanced CACs began to be widely adopted in newly issued sovereign bonds, particularly under New York and English law, which are the most frequently used governing laws for sovereign bonds. The IMF continued to monitor the implementation and effectiveness of enhanced CACs, encouraging their use in sovereign issuances to build a more resilient restructuring architecture.

326. The IMF's approach to sovereign debt evolved significantly during the COVID-19 crisis, both in response to the scale of the shock and the emerging vulnerabilities in low-income countries. While the IMF did not formally abandon its earlier positions, the crisis prompted a more flexible and proactive stance. In particular, the IMF strongly supported the G-20 Debt Service Suspension Initiative (DSSI) (2020–2021), which allowed seventy-three eligible low-income countries to temporarily suspend debt service payments to official bilateral creditors (including China, which despite being one of the largest lenders is not a member of the Paris Club), thereby freeing up resources for pandemic-related spending. In addition, the IMF activated and expanded the CCRT to provide outright debt service relief for the poorest and most vulnerable countries hit by catastrophic natural disasters or public health disasters (*see also infra*, paragraph 344). In November 2020, the IMF backed the creation of the Common Framework for Debt Treatments beyond the DSSI, designed to facilitate a more coordinated restructuring process among Paris Club and non-Paris Club creditors (especially China); the Framework aims to ensure fair burden-sharing among all official creditors and encourages comparable treatment by private creditors, with the IMF and World Bank involved to assess debt sustainability and monitor programme implementation; so far, it has been used only by a few countries (Chad, Ethiopia, Ghana, and Zambia), revealing critical flaws such as delays, lack of transparency, and coordination difficulties, which have prompted calls for further reform.

327. More recently, in April 2025, the Global Sovereign Debt Roundtable released a new Restructuring Playbook to guide debtor country authorities considering a debt restructuring. The Global Sovereign Debt Roundtable is a joint initiative of the IMF, the World Bank, and the G-20 aimed at enhancing the effectiveness and timeliness of sovereign debt restructurings, particularly for low-income and vulnerable countries facing unsustainable debt burdens. The Playbook outlines the key steps, concepts and processes typically followed in such operations, particularly in the context of IMF-supported programmes and restructurings conducted under the Common Framework. While offering a general overview of standard practices, the Playbook recognises that each case involves unique circumstances and challenges. It is a non-binding document, intended neither to prescribe specific actions nor to constrain how debtor countries and creditors would handle a specific case, under or outside the Common Framework.

328. The preceding analysis of the IMF's role in sovereign debt governance helps explain why, in his seminal 1989 course at The Hague, François Gianviti observed that 'Although the Fund has no jurisdiction over the contracting or discharge of external debt, some of the measures affecting external debt are subject to its jurisdiction.' Today, the IMF has indeed become a central actor in the field of sovereign debt, performing several critical functions despite the formal limits of its mandate.

329. First, the IMF plays a central role in sovereign debt restructuring by conducting Debt Sustainability Analyses (DSAs, on which *see infra*, paragraphs 330 ff.) to determine whether a country's debt is sustainable or requires restructuring as a prerequisite for receiving financial assistance. Although the Fund does not directly negotiate with creditors, its assessments shape the scope of debt relief and fiscal adjustment, thereby heavily influencing the restructuring process. Second, IMF-supported programmes provide both a policy anchor and financial backing to help countries restore or maintain external viability, and the Fund's endorsement of the borrowing country's reform programme serves as a signal of credibility to official and private creditors. Moreover, the IMF leverages its position to encourage debtor countries to reach timely agreements with creditors, facilitating the restoration of market access. Third, beyond individual cases, the Fund contributes to the development of the broader sovereign debt architecture through its support for initiatives such as the design of enhanced CACs (on which *see supra*, paragraphs 320 ff.) and the Common Framework for Debt Treatments (*see supra*, paragraph 326). Fourth, the IMF – which is recognised preferred creditor status (*see infra*, paragraphs 336 ff.) – has exceptionally agreed to provide debt relief to HIPC and countries affected by catastrophes (*see infra*, paragraph 340). Finally, through surveillance, technical assistance, and policy dialogue, the Fund helps countries build institutional capacity for sound debt management, strengthen fiscal frameworks, and adopt transparent borrowing practices to prevent the accumulation of excessive debt burdens in the future.

III. The IMF's Debt Sustainability Frameworks

330. A cornerstone of the IMF's role in sovereign debt issues is its responsibility for conducting Debt Sustainability Analyses (DSAs), which evaluate a country's current and projected debt burden relative to its capacity to service debt under various macroeconomic scenarios. Introduced in 2002, the DSA framework serves as a key tool to detect, prevent, and resolve potential debt crises. It functions both as a standard instrument of fiscal surveillance and as a basis for making informed decisions on IMF financial support. DSAs help identify the risk of debt distress, guide the design of conditionality in IMF-supported programmes, and inform creditors and stakeholders about the sustainability of a country's debt and the potential need for restructuring.

331. DSAs are conducted in the context of Article IV surveillance or when a country approaches the IMF for financing (both during the design of an IMF-supported programme and when the Fund undertakes programme reviews). The Fund carries out projections on a country's debt burden, assessing exposures to external and policy shocks, usually recommending borrowing strategies aimed at limiting the risk of debt distress. Country-specific circumstances are duly taken into account, and a distinction is made between market-access countries (which have access to international capital markets) and LICs (which meet their external financing needs mostly through concessional resources), reflecting their different vulnerabilities and financing conditions.

332. The Sovereign Risk and Debt Sustainability Framework for Market Access Countries (SRDSF) is one of the two debt sustainability frameworks used by IMF's staff. The Executive Board approved this new framework for market access countries in 2021, encompassing all advanced economies and most emerging market economies. The SRDSF supports the IMF's surveillance by identifying countries at risk of sovereign stress early on. In precautionary arrangements, it also helps assess whether a country meets debt sustainability criteria. In non-precautionary programmes – typically initiated after stress has emerged – the SRDSF guides decisions on whether adjustment and new financing are sufficient or if debt restructuring is required. When restructuring is necessary, it helps define the required debt relief and restructuring targets to restore medium-term debt sustainability, a key condition for IMF lending. SRDSFs provide both a sovereign risk assessment and a debt sustainability assessment. These assessments aim to capture vulnerability to sovereign stress events, risks that debt could become unsustainable, and prospects for stabilising the debt trajectory.

333. The second debt sustainability framework used by IMF's staff is the IMF-World Bank Debt Sustainability Framework for Low-Income Countries (LIC DSF). It was introduced in April 2005 in recognition of the considerable challenges LICs face in achieving their development goals (including the Sustainable Development Goals (SDGs)), while maintaining sustainable levels of external debt. Jointly developed by IMF and World Bank staff, the LIC DSF is designed to assess public and external debt sustainability in LICs. Their primary objective is to guide LICs in making prudent borrowing decisions that align with their current and projected capacity to service debt, taking into account country-specific circumstances. Given the crucial role of official creditors and donors in financing development in these countries, the LIC DSF also informs lending and grant-allocation decisions, helping ensure that financial support is consistent with long-term debt sustainability and the pursuit of the SDGs. As a forward-looking tool, the LIC DSF functions as an early warning mechanism, allowing policymakers and stakeholders to identify and address potential risks of debt distress before they escalate.

334. Usually a DSA includes: an analysis of a country's projected debt burden over a 20-year horizon; an assessment of the baseline macroeconomic scenario and key fiscal and external indicators; an evaluation of the country's vulnerability to external and policy shocks; an assessment of the risk of external debt distress; and tailored policy recommendations for a borrowing strategy aimed at minimising the risk of future debt distress. However, it is worth noting that DSAs do not take into account the impact of debt service on economic, social and cultural rights. In this regard, numerous appeals have been made on the need to address this shortcoming either by incorporating human rights aspects into debt sustainability analyses or by making separate human rights impact assessments.

335. L.C. Buchheit and J. Zettelmeyer describe DSAs as a 'trigger': 'Whether a country requires a debt restructuring will depend on a DSA, which assesses the feasibility of policy adjustment and the availability of financing from all available sources. The IMF's DSA hence plays a role in the decision on whether a debt restructuring will take place (whether in the context of an IMF – or outside – supported adjustment program).' Moreover, the country's DSA and the scale of financing that the Fund is willing to provide help determine both the amount of debt relief requested from creditors and the extent of fiscal adjustment required from the debtor country. Therefore, the Fund's analysis shapes the restructuring expectations of both the debtor and its creditors. In practice, 'the IMF's DSA also effectively identifies the envelope of resources available for debt service payments to official and private creditors, which is crucial to anchor deliberations between the debtor and its creditors'.

IV. The IMF's Preferred Creditor Status

336. The IMF, the World Bank, and all the multilateral development banks enjoy preferred creditor status, meaning that countries borrowing from these international organisations are expected to prioritise repayment to them over other public or private creditors. Some authors argue that the privileged status of the IMF stems from a norm of customary international law. Others, however, contend that no such general rule of international law has emerged, and that decisions by certain creditor countries (particularly, the members of the Paris Club) to grant the IMF *de facto* preferential status differ fundamentally from recognising a legal entitlement. Notably, the IMF Articles of Agreement make no explicit reference to the Fund's preferred creditor status. During the protracted arrears crisis of 1983–1992, the Fund acknowledged the weak legal basis for its seniority and 'urged all members, within the limits of their laws, to treat the Fund as a preferred creditor'. Nonetheless, it is now almost undisputed that, when the Fund provides financial assistance to a Member State, its claims are senior to those of all the other creditors. The Paris Club and G-20 countries consistently grant the IMF such seniority.

337. It can be argued that preferred creditor status is essential to ensure that the IMF's reserve assets remain risk-free. Without such seniority, the IMF's ability to lend – particularly to countries facing debt crises – would be significantly constrained. This 'adequate safeguard' (within the meaning of IMF Article V, section 3) reflects the global public good nature of the IMF financing.

338. It is also worth noting that certain experts still question the preferred creditor status of international financial institutions. For instance, the 2012 Human Rights Council's Guiding Principles on Foreign Debt and Human Rights contend that 'The renegotiation and restructuring should be conducted in good faith and should cover all types of external debts owed to all types of external creditors, including international financial institutions.' In the Draft Commentary to the Guiding Principles, the Independent Expert argued that 'There should be a balance between protecting a debtor country's access to a "lender of last resort" and the need to restructure a significant portion of a debtor country's total external debts to produce an effective outcome.' The commentary emphasised that 'the downside of giving preference to all types of loans extended by the World Bank and IMF is that it leaves many low-income debtor countries with only a limited portion of their total external debt stock to restructure, because the bulk of their external debts is owed to the World Bank and IMF. This defeats the purpose of an international debt restructuring, which aims to avoid a default on the part of a debt-distressed country in the short term, and to give it a "fresh start" that enables it to return to the path of economic growth in the long run. This is possible if, and only if, a significant portion of its total external debts is restructured'. In other words, since the seniority of international financial institutions may hinder the recovery and development of debtor countries, the preferred creditor status of these institutions should be reconsidered – at least in exceptional circumstances – in favour of a more inclusive approach involving multilateral sector participation.

V. The IMF's Debt Relief Initiatives: From the HIPC to the CCRT

339. The preservation of the IMF's preferred creditor status becomes especially relevant when considering the IMF's own engagement in debt relief through initiatives such as the HIPC Initiative, the Multilateral Debt Relief Initiative (MDRI), the CCRT, and the DSSI. These efforts have, apparently, required the Fund to temporarily depart from protecting its seniority to provide debt relief to countries facing unsustainable debt burdens or external shocks.

340. In 1996, after the debt crisis of the 1980s, the IMF and the World Bank launched the HIPC initiative. The goal of this initiative was to reduce to sustainable levels the external debt burden of eligible low-income countries, contingent on their implementation of strong economic adjustment programmes. To qualify for the HIPC Initiative, a country had to be eligible for concessional lending from both the World Bank and the IMF, face an unsustainable debt burden that could not be addressed through traditional mechanisms, demonstrate a proven record of policy reform under IMF and World Bank programmes, and prepare a Poverty Reduction Strategy Paper (PRSP) through a participatory process. Countries that successfully implemented key reforms agreed under the HIPC Initiative and reached the so-called completion point were allowed to receive debt relief. The amount of debt cancelled varied based on each country's specific debt burden and the arrangements made with other creditors. In fact, to ensure comprehensive debt relief, the initiative involved coordinated action among the IMF, the World Bank, official bilateral creditors, and commercial creditors.

341. In 2005, to accelerate progress towards the Millennium Development Goals (MDGs), the IMF, the World Bank and the African Development Fund established the MDRI. Under the MDRI, these organisations committed to cancelling 100% of their claims for countries that reached the completion point under the HIPC initiative. The MDRI covered the full stock of debt owed to participating multilateral institutions that was outstanding as of end-2004, and remained unpaid at the time the country reached the HIPC completion point and qualified for MDRI relief.

342. The HIPC and MDRI initiatives benefited a considerable number of countries, mostly in sub-Saharan Africa. Of the thirty-nine countries eligible for debt relief, thirty-seven reached the completion point, with Somalia being the last to do so in 2023. Sudan is slowly progressing towards the completion point, while Eritrea has not yet reached the decision point, primarily due to its limited engagement with international financial institutions. However, while official creditors provided their full share of debt relief under the HIPC initiative and even went beyond it through the MDRI, private creditors did not follow suit. The HIPC and MDRI initiatives have been phased out, and no comprehensive successor initiative has been established to address unsustainable debt burdens in low-income countries, leaving current efforts to rely on more *ad hoc* or case-by-case mechanisms such as the Common Framework.

343. Even in the context of the HIPC initiative, however, the IMF and the IDA retained their preferred creditor status. Debt relief was, in fact, provided through a mechanism that ensured that payments to the IMF/IDA were made as they fell due. In practice, much of the debt relief was disbursed by a special Debt Relief Trust Fund, financed by IBRD income, or by special grants provided by the IMF. Additionally, a portion of the HIPC-related debt was covered by IDA member countries through their replenishment contributions. These funds were used either to buy back or repay portions of the debt owed by HIPC countries to the IMF and IDA, or the Trust Fund committed to cover portions of future debt-service owed to multilateral creditors as it came due. Similar arrangements were adopted under the MDRI to ensure continued recognition of preferred creditor status. In practice, international financial institutions were still repaid, not by the debtor countries themselves, but through special funds largely provided by advanced economies. In other words, the debt was effectively repaid by donor countries on behalf of the debtors.

344. A similar financial structure was used to fund the CCRT, the trust created in 2015 to provide debt relief to low-income countries affected by natural disasters or fast-spreading epidemics or pandemics. To qualify for CCRT assistance, countries must be eligible to borrow from the IMF PRGT and have a per capita income below the operational threshold set by the IDA. For natural disasters, relief is granted if the event impacts at least one-third of the population, destroys over 25%

of productive capacity, or causes damage exceeding 100% of GDP. Eligible countries receive debt service relief on IMF obligations for up to two years following the disaster. In the case of epidemics, relief is available if a life-threatening outbreak affects multiple regions, spreads internationally, and disrupts the economy significantly. In the event of a global pandemic causing widespread economic disruption, countries can receive substantial additional grant support and debt service relief. Countries experiencing public health disasters may be granted up-front assistance to cover IMF debt service payments due for up to two years from the initial decision, contingent on the availability of sufficient resources in the dedicated trust. In 2015, Guinea, Liberia, and Sierra Leone, which were severely affected by the Ebola outbreak, received relief under the Catastrophe Containment window. More recently, thirty-one countries benefited from CCRT assistance during the COVID-19 pandemic, with multiple rounds of debt service relief provided in 2020–2021.

§8. The IMF and Climate Change

345. Over the past three decades, the IMF has progressively expanded its role in addressing climate change, recognising it as a macro-critical issue with significant implications for countries' economic and financial stability and balance of payments. Supported by the development of a dedicated legal and institutional framework, climate-related considerations are now an integral part of the Fund's engagement across its three core pillars: surveillance, lending, and capacity development.

346. Regarding surveillance, since the 2021 Climate Strategy, the IMF has systematically integrated climate-related risks and policies into its bilateral and multilateral surveillance activities. Article IV consultations (*see supra*, paragraphs 235 ff.) now include climate adaptation, transition risks, and resilience building, when relevant. Climate considerations are also included in FSAPs (*see supra*, paragraphs 262 ff.) and multilateral surveillance reports like the WEO and Fiscal Monitor.

347. Regarding lending, in 2022, the IMF established the RST (*see supra*, paragraph 159) to help low-income and vulnerable middle-income countries address long-term structural challenges – particularly those related to climate change and pandemic preparedness – that pose risks to macroeconomic stability. Through the RSF, the RST provides affordable, longer-term financing to support reforms that strengthen resilience and promote sustainable growth. To access RSF support, countries must already have an IMF-supported programme and demonstrate a credible reform agenda aligned with climate or health-related objectives. Up to mid-2025, all twenty-three approved RSF arrangements had focused on climate-related reforms, reflecting growing global recognition of the macroeconomic impacts of climate change and the IMF's evolving role in supporting the green transition. For example, Rwanda's RSF-supported programme included reforms aimed at enhancing climate-resilient agriculture and improving public investment planning to better address climate risks.

348. Regarding capacity development, the IMF has significantly scaled up technical assistance to help member countries build climate-resilient public financial management, improve climate data and design mitigation and adaptation policies. Tools like the Climate Policy Diagnostic (CPD) contribute to this effort. CPDs help member countries evaluate and develop effective climate mitigation and adaptation strategies. They provide a structured assessment of a country's climate-related policy landscape, identifying key vulnerabilities, gaps in policy or implementation, and reform priorities. CPDs focus on the alignment of national policies with climate objectives, the integration of climate considerations into fiscal frameworks, and the readiness of institutions to implement climate action. They offer a platform for policy dialogue between the IMF and member countries and often inform the design of RST programs.

349. Additionally, the IMF is increasingly active in the global climate governance landscape, cooperating with institutions like the World Bank, the OECD and others, and participating in international initiatives and forums such as the Conference of the Parties to the UN Framework Convention on Climate Change and the Coalition of Finance Ministers for Climate Action. For instance, Climate Change Policy Assessments are a joint IMF-World Bank initiative introduced on a pilot basis in 2017 to provide an overarching assessment of countries' climate strategies, as articulated in their Nationally Determined Contributions and other government documents.

Chapter 5. The IMF in the Global Context

§1. The Duty of Cooperation with Other International Organisations

350. The IMF cannot be examined in isolation from the global context. Article X of the IMF Articles of Agreement explicitly requires the Fund to cooperate 'with any general international organisation and with public international organisations having specialised responsibilities in related fields'. This duty of cooperation fosters interaction between the IMF and other institutions, shaping the IMF's policies and influencing its decision-making process, while also enabling the Fund's objectives to inform the work of its counterparts.

351. How 'related fields' should be understood depends largely on how the IMF interprets its own purposes. A broader or evolving interpretation of its mandate can expand the range of 'related fields', prompting cooperation in new areas. Certainly, in areas where the IMF operates but lacks the necessary expertise, cooperation with other organisations becomes not just appropriate but essential. Moreover, to the extent that the IMF views the promotion of sustained economic growth as a core component of its macroeconomic adjustment programs, it must seek effective forms of collaboration with institutions possessing complementary mandates and expertise.

352. Cooperation is also possible in a range of areas that are closely connected to the IMF's mandate. The more the IMF becomes concerned with broader aspects of economic adjustment – such as trade liberalisation, anti-corruption measures, the protection of human rights and climate change – the more it is reasonable to expect that it will rely on the expertise of organisations with a specific mandate in these fields.

353. Cooperation may take place informally, with Fund representatives attending meetings of other organisations and staff members participating in working groups and seminars. The IMF Managing Director delivers an annual address to the UN Economic and Social Council (ECOSOC), and the IMF is represented at various UN meetings and cooperation bodies. The IMF Managing Director also participates in informal consultative forums and in the G-7 and G-20. Conversely, representatives of other organisations attend the IMF's annual meetings as well as sessions of the IMFC.

354. Cooperation is formalised through an international agreement only with a few organisations (namely, the United Nations, the World Bank and the WTO). With other organisations, cooperation has evolved into more permanent, albeit less formalised, arrangements (e.g., through the opening of the IMF's European Offices in Brussels and Paris, which were primarily established to liaise with the EU and the OECD). The Fund also cooperates closely with regional development banks, as shown by the HIPC and MDRI initiatives (*see supra*, paragraphs 340 ff.). One notable example of effective cooperation is the joint publication of statistics on external debt by the IMF, the World Bank, the BIS and the OECD.

§2. The IMF, Intergovernmental Groups and the Financial Stability Board

I. The G-7, G-20, G-10 and G-24

355. Since the 1970s, countries have engaged in extensive informal consultations on major political and economic issues through various intergovernmental fora. The so-called Gs (such as the G-7 and G-20) lack a formal institutional structure and operate without conferred powers or permanent administrative bodies, and their composition is determined by mutual agreement among participating States. As such, they do not constitute international organisations. Administrative and secretarial support is typically provided by the government that periodically hosts the group's meetings. Despite their informal nature, these intergovernmental fora play a significant role in fostering international coordination on a wide range of economic issues.

356. The G-7 consists of Canada, France, Germany, Italy, Japan, the United Kingdom, and the United States, with some additional observers. Russia joined the group as a full participant in 1998, thus marking the formation of the G-8. However, in 2014, in response to Russia's violations of international law in Ukraine (including the illegal annexation of Crimea), G-7 leaders announced they would no longer hold summits with Russia. The G-7 Summit meets at the level of Head of State or Government and issues Final Communiqués that, while not legally binding, reflect the leaders' political commitments.

357. Since 1998, in light of its expanding working agenda, the G-7 has increasingly convened ministerial meetings, independent from the annual Summit of the Heads of State or Government. The conclusions reached at ministerial meetings are usually reflected in the Summit Final Communiqué. The country holding the Presidency decides upon the number, scope and agenda of ministerial meetings, among which the meetings of the Foreign Ministers and of the Finance Ministers and Central Bank Governors are the most influential. The G-7 usually convenes immediately prior to the IMF's semi-annual meetings, often including in the agenda of G-7 Finance Ministers issues that fall within the IMF's mandate. In this case, the consensus reached among G-7 members may influence – or even supersede – consultations within the Fund. In fact, G-7 countries collectively hold 41.24% of total voting power in the IMF, giving them significant influence over its decisions.

358. The G-7 has lost much of its prominence with the rise of the G-20, a group established in 1999 in the wake of the Asian financial crisis as a meeting of the Finance Ministers and Central Bank Governors of systemically important economies, with the aim of stabilising global financial markets. Since 2008, the G-20 has also convened at the level of Heads of State or Government. The G-20 brings together major advanced and emerging economies (Argentina, Australia, Brazil, Canada, China, France, Germany, India, Indonesia, Italy, Japan, Korea, Mexico, Russia, Saudi Arabia, South Africa, Turkey, the United Kingdom, and the United States) along with the EU (represented by the President of the European Council and the President of the European Commission) and the African Union (represented by the member that holds the Union's rotating chair and supported by the Chairperson of the African Union Commission). Spain is a permanent invited guest to the G-20. The IMF Managing Director (together with the Chair of the IMFC and of the Development Committee) and the President of the World Bank are also invited to attend. In addition, countries chairing key regional groups – such as the Association of Southeast Asian Nations, the New Partnership for Africa's Development and the Caribbean Community – are generally invited to the summit.

359. During the global financial crisis, the G-20 assumed a prominent role in promoting economic cooperation and advancing reforms to the international monetary and financial system. At the Pittsburgh Summit of 2009, the leaders designated the G-20 as their 'premier forum' for international economic cooperation. Today, G-20 countries collectively represent around the 64.82% of the total voting power in the IMF, and when the group reaches a consensus, there are high expectations that the IMF will reflect it in its policy actions. The G-20 Finance Ministers and Central Bank Governors meet annually to discuss measures aimed at promoting global financial stability.

360. The G-10 was originally formed in 1962 by the G-7 countries plus Belgium, the Netherlands, and Sweden in order to coordinate participation in the GAB (*see supra*, paragraph 102), a mechanism for providing additional resources to the Fund. Switzerland joined the group in 1964 (despite not yet being a member of the Fund), bringing the membership to eleven countries but the G-10 name was retained. The group contributed to the discussions that led to the creation of SDRs in 1969 (*see supra*, paragraphs 293 ff.). Today, the G-10 plays a technical and advisory role, especially within the BIS, where G-10 central banks are heavily involved.

361. The G-24 was established in 1971 as a coalition of emerging markets and developing countries from Africa, Asia, and Latin America. Originally, it operated as a subgroup within the G-77, a broader coalition of developing countries that now comprises 134 members. The primary aim of the G-24 is to coordinate the positions of developing countries and emerging markets on key issues related to international monetary policy and development finance. The IMF provides secretarial support to the G-24 and facilitates its research and meetings. The group typically meets twice a year, just before the semi-annual meetings of the IMF and the World Bank. The G-24 has been instrumental in IMF policymaking by issuing communiqués, studies, and reports that help shape the discourse on international economic and financial matters, particularly from the perspective of developing countries.

II. The Financial Stability Board

362. In February 1999, the G-7 established the Financial Stability Forum (FSF), assigning it the task of promoting global financial stability through the exchange of information and international cooperation in financial supervision and surveillance. In 2009, the G-20 created the Financial Stability Board (FSB) as the successor of the FSF. To address concerns around participation and legitimacy issues, membership in the FSB was expanded to include all G-20 countries as well as Hong Kong SAR, Singapore, Spain and Switzerland. Each member is represented by its central bank, finance ministry, and relevant regulatory authorities. In addition to member countries, the FSB includes major international organisations and standard-setting bodies, among which are the BIS, the OECD, the World Bank and the IMF. The EU is represented by the ECB, the ECB Banking Supervision Single Supervisory Mechanism (SSM), and the European Commission. The FSB coordinates the work of national financial authorities and international standard-setting bodies at the international level, and develops and promotes the implementation of effective regulatory, supervisory and financial sector policies. It brings together national authorities responsible for financial stability in key international financial regions, along with international financial institutions, international groupings of sector-specific regulators and supervisors, and committees of central bank experts.

363. The 2010 IMF Executive Board's decision to approve the Fund's participation in the FSB made it clear that such participation would not amount to membership in an international organisation and that, therefore, the Fund would not be legally bound by decisions adopted within the FSB, but would only be politically accountable to the other FSB members. The Board further emphasised that the IMF's participation in the FSB would not affect its existing rights and obligations, and that the Fund would retain the right to opt out of any FSB decisions that might conflict with its legal or policy framework.

364. In 2013, the IMF Executive Board renewed its decision concerning the Fund's participation in the FSB, which in the meantime had become an association under Swiss law. This decision reaffirmed the same caveats set out in 2010, confirming that the IMF's participation would not entail legal obligations and would remain aligned with the Fund's existing mandate and rights. Within the framework of the new association, the collaboration between the IMF and the FSB continues to be guided by the respective mandates of each institution. While the IMF is principally responsible for the supervision of the international monetary system and of its members' domestic policies with an impact on external stability (through Article IV consultations, FSAPs, and ROSCs), the FSB is primarily concerned with regulatory and supervisory matters: it coordinates standard-setting bodies, identifies vulnerabilities and gaps, exercises peer pressure through its monitoring mechanisms and promotes adherence to international financial standards.

365. On the one hand, the IMF monitors the economic and financial policies of its members through mandatory Article IV consultations, which now include mandatory FSAP assessments for systemically important countries (*see supra*, paragraphs 262 ff.). On the other hand, FSB members commit to pursuing financial stability, maintaining openness and transparency in their financial sectors, implementing international financial standards (including the twelve key International Standards and Codes, on which *see supra*, paragraph 271) and undergoing periodic peer reviews. The leverage exerted by both the IMF and the FSB over their members largely relies on peer pressure and the fear of reputational costs, as neither institution has the authority to impose sanctions on members that fail to comply with their recommendations.

366. The IMF and the FSB share responsibility for conducting the Early Warning Exercise, which assesses low-probability, high-impact risks to the global economy. This exercise aims to identify vulnerabilities that could trigger systemic crises and provides policy recommendations to mitigate these risks. It remains a crucial tool for both institutions in strengthening global financial stability.

367. Both the IMF and the FSB report to the IMFC and to the G-20 Finance Ministers and Central Bank Governors. For instance, in September 2023, in response to a request from the Indian G-20 Presidency, the IMF and the FSB released a comprehensive synthesis paper on policies for crypto-assets. This document did not introduce new policies but rather clarified how existing policy recommendations and standards interact, with the aim of addressing macroeconomic and financial stability risks associated with crypto-asset activities. The paper emphasised the importance of cross-border cooperation and information sharing to ensure consistent regulation of crypto-assets, and it even outlined an implementation roadmap.

§3. The IMF and the United Nations

I. The IMF as a UN Specialised Agency

368. The IMF Articles of Agreement entered into force on 27 December 1945, just two months after the UN Charter. In November 1947, the IMF became a specialised agency of the United Nations. According to Article 57 of the UN Charter, specialised agencies are intergovernmental organisations established by treaty, entrusted with broad international responsibilities – as defined in their founding instrument – in economic, social, cultural, educational, health, or related fields, and which have entered into a formal relationship with the United Nations. Pursuant to Article 63 of the UN Charter, relationship agreements are negotiated with the ECOSOC and must be approved by the General Assembly. These agreements establish both reciprocal and non-reciprocal obligations: while both parties commit to mutual duties – such as exchanging information, participating in debates and cooperating on administrative and financial matters – the United Nations retains certain unilateral rights, including the power to issue recommendations and request reports or assistance. Currently, there are seventeen specialised agencies, most of which negotiated their relationship agreement with the United Nations between 1946 and 1977.

369. The relationship agreement between the United Nations and the IMF, known as the 'Agreement Between the United Nations and the International Monetary Fund', was approved by the UN General Assembly through Resolution 124

(II). Under this treaty, the Fund 'is required to function as an independent international organisation' while cooperating with the United Nations and reporting on its activities. The Fund's independence is recognised because of the nature of its 'wide international responsibilities … in economic and related fields', as defined by the IMF Articles. An excessively close involvement with the United Nations was seen as potentially leading to politicisation and at risk of jeopardising the Fund's primarily technical character. The relationship agreement therefore grants the Fund a greater degree of autonomy compared to other specialised agencies. The United Nations and the IMF may also make formal recommendations to each other but only after prior consultation.

370. As a specialised agency part of the United Nations system, the IMF operates within the broader framework established by the UN Charter. Article 103 of the Charter plays a pivotal role in defining the legal hierarchy between the Charter and other international agreements. It stipulates that in the event of a conflict between the obligations of UN Member States under the Charter and their obligations under any other international agreement, the Charter obligations must prevail. This provision affirms the primacy of the UN Charter in the international legal order and carries implications for the interpretation and application of the IMF Articles of Agreement. Although the IMF maintains institutional independence, its operations must be conducted in a manner consistent with the purposes and principles of the United Nations. In practice, this means that the IMF's policies and actions should be aligned with the overarching legal framework of the UN Charter.

371. Cooperation between the IMF and the United Nations has often proved challenging, marked by significant differences in policy approaches. At times, initiatives launched at the UN level received limited consideration from the IMF. A notable example is the 2008 initiative of the President of the UN General Assembly, who convened a Commission of experts chaired by Joseph E. Stiglitz to examine the causes of the global financial crisis, assess its impact across countries and recommend appropriate responses. The Final Report of the Commission of Experts (commonly referred to as 'the Stiglitz Report') was released on 21 September 2009. The report contended that only the United Nations possess the political legitimacy required to lead discussions on the reform of the international economic and financial architecture, due to its more inclusive representation of middle-income countries and low-income countries. The report proposed the creation of a Global Economic Coordination Council, which would oversee and coordinate the work of specialised agencies, including the IMF and the World Bank. Although the proposal was ultimately deemed politically unfeasible, it highlighted persistent concerns about the limited voice and participation of developing countries within international financial institutions. The IMF did not participate in the discussions leading to the Stiglitz Report, nor did it directly address the report's recommendations, opting instead to pursue its own internal reform agenda independently.

372. More recently, in 2015, the UN General Assembly adopted Resolution 69/319, which sets forth Basic Principles on Sovereign Debt Restructuring Processes. These principles include the sovereign's right to initiate the debt restructuring process, sovereign immunity, equitable treatment of creditors, supermajority restructuring, transparency, impartiality, legitimacy, sustainability, and good faith in negotiations. The resolution urges all Member States and international financial institutions – the IMF in particular – to support and promote the principles. Despite this call, the IMF has not taken a formal position on the resolution, underscoring its cautious approach when UN activities intersect with its own mandate and policy framework (on the IMF and sovereign debt *see supra*, paragraphs 310 ff.).

II. The IMF and Peace and Security

373. The 1947 UN-IMF Relationship Agreement addresses the relationship between the UN Security Council and the IMF. Article VI states that the Fund 'takes note' of its members' obligations to comply with the UN Security Council's resolutions and that, in conducting its activities, the Fund will 'have due regard' for decisions adopted by the Security Council under Articles 41 and 42 of the UN Charter. These terms – 'takes note' and 'due regard' – fall short of establishing a legal obligation of strict compliance or a relationship of subordination. According to the letter of this provision, the Fund may continue to provide balance of payments support to a member country subject to an embargo or other sanctions imposed by the UN Security Council under Chapter VII of the UN Charter. The IMF's distinctive position is difficult to reconcile with the obligation of UN members to accept and carry out the decisions of the Security Council established by Article 25 of the UN Charter. This notwithstanding, the IMF consistently maintains that under no circumstances can it act in a manner that conflicts with its own Articles of Agreement and, as a result, it does not consider itself *ipso jure* bound by UN Security Council resolutions.

374. It is reasonable to question whether the ECOSOC and the General Assembly acted *ultra vires* by endorsing the provision of the UN-IMF Relationship Agreement requiring the IMF to 'have due regard for the decisions of the Security Council'. It is indeed difficult to reconcile this wording with the intent of the authors of the UN Charter, which empowers the Security Council to impose binding sanctions on Member States. It seems paradoxical that a State targeted by UN multilateral sanctions could, at the same time, receive financial assistance from the IMF. It may be argued that this formulation was a concession made to secure the IMF's participation in the UN system as a specialised agency. However, this overlooks the fact that the Relationship Agreement potentially enables the IMF to provide financial assistance against the spirit of the Charter. In practice, though, conflicts are unlikely to arise as the permanent members of the Security Council – which play a central role in shaping and enforcing sanctions – also wield important voting power in the IMF. It is therefore reasonable to expect that these actors will ensure alignment between the two organisations when such critical decisions are made.

375. Furthermore, under the IMF Executive Board Decision No. 144-(52/51), Fund members are allowed to introduce exchange restrictions on grounds of national or international security (*see supra*, paragraphs 279 ff.). Decision No. 144-(52/51) is based on the recognition that the Fund is 'not a suitable forum for discussion of the political and military considerations leading to actions of this kind', and therefore, it cannot investigate the reasons underlying the adoption of security restrictions. Notably, the Fund has never formally distinguished between multilateral security restrictions imposed under UN Security Council resolutions and unilateral sanctions adopted independently by individual States. More precisely, the Fund has never adopted specific criteria to assess the legitimacy of unilateral restrictions, shielding itself behind the fact that it is not the appropriate forum for discussions on members' foreign policy and national security strategies.

376. The absence of a clear distinction between multilateral and unilateral security restrictions is evident in the notification practice of IMF members. Even if Decision No. 144-(52/51) requires notification of all restrictions that 'in the judgment of the member, are solely related to the preservation of national or international security', data available in the AREAER indicate that the practice of member countries is far from uniform. For instance, it is not the standard practice of the United States to notify the Fund of restrictions adopted in compliance with the obligations arising from its UN membership. By contrast, most EU Member States notify the Fund of both restrictions imposed under their autonomous sanctions regimes and those implemented in accordance with UN Security Council resolutions and EU regulations.

III. The IMF and Human Rights

377. The international human rights framework is grounded in the Universal Declaration of Human Rights and in the two 1966 International Covenants on Human Rights – the International Covenant on Civil and Political Rights (ICCPR) and the International Covenant on Economic, Social and Cultural Rights (ICESCR). These instruments have given rise to a number of other multilateral human rights treaties, such as those prohibiting racial discrimination and torture. In addition, regional human rights treaties constitute an independent but complementary set of legal instruments. The IMF Articles do not explicitly establish a link between the provision of financial assistance and the protection of human rights. However, this does not preclude IMF organs from acknowledging that they are bound by customary international law and peremptory norms (*ius cogens*) related to human rights.

378. Nevertheless, in a 2002 paper addressing the relationship between the 1966 ICESCR and the IMF Articles, the General Counsel François Gianviti adopted a restrictive interpretation, arguing that the IMF is primarily a monetary institution and should not be held responsible for upholding human rights. He noted that 'the norms contained in the Covenant have not attained the status under general international law that would make them applicable to the Fund independently of the Covenant'. He also underscored that the IMF is not a party to the ICESCR and emphasised that the IMF may not exceed its mandate: if members believe that the IMF should integrate human rights considerations in its decision-making, they should amend the IMF Articles of Agreement accordingly. As a caveat, it should be noted that Gianviti's paper has never been officially endorsed by the IMF, nor has the IMF Legal Department issued any formal recommendation on the subject matter.

379. IMF Article IV, section 3 (b) provides that: 'In helping members to devise economic and financial programs, the Fund shall respect the domestic social and political policies of members.' This provision, commonly known as 'the political prohibition', is generally interpreted to mean that the IMF does not take into account whether borrowing countries respect or violate human rights when making lending decisions. Rather, the prohibition is understood to affirm the borrowing country's ownership of its reform programme, meaning that the IMF focuses on ensuring that the country is responsible for and takes ownership of the policies and measures it adopts in its reform agenda. However, it is worth noting that, during the 1960s, the UN General Assembly repeatedly urged the IMF to cease providing financial assistance to the apartheid regime in South Africa, yet the Fund continued lending until 1983.

380. Gross and systematic human rights violations lead to the following considerations. The Fund may refuse or withdraw financial support to States involved in gross human rights violations only when these abuses would hinder the performance of the adjustment programme. In such cases, the political and economic consequences of the violations make the successful implementation of the programme unlikely. The situation is entirely different when human rights violations do not undermine a member's capacity to successfully implement a programme. In such cases, while the IMF's refusal to provide balance of payments support might indeed put pressure on a government to improve its human rights record, it could just as easily worsen the situation. For this reason, any decision to suspend or not to disburse financial support should be adopted with the greatest caution and be justified on purely economic grounds. In fact, it is a highly debatable assumption that withholding balance of payments support will result in greater respect for human rights. On the contrary, withholding assistance might plunge the economy deeper into the mire, which is hardly likely to prompt improved observance of human rights. Besides, this kind of decision would only affect member countries that no longer have access to other sources of financing apart from the Fund.

381. From a different perspective, the impact of IMF conditionality on human rights protection raises significant concerns. The IMF's Guidelines on Conditionality make no reference to whether Member States should uphold international human rights standards while implementing economic adjustment programs, leaving the relationship between IMF conditionality and human rights obligations unclear. In general, the Fund tends to avoid engaging with the potential human rights impacts of its policy recommendations.

382. In 2016, the IEO published a report titled 'The IMF and Social Protection' affirming that, while social protection is not an explicit part of the Fund's mandate, it is nonetheless indirectly affected by policy advice and conditionality. The report identified some key areas in which the IMF recently changed its stance, incorporating social protection concerns into its policy advice, such as the design of 'social safety nets and their financing, the fiscal consequences of publicly mandated pension and health insurance schemes in countries with ageing populations, and the impact of food and energy subsidy reform on vulnerable groups'. The report also acknowledged that the 2014 Revised Operational Guidance to IMF Staff on Conditionality (*see supra*, paragraphs 197 ff.) had already highlighted the need to incorporate macro-social aspects in Fund-supported programs. Despite this progress, the IEO noted that poverty and social impact assessments remained underutilised and emphasised the need for stronger collaboration with other international partners – such as the World Bank and UN agencies – possessing specialised expertise in these domains. It has been argued that the IMF should strengthen its collaboration with human rights bodies, to identify areas where public expenditure must be safeguarded or, where necessary, increased.

383. In recent years, the Fund has gradually begun to pay greater attention to the promotion of economic, social and cultural rights. These rights include obligations to promote full employment, just and favourable working conditions, social security, adequate living standards (including access to food and housing), health and education. Advancing these rights often requires targeted public spending and deliberate allocation of financial resources to the relevant sectors. The Fund has acknowledged that protecting vulnerable groups during the implementation of IMF-supported programmes is crucial. In fact, social exclusion and inequality can lead to political instability, which may in turn undermine the success and sustainability of economic adjustment efforts. At the same time, as noted by the Special Rapporteur on Extreme Poverty and Human Rights in his 2018 report, the Fund should address non-productive spending, such as military expenditures, to ensure that investments in human capital – especially in basic health care and primary education – are not displaced. Many argue that, by integrating a more comprehensive socio-economic human rights dimension in its adjustment programmes, the Fund will enhance its contribution to sustainable development.

IV. The IMF and Sustainable Development

384. Sustainable development has been defined as 'development that meets the needs of the present without compromising the abilities of future generations to meet their own needs' (Brundtland Report, 'Our Common Future', 1987). While this definition is frequently applied in the context of environmental protection – emphasising that future generations should not bear the consequences of environmental degradation and climate change caused by the careless policies of the present generation – the concept has broader dimensions. As recognised by the UNDP, sustainable development also includes: (a) avoiding the financing of current consumption through sovereign debt that future generations will be required to repay; (b) investing in the health and education of today's population to prevent the accumulation of a social debt; and (c) managing natural resources responsibly and avoiding the creation of an ecological debt through the overexploitation of the Earth's productive and regenerative capacities.

385. In September 2000, the leaders of 189 countries gathered at the United Nations to sign the Millennium Declaration, whereby they committed to achieving the MDGs – a set of eight measurable goals ranging from halving extreme poverty and hunger to promoting gender equality and reducing child mortality – by the target date of 2015. In September 2015, the United Nations adopted the SDGs as a new set of seventeen global development targets to succeed the MDGs for the period 2015–2030. The SDGs are broader in scope and reflect the view that development needs to be economically, socially and environmentally sustainable. SDGs focus on five pillars: people, planet, peace, prosperity and partnership. To mobilise the financial resources needed to achieve these targets, the 2015 Third UN Conference on Financing for Development adopted the Addis Ababa Action Agenda on a sustainable financing strategy. In July 2025, the Fourth International Conference on Financing for Development addressed the financing challenges hindering the urgently needed investment push for the SDGs and further supported efforts to reform the international financial architecture.

386. Within its mandate, the IMF contributes to sustainable development primarily through: (a) providing financial assistance to low-income developing countries; (b) engaging with countries in fragile and conflict-affected situations (FCSs) to help them restore macroeconomic stability, build core macroeconomic policy institutions and catalyse donor support (*see supra*, paragraphs 212 ff.); (c) providing technical assistance, in particular on tax policy and administration, to help developing countries to boost domestic revenues mobilisation; (d) offering policy advice and capacity development to improve the efficiency of public spending on infrastructure, reduce income and gender inequality, and enhance environmental sustainability.

387. An important recent contribution by the IMF to sustainable development is the establishment of the RST in 2022 (*see supra*, paragraph 159). The RST is a key initiative designed to assist low-income and vulnerable middle-income countries in building resilience to long-term challenges that pose macroeconomic risks, particularly those related to climate change and pandemic preparedness. Unlike traditional IMF programs focused on short-term balance of payments needs, RST-supported programs are intended to facilitate policy reforms and investments that strengthen a country's resilience and sustainability. Although still in its early stages, the RST marks a significant step by the IMF towards integrating climate change and other long-term vulnerabilities into its core mandate of promoting global financial stability and economic growth.

§4. THE IMF AND THE WORLD BANK

I. The Institutional Relationship Between the IMF and the World Bank

388. The relationship between the IMF and the World Bank encompasses several important institutional and legal dimensions. To begin with, membership in the IBRD and IDA is open only to countries that are members of the Fund. This requirement reflects the original intention of the Bretton Woods architects, who sought to ensure that only countries accepting the IMF's Articles of Agreement – and thus the stability of the par value system – could access the benefits of World Bank membership. Although the fixed exchange rate system was effectively dismantled with the 1978 Second Amendment to the IMF Articles, the requirement of IMF membership as a condition for World Bank membership remained in place.

389. Furthermore, Article V, section 8 of the IBRD Articles of Agreement contains a cooperation clause that implicitly points to the IMF as a key institutional partner. Specifically, paragraph (a) commits the Bank to 'cooperate with any general international organisation and with public international organisations having specialised responsibilities in related fields'; in addition, paragraph (b) requires the Bank to consider 'the views and recommendations of such organisation' when addressing matters that fall directly within their competence. The language in paragraph (a) mirrors the cooperation clause found in the IMF Articles, although paragraph (b) has no counterpart in the Fund's foundational document.

390. In this context, the term 'international organisation' clearly refers to the IMF. The World Bank is thus expected to take the Fund's assessments into account when its activities touch on matters within the IMF's jurisdiction. The drafters of the Bretton Woods Agreements anticipated the possibility of overlap, particularly with respect to the Bank entering the domain of the IMF, but not the other way around. This asymmetry is reflected in the absence of a reciprocal obligation in the IMF Articles.

II. Division of Competences

391. To clarify the boundaries of their respective jurisdictions and avoid conflicting policy advice, the IMF and World Bank have established various arrangements aimed at enhancing coordination and mutual understanding. These efforts are intended to ensure that each institution operates within its mandate while respecting the competencies of the other. In practice, this means that the IMF focuses on short-term macroeconomic stabilisation and balance of payments issues, while the World Bank emphasises long-term development and structural reform. Nonetheless, tensions can still arise when both organisations are engaged simultaneously in the same country, potentially leading to diverging policy recommendations or incompatible conditionalities.

392. In an effort to mitigate such risks, the two institutions adopted formal arrangements aimed at fostering coherence and coordination in their activities. In 1966, the IMF Managing Director and the President of the World Bank jointly issued the 'Fund–Bank Collaboration Memorandum', which outlined the procedures for collaboration between the two sister organisations. In 1989, after several reviews of the Memorandum, the 'IMF–World Bank Concordat' was adopted to further strengthen cooperation and reduce inconsistencies in the policy advice given to member countries. This step was particularly necessary as the overlap between the activities of the two organisations had increased significantly during the 1980s, especially with the rise of structural adjustment programs and the emergence of the Latin American debt crisis.

393. The key element of the Concordat is the delineation of the main responsibilities of the IMF and the World Bank. The Bank has 'primary responsibility for the composition and appropriateness of development programs and project evaluation, including development priorities'. The Bank is expected to focus on the efficient allocation of resources in both the public and private sectors, setting priorities in government expenditures and supporting reforms of administrative systems as well as in the production, trade and financial sectors, including the restructuring of State enterprises. The Fund has 'primary responsibility for exchange rates and restrictive systems, for adjustment of temporary balance of payments disequilibria, and for evaluating and assisting members to work out stabilisation programs as a sound basis for economic advance'. This responsibility extends to the aggregate aspects of macroeconomic policies and their associated instruments, including public sector spending and revenues, aggregate wage and price policies, monetary and credit policies, interest rates, and exchange rates.

394. In 2007, the IMF–World Bank collaboration was further streamlined through the adoption of the Joint Management Action Plan (JMAP). Building on the Concordat, the JMAP provides a framework to enhance coordination on country issues, improve communication on common thematic issues, and promote information sharing between the staff of the two organisations at the earliest possible stage. IMF and World Bank country teams should meet at least once a year to discuss their country-level work programme, identifying the key macroeconomic challenges that the country is facing and the necessary macro-critical sectoral reforms. The new framework for collaboration was first and effectively applied by many country teams in the aftermath of the global financial crisis.

395. The IMF and the World Bank collaborate closely in providing financial support to LICs with protracted balance of payments problems, limited access to private financial markets, and persistent debt sustainability challenges. Through initiatives like the HIPC and the MDRI (*see supra*, paragraphs 340 ff.), the IMF and the Bank have helped the poorest countries reduce their external debt burdens towards achieving debt sustainability. Under the joint Debt Sustainability Framework for Low-Income Countries, the IMF and the World Bank assist countries and donors in mobilising financing while mitigating the risk of excessive debt accumulation. The DSF enables the Bretton Woods organisations to integrate debt issues in their policy advice. To this end, DSAs are regularly conducted to assess a country's projected debt burden, its vulnerability to external and domestic shocks, and the risk of debt distress (*see supra*, paragraphs 333 ff.). More recently, recognising the escalating debt challenges faced by low- and middle-income countries, the IMF and World Bank have intensified their collaboration on debt sustainability, in particular by releasing in April 2025 a new 'Restructuring playbook', which aims to provide debtor country authorities considering a debt restructuring with the key steps, concepts and processes for such an operation (*see supra*, paragraph 327).

396. The FSAP – aimed at appraising the stability of the financial sector in a given country – is another joint responsibility of the IMF and the Bank (*see supra*, paragraphs 262 ff.). More recently, the IMF and the World Bank and the World Health Organization (WHO) have agreed on broad principles for cooperation on pandemic preparedness. This collaboration aims to scale up support to countries to prevent, detect, and respond to public health threats. The IMF's RST (*see supra*, paragraph 159), the World Bank Group's financial and technical support, and the WHO's technical expertise and in-country capabilities are central to this joint effort.

397. In 2024, the IMF and the World Bank launched the Enhanced Cooperation Framework for Climate Action, designed to support countries in scaling up efforts to confront climate change. This framework promotes an integrated, country-led approach to policy reforms and climate investments, leveraging both institutions' analytical, technical, and financial resources. Under this initiative, countries like Madagascar and Tanzania have begun implementing programs that combine IMF-supported RSF arrangements (*see supra*, paragraph 159) with active World Bank engagement on climate-related projects.

III. Cross-Conditionality

398. Cross-conditionality refers to a situation where one of the two Bretton Woods institutions (the IMF or the World Bank) provides or continues financial assistance on the condition that the borrower complies with conditions set by the other, and it is legally prohibited. IMF Executive Board Decision No. 12864-(02/102), adopted in September 2002, states that 'the Fund is fully responsible for the establishment and monitoring of all conditions attached to the use of its resources. There will be no cross-conditionality, under which the use of the Fund's resources would be directly subjected to the rules or decisions of other organisations'. Cross-conditionality may have in fact a potential domino effect: if the IMF suspends credit due to non-compliance with the programme performance criteria, the World Bank may follow suit. Subsequently, international financial markets may also lose confidence in the country. This loss of confidence can trigger a broader withdrawal of support by other creditors, including regional development banks, commercial lenders, and bilateral donors. As a result, even a seemingly minor failure – such as not reducing inflation below a specific threshold – can escalate into a comprehensive block on international credit.

399. Even if cross-conditionality is not formally allowed, it is often operationalised indirectly: the Bank provides support based on policies and strategies 'agreed' with the Fund, while the Fund extends credit after confirming that investment priorities and other factors 'agreed' with the Bank – particularly those related to the efficient allocation of government resources – are satisfactory. Furthermore, the Bank incorporates relevant Fund conditions into its own loan agreements, and the Fund ensures compliance with the Bank's conditions during its programme reviews. Officially, this is not framed as cross-conditionality, but rather as joint conditionality – the mutual transfer or recognition of conditions between the two organisations.

§5. The IMF and the World Trade Organization

I. Exchange Policies and Trade Liberalisation

400. The multilateral system envisioned at Bretton Woods presupposed the return to full current account convertibility and emphasised the importance of the freedom of payments and transfers to restore international commercial relations. After years of war and economic depression, maintaining the existing exchange restrictions would have hampered the reconstruction process and slowed the growth of world trade. The Bretton Woods founding fathers therefore agreed that the IMF would have jurisdiction over exchange restrictions, while the ITO – and afterwards the GATT and WTO – would be responsible for measures restricting trade, with both types of measures being, in principle, prohibited (on the ITO, *see supra*, paragraph 22).

401. Acknowledging that exchange restrictions have a highly detrimental effect on international trade, GATT Article XV makes IMF and WTO provisions complementary, delineating the respective competences of the two organisations. Two paragraphs are particularly relevant. First, Article XV, paragraph 2 of the GATT provides that in all cases in which WTO members are called upon to consider or deal with problems concerning monetary reserves, balances of payments or foreign exchange arrangements, they 'shall consult fully with the IMF'. In such consultations they: 'shall accept all findings of statistical and other facts presented by the Fund relating to foreign exchange, monetary reserves and balances of payments, and shall accept the determination of the Fund as to whether action by a contracting party in exchange matters is in accordance with the IMF Articles'. Second, GATT Article XV, paragraph 9(a) establishes that 'nothing in this Agreement shall preclude: (a) the use by a Contracting Party of exchange controls or exchange restrictions in accordance with the IMF Articles of Agreement … '.

402. The first provision focuses on the shared areas of concern for both organisations: balance of payments, exchange rates and monetary reserves. Essentially, GATT Article XV, paragraph 2 stipulates that, when addressing monetary issues, the WTO must give due regard to the opinion of the IMF. However, the terminology concerning the scope of IMF-WTO cooperation is somewhat inconsistent: while paragraph 2 of Article XV GATT refers to 'exchange matters', the IMF Articles of Agreement use the term 'exchange policies'. The second provision makes clear that any exchange measure that is permitted under the IMF Articles would be considered legitimate also under the GATT. Reference is implicitly made to exchange restrictions adopted for balance of payments reasons, for security reasons or under the transitional period (*see supra*, paragraphs 273 ff.): these measures would not amount to a breach of the GATT Agreement when introduced or maintained in accordance with the IMF Articles.

403. In 1995, the WTO was established with an expanded mandate, which included trade in services and a stronger focus on the liberalisation of capital movements. During the negotiations, concerns were raised about potential overlaps in jurisdiction between the General Agreement on Trade in Services (GATS) and the IMF. As a result, the Declaration on the Relationship of the WTO with the IMF, adopted as part of the Uruguay Round Final Act, reaffirmed the IMF's jurisdiction over exchange matters. Moreover, a provision analogous to GATT Article XV was introduced in the GATS. Pursuant to GATS Article XI, paragraph 2: 'nothing shall affect the rights and obligations of the IMF members under the Articles of Agreement of the Fund, including the use of exchange actions which are in conformity with the Articles of Agreement, provided that a member shall not impose restrictions on any capital transactions inconsistently with its specific commitments regarding such transactions, except under [GATS] Article XII or at the request of the Fund'.

II. Trade Restrictions for Balance of Payments Reasons and Monetary Measures

404. The IMF also comes into focus when WTO members are allowed to introduce balance of payments restrictions. The WTO recognises that, under certain circumstances, imports can place significant pressure on a country's balance of payments. When a balance of payments deficit cannot be financed, a country may decide to resort to restrictive import measures in order to contain the deficit.

405. According to GATT Article XII, paragraph 2, any contracting party may impose restrictions on the quantity or value of merchandise permitted to be imported in order to safeguard its external financial position and balance of payments. The restrictions instituted, maintained or intensified by a contracting party 'shall not exceed those necessary: (i) to forestall the imminent threat of, or to stop, a serious decline in its monetary reserves; or (ii) in the case of a contracting party with very low monetary reserves, to achieve a reasonable rate of increase in its reserves'. This provision does not cover the introduction of exchange restrictions for balance of payments reasons, as such measures are already regulated by the IMF Articles. Judgments regarding the necessity of trade restrictions fall within the mandate of the WTO, which applies more flexible conditions for developing countries. A WTO member that introduces a new restriction or intensifies existing ones must consult the Committee on Balance of Payments Restrictions. The Committee is required to open an investigation and report to the General Council on the legitimacy of the restriction. The IMF plays a central role in this procedure. The WTO asks the Fund for information about the country's adjustment strategy and monetary position. In particular, the IMF assesses the underlying causes of the balance of payments problem so that the WTO can judge if the restrictions are legitimate. The WTO is obligated to respect the Fund's views.

406. The GATS sets forth a balance of payments clause that allows members not only to impose temporary trade restrictions on service sectors for which they have undertaken specific commitments but also to introduce exchange restrictions and capital controls on services-related payments. Pursuant to GATS Article XII, paragraph 1, in the event of serious balance of payments and external financial difficulties or threat thereof, a member may adopt or maintain restrictions on trade in services on which it has undertaken specific commitments, including on payments or transfers for transactions related to such commitments. Article XII, paragraph 5(e) of the GATS establishes the procedure for consultations with the Committee on Balance of Payments Restrictions, which is required to accept the IMF's assessment of the member's situation in terms of foreign exchange, monetary reserves and balance of payments.

III. The IMF and Trade Liberalisation

407. Although the IMF's Articles of Agreement do not provide detailed guidance on trade policy, they allow for the IMF's engagement in this area. In fact, while primarily focused on monetary issues, the IMF is mandated by Article I to facilitate the expansion and balanced growth of international trade and has consistently urged its members to promote trade liberalisation. In addition, the IMF is widely regarded as the organisation best placed to quantify and analyse the macroeconomic effects of trade policies, both at national and international levels.

408. Generally, the IMF advocates for open, rules-based international trade, as it considers trade restrictions – such as tariffs and quotas – as obstacles to economic growth and development. In the 1990s, trade liberalisation became a key component of Fund-supported programs, often accompanied by structural conditions aimed at the removal of both tariff and non-tariff barriers. Through trade-related conditionality, the obligations established by the WTO could effectively be integrated into IMF-supported programs. Following the establishment of the WTO in 1995, however, the IMF began refraining from taking strong positions on trade policy, even when such measures had significant macroeconomic implications. The IMF also recognised that certain trade measures, such as temporary restrictions, may be necessary to protect national economies from external shocks or to address balance of payments problems.

409. In 2009, an IEO evaluation report on the 'IMF Involvement in International Trade Policy Issues' found that, while the Fund's guidance on traditional trade policy issues was generally clear and focused, it was less so on newer topics such as preferential trade agreements and trade in services. Moreover, the report noted that the IMF's involvement in trade policy through surveillance had been uneven across countries and over time. Three areas were highlighted as receiving insufficient attention despite their importance for macroeconomic stability and spillovers: trade in financial services, preferential trade agreements, and trade finance. The evaluation also found that the IMF had missed the opportunity to address the growing multilateral dimensions of trade policy.

410. In 2019, the IEO released an update report on the IMF's involvement in international trade policy issues, highlighting the IMF's strong response to changes in the global trade environment, particularly the rise in trade tensions since the global financial crisis. The report found that the IMF had significantly expanded its focus on trade policy, especially in bilateral and multilateral surveillance, and had become a key advocate for an open, rules-based multilateral trading system. In particular, the 2012 Integrated Surveillance Decision (*see supra*, paragraphs 244 ff.) acknowledged the increasing importance of trade and financial interconnections, allowing the IMF to address trade issues in bilateral surveillance when serious trade distortions threaten stability or when the balance of payment is vulnerable to adverse trade developments. In addition, trade issues had become increasingly prominent in the IMF's multilateral surveillance, particularly in response to shifting global trade dynamics and rising protectionist pressures. In contrast, trade-policy-related conditionality had virtually disappeared from Fund-supported programs.

411. In recent years, the IMF has made significant contributions to trade-related multilateral efforts under the G-20 framework. Since May 2016, the IMF has produced three high-profile reports, either independently or in collaboration with the WTO and World Bank, emphasising the critical role of trade as a driver of inclusive growth and underscoring the importance of a well-functioning, rules-based multilateral trading system.

IV. The IMF-WTO Institutional Cooperation

412. The establishment of the WTO in 1995 marked a pivotal evolution in the global trading system, moving beyond the GATT to create a more comprehensive and institutionalised framework that includes not only trade in goods but also services and intellectual property. This broadened scope reflected the growing complexity of global trade, as it increasingly intersected with other policy areas such as investment, competition, and regulatory standards – highlighting the deepening links between international trade and economic development.

413. In this context, closer cooperation between international economic institutions like the WTO and the IMF became essential to ensure coherence between trade liberalisation efforts and broader macroeconomic stability objectives. Recognising this need, the IMF and the WTO formalised their collaboration through the 1996 Cooperation Agreement. This agreement provides for the participation of staff from each institution in selected meetings of the other's governing bodies and establishes procedures for the exchange of documents and information to ensure greater policy coordination and transparency. Cooperation is particularly strong in areas such as the WTO's Trade Policy Reviews, Trade Monitoring Reports, and accession processes.

414. Despite the current challenges facing the WTO, particularly the rise in protectionist trade measures and the resulting economic fragmentation, there has been a substantial increase in cooperation between the IMF and the WTO. At the IMF Spring Meetings in April 2025, finance ministers and central bank governors expressed concerns over escalating trade tensions and their impact on global economic stability. The IMF's chief economist highlighted that the global economic system is undergoing profound changes, marked by heightened uncertainty and increased risks to growth and financial stability. The meetings underscored the critical role of the IMF in navigating these challenges and emphasised the importance of strengthening multilateral cooperation.

§6. The IMF and the European Union

415. As seen above (*see supra*, paragraphs 41 ff.), since the introduction of the single currency in 1999, euro area countries have transferred key monetary and exchange rate policy powers to the EMU level. This delegation of core sovereign monetary functions has created a dichotomy in the Fund's relationship with EU Member States, distinguishing between those that are already part of the euro area and those that have not yet adopted the euro. Despite its deep economic and monetary integration, the euro area is not represented as a single entity within the IMF, and each euro area country retains individual membership and voting rights. However, the unique features of the euro area have made the IMF's surveillance and provision of financial assistance particularly complex.

I. Surveillance

416. As far as surveillance is concerned, the IMF conducts bilateral Article IV consultations with individual EU member countries as well as with the euro area as a whole (on surveillance over currency unions *see supra*, paragraphs 256 ff.). Developments in the EU and the euro area are also analysed in the WEO, in the GFSR, in the Fiscal Monitor and in the Spillover Report, all of which form part of the IMF's multilateral surveillance framework. Before the global financial crisis, there was no FSAP (*see supra*, paragraphs 262 ff.) for the EU; the first FSAP exercises for the EU and the euro area were respectively completed in March 2013 and July 2018.

417. Modalities for conducting IMF surveillance over the euro area were established with the introduction of the euro. Every six months, IMF staff exchange views with the ECB, the European Commission and other European institutions and bodies. Surveillance over the euro area does not involve EU and national authorities simultaneously. The resulting IMF Euro Area Policies Report complements the Article IV reports covering the national policies of individual euro area Member States.

418. A general issue is the overlap of oversight responsibilities between the IMF and the EU. In the aftermath of the financial crisis, the EU adopted a set of regulations aimed at strengthening the surveillance of budgetary position as well as the surveillance and coordination of economic policies. EU surveillance currently operates according to a defined schedule under the so-called EU Semester. As a result, both organisations independently and simultaneously seek to oversee and supervise the economic policies of euro area Member States. In the absence of a formal agreement on coordination or a clear delineation of responsibilities, the potential for conflict is significant. To date, however, the enhanced EU surveillance framework has not led to changes to the scope or modalities of IMF surveillance. Nevertheless, the growing complexity of the EU framework may pose challenges to the Fund's ability to effectively conduct Article IV bilateral consultations with euro area members.

419. In addition, the different nature of IMF and EU surveillance can lead to tensions. IMF surveillance is based on cooperation between the Fund's staff and national authorities, with its influence deriving primarily from the perceived impact of the Fund's assessment on capital markets and pressure exerted by peers. In contrast, EU surveillance is a continuous process governed by a precise calendar. The Stability and Growth Pact and the Macroeconomic Imbalances Procedure establish procedures to be followed and provide for sanctions in cases of non-compliance with EU rules. Furthermore, the so-called Fiscal Compact (i.e., the Treaty on Stability, Coordination and Governance, signed by all EU members and partially incorporated into EU law in 2024) imposes additional obligations on participating States. These include the requirement to introduce a balanced-budget rule into their domestic legal system and provisions that facilitate the eventual application of sanctions. As a result, in the event of diverging policy advice from the two organisations, a European country would be compelled to follow the EU's recommendations to avoid sanctions.

II. Co-financing

420. The 2012 European sovereign debt crisis brought to the forefront the issue of providing financial assistance to an IMF advanced economy for the first time in decades. At that time, under the EU legal framework, only countries outside the euro area were eligible to receive balance of payments assistance from the Union, while no comparable mechanism existed for euro area Member States. Moreover, the Treaty on the Functioning of the European Union (TFEU) prohibited any form of monetary financing or privileged access to financial institutions, while the no-bailout clause of Article 125 TFEU made it unlawful for EU institutions or Member States to assume the debts of another member. As the EU was in the process of developing a new legal framework to provide financial assistance to euro area countries, procedures were also established to enable a closer collaboration with the Fund.

421. Cooperation between the IMF and the EU initially developed in the context of providing financial assistance to non-euro countries, specifically Hungary (2008), Latvia (2008) and Romania (2009). Although the existing EU balance of payments facility did not formally envisage the involvement of the IMF, the EU adopted internal guidelines outlining the operational procedures for coordination with the IMF. These guidelines aimed to ensure early consultation, continuous exchange of information, consistency in policy advice, synchronisation of disbursements, and alignment of programme reviews. This collaboration gave rise to the institutional arrangement commonly referred to as 'the Troika' (more recently, 'the Institutions'), composed of the IMF, the ECB and the European Commission. The members of the Troika were expected to act in accordance with the group's decisions and to refrain from disclosing internal disagreements.

422. At a later stage, when the crisis spread to euro area Member States and in particular to Greece, EU-IMF co-financing was explicitly envisaged in the newly established mechanisms: the European Financial Stabilisation Mechanism (EFSM), the European Financial Stability Facility framework agreement (EFSF) and the Treaty establishing the European Stability Mechanism (ESM).

423. Article 13(3) of the ESM Treaty assigns the task of negotiating a Memorandum of Understanding (MoU) – which outlines the conditions attached to financial assistance provided to a euro area Member State – to the European Commission, in liaison with the ECB and, 'wherever possible', with the IMF. The same wording is used in paragraph 7, which concerns the monitoring of compliance with the conditionality attached to the financial assistance facility. These provisions, however, do not elaborate on the scope or modalities of the cooperation between the EU and the IMF and, therefore, offer little clarification of the applicable legal framework. It is also worth underlining that the ESM Treaty is not binding upon the IMF, which did not take part in its drafting. In fact, the IMF Executive Board did not adopt any formal decision regarding the Fund's participation in the Troika or the terms of its involvement.

424. The Troika arrangement raised many concerns. Some critics argued that it could undermine the IMF's independence and the principle of uniform treatment of its member countries. European Executive Directors, though, viewed the arrangement more positively, especially because at the time the ECB and the European Commission lacked experience in designing crisis-response programs. Commentators also highlighted the ECB's 'dual role' and the resulting conflict of interest: in fact, the ECB played a key role in drafting programme conditions while simultaneously being tasked with monitoring the implementation of conditionality. In addition, the Troika arrangement gave rise to a substantial asymmetry within the IMF Executive Board, with information skewed in favour of euro area Directors, who collectively held more than one-third of the IMF's voting power.

425. Four euro area Member States received joint financial assistance from the IMF and the EU: Greece (2010), Ireland (2010), Portugal (2011) and Cyprus (2013). Interestingly, the primary issue for these countries was not a traditional balance of payments deficit, but rather an unsustainable sovereign debt and the inability of their governments to access capital markets to finance budget deficits. The IMF staff argued that urgent budgetary financing needs could justify the Fund's intervention under the guise of balance of payments support. However, this rationale met resistance within the IMF Executive Board, where some Directors questioned the appropriateness of using Fund resources primarily to finance a budget deficit. Further concerns were raised over the exceptional access to IMF resources granted to EU countries (*see supra*, paragraphs 171 ff.), a model that the IMF was unwilling to extend to other regional groupings and which was subsequently repealed.

§7. The IMF and Regional Financing Arrangements

426. Regional Financing Arrangements (RFAs) are mechanisms for crisis prevention or resolution established by a group of countries within a specific geographic area or sharing similar economic characteristics (e.g., BRICS). Under an RFA, members commit to provide common financial support to any member of the group that is experiencing balance of payments problems or external liquidity needs, either through a pool of financial resources or through a swap of foreign exchange reserves. Their financial resources either derive from member countries' contributions – in the form of paid-in capital or financial commitments – or from borrowing in the financial markets. Some RFAs also perform a surveillance function aimed at detecting emerging risks that would affect a member country's financing needs. A few RFAs also have a mandate for economic development and regional integration. In general, despite the heterogeneity in their mandates, histories, and operational modalities, crisis prevention and financing are the common denominator of these mechanisms.

427. Currently, there are eight RFAs: the Arab Monetary Fund; the BRICS Contingent Reserve Arrangement; the Chiang Mai Initiative Multilateralisation together with its surveillance unit (the ASEAN+3 Macroeconomic Research Office); the Eurasian Fund for Stabilization and Development; the ESM; the EU Balance of Payments Facility together with the EU Macro-Financial Assistance (both administered by the European Commission); and the Latin American Reserve Fund.

428. By the end of the Millennium, the increasing competition between RFAs and the IMF started to raise serious concerns about the effectiveness of the global financial safety net (GFSN), with many observers fearing its fragmentation. Such concerns first emerged after the 1997–1998 Asian financial crisis, when the IMF's conditionality and role in safeguarding financial stability in the region were questioned. In response, several countries decided to establish or strengthen their own RFAs to complement or, in some cases, provide alternatives to the IMF's financial assistance. Concerns intensified further during the global financial crisis of

2007–2008 as RFAs became more active in crisis prevention and resolution, potentially duplicating or conflicting with the IMF's role.

429. In 2011, this led the G-20 to adopt the 'Principles for Cooperation between the IMF and RFAs', which the Fund also endorsed. The Principles acknowledged the importance of cooperation between the IMF and RFAs to promote regional and global financial stability, but the document merely recommended the sharing of information and timely consultations (not only during crisis resolution joint missions but also in surveillance activities) as well as an alignment of lending conditions to prevent arbitrage and facility shopping. By taking this cautious approach, the G-20 Principles also pointed out the need to respect the roles, independence and decision-making processes of each RFA. Although the IMF was not granted hierarchical authority over RFAs, the Principles clarified that RFAs have to respect the IMF's preferred creditor status (*see supra*, paragraphs 336 ff.).

430. In July 2017, building upon the G-20 Principles and on lessons learnt from co-financing in Europe (*see supra*, paragraphs 420 ff.), the Fund adopted a new framework to guide its collaboration with RFAs. This initiative aimed to increase the effective firepower of the GSFN and ensure the timely deployment of financial resources. The IMF Executive Board endorsed Six Operational Principles for Strengthening IMF-RFA Collaboration, designed to enhance the transparency, predictability, and effectiveness of collaboration in an increasingly multi-layered GFSN, with the Fund firmly at its core. In reviewing its relationship with RFAs, the IMF was guided by two institutional imperatives. First, while it generally welcomes the development of RFAs, the Fund seeks to pre-empt competition over the design of programs. Second, the IMF aims to avoid the nightmare scenario in which a region misdiagnoses a crisis, intervenes ineffectively, and the country only turns to the Fund belatedly.

431. The IMF's Six Principles can be summarised as follows: (a) *Independence*: the IMF and RFAs must respect each other's autonomy, with decisions guided by their own policies and governance structures; (b) *Mandates and technical expertise*: roles in collaboration should align with each institution's mandate, legal framework, and comparative technical strengths; (c) *Early and ongoing cooperation*: continuous engagement is encouraged to strengthen crisis prevention and ensure coordinated, transparent action during crises; (d) *Consistency and limited arbitrage*: lending arrangements should be consistent, with a single country programme supported by multiple creditors, avoiding duplication or policy shopping; (e) *Even-handedness*: the IMF should engage fairly across different RFAs and their members, applying consistent principles based on the nature of the activities; (f) *IMF preferred creditor status*: the IMF's status as a preferred creditor must be upheld, reflecting its central role in the GFSN and shielding it from debt restructuring processes.

432. When discussing the Six Principles, Executive Directors underlined that when an RFA has limited capacity or its areas of responsibility do not significantly overlap with those of the Fund, the IMF should take the lead in establishing the macroeconomic framework, policy design, and conditionality (the 'lead agency model'). Conversely, where the RFA has relevant expertise and there is substantial overlap between the capabilities and mandates of the two institutions, collaboration should, in principle, be based on a single, coherent, and consistent programme framework that respects the independence of all parties involved (the 'coherent program design model'). The IMF generally expects to follow the coherent programme design model in Europe and the lead agency model everywhere else. However, RFA staff have suggested that in some cases, an RFA could take the lead instead.

433. IMF Executive Directors also noted that co-financing by the Fund would proceed only when the member's programme is consistent with the Fund's policies, and that the Fund's role in programme design and monitoring would not be contingent upon the extent of its financial contribution. Lastly, they warned that, in order to protect its independence, the Fund must be prepared to withhold its participation whenever core areas of its mandate would be otherwise compromised.

Appendix. Articles of Agreement of the International Monetary Fund (as lastly amended on 2016)

Adopted at the United Nations Monetary and Financial Conference, Bretton Woods, New Hampshire, July 22, 1944. Entered into force December 27, 1945. Amended effective July 28, 1969, by the modifications approved by the Board of Governors in Resolution No. 23–5, adopted May 31, 1968; amended effective April 1, 1978, by the modifications approved by the Board of Governors in Resolution No. 31–4, adopted April 30, 1976; amended effective November 11, 1992, by the modifications approved by the Board of Governors in Resolution No. 45–3, adopted June 28, 1990; amended effective August 10, 2009, by the modifications approved by the Board of Governors in Resolution No. 52–4, adopted September 23, 1997; amended effective February 18, 2011, by the modifications approved by the Board of Governors in Resolution No. 63–3, adopted May 5, 2008; and amended effective March 3, 2011, by the modifications approved by the Board of Governors in Resolution No. 63-2, adopted April 28, 2008; amended effective January 26, 2016 by the modifications approved by the Board of Governors in Resolution No. 66-2, adopted December 15, 2010.

The Governments on whose behalf the present Agreement is signed agree as follows:

Introductory Article

(i) The International Monetary Fund is established and shall operate in accordance with the provisions of this Agreement as originally adopted and subsequently amended.

(ii) To enable the Fund to conduct its operations and transactions, the Fund shall maintain a General Department and a Special Drawing Rights Department. Membership in the Fund shall give the right to participation in the Special Drawing Rights Department.

(iii) Operations and transactions authorised by this Agreement shall be conducted through the General Department, consisting in accordance with the provisions of this Agreement of the General Resources Account, the Special Disbursement Account, and the Investment Account; except that operations and transactions involving special drawing rights shall be conducted through the Special Drawing Rights Department.

Appendix

Article I: Purposes

The purposes of the International Monetary Fund are:

(i) To promote international monetary cooperation through a permanent institution which provides the machinery for consultation and collaboration on international monetary problems.
(ii) To facilitate the expansion and balanced growth of international trade, and to contribute thereby to the promotion and maintenance of high levels of employment and real income and to the development of the productive resources of all members as primary objectives of economic policy.
(iii) To promote exchange stability, to maintain orderly exchange arrangements among members, and to avoid competitive exchange depreciation.
(iv) To assist in the establishment of a multilateral system of payments in respect of current transactions between members and in the elimination of foreign exchange restrictions which hamper the growth of world trade.
(v) To give confidence to members by making the general resources of the Fund temporarily available to them under adequate safeguards, thus providing them with opportunity to correct maladjustments in their balance of payments without resorting to measures destructive of national or international prosperity.
(vi) In accordance with the above, to shorten the duration and lessen the degree of disequilibrium in the international balances of payments of members.

The Fund shall be guided in all its policies and decisions by the purposes set forth in this Article.

Article II: Membership

Section 1 Original Members

The original members of the Fund shall be those of the countries represented at the United Nations Monetary and Financial Conference whose governments accept membership before December 31, 1945.

Section 2 Other Members

Membership shall be open to other countries at such times and in accordance with such terms as may be prescribed by the Board of Governors. These terms, including the terms for subscriptions, shall be based on principles consistent with those applied to other countries that are already members.

Article III: Quotas and Subscriptions

Section 1 Quotas and Payment of Subscriptions

Each member shall be assigned a quota expressed in special drawing rights. The quotas of the members represented at the United Nations Monetary and Financial Conference which accept membership before December 31, 1945 shall be those set forth in Schedule A. The quotas of other members shall be determined by the Board of Governors. The subscription of each member shall be equal to its quota and shall be paid in full to the Fund at the appropriate depository.

Section 2 Adjustment of Quotas

(a) The Board of Governors shall at intervals of not more than five years conduct a general review, and if it deems it appropriate propose an adjustment, of the quotas of the members. It may also, if it thinks fit, consider at any other time the adjustment of any particular quota at the request of the member concerned.
(b) The Fund may at any time propose an increase in the quotas of those members of the Fund that were members on August 31, 1975 in proportion to their quotas on that date in a cumulative amount not in excess of amounts transferred under Article V, Section 12(f)(i) and (j) from the Special Disbursement Account to the General Resources Account.
(c) An eighty-five per cent majority of the total voting power shall be required for any change in quotas.
(d) The quota of a member shall not be changed until the member has consented and until payment has been made unless payment is deemed to have been made in accordance with Section 3(b) of this Article.

Section 3 Payments when Quotas are Changed

(a) Each member which consents to an increase in its quota under Section 2(a) of this Article shall, within a period determined by the Fund, pay to the Fund twenty-five per cent of the increase in special drawing rights, but the Board of Governors may prescribe that this payment may be made, on the same basis for all members, in whole or in part in the currencies of other members specified, with their concurrence, by the Fund, or in the member's own currency. A non-participant shall pay in the currencies of other members specified by the Fund, with their concurrence, a proportion of the increase corresponding to the proportion to be paid in special drawing rights by participants. The balance of the increase shall be paid by the member in its own currency. The Fund's holdings of a member's currency shall not be increased above the level at which they would be subject to charges under Article V, Section 8(b)(ii), as a result of payments by other members under this provision.
(b) Each member which consents to an increase in its quota under Section 2(b) of this Article shall be deemed to have paid to the Fund an amount of subscription equal to such increase.
(c) If a member consents to a reduction in its quota, the Fund shall, within sixty days, pay to the member an amount equal to the reduction. The payment shall be made in the member's currency and in such amount of special drawing rights or the currencies of other members specified, with their concurrence, by the Fund as is necessary to prevent the reduction of the Fund's holdings of the currency below the new quota, provided that in exceptional circumstances the Fund may reduce its holdings of the currency below the new quota by payment to the member in its own currency.
(d) A seventy per cent majority of the total voting power shall be required for any decision under (a) above, except for the determination of a period and the specification of currencies under that provision.

Section 4 Substitution of Securities for Currency

The Fund shall accept from any member, in place of any part of the member's currency in the General Resources Account which in the judgment of the Fund is not needed for its operations and transactions, notes or similar obligations issued by the member or the depository designated by the member under Article XIII, Section 2, which shall be non-negotiable, non-interest bearing and payable at their face value on demand by crediting the account of the Fund in the designated depository. This Section shall apply not only to currency subscribed by members but also to any currency otherwise due to, or acquired by, the Fund and to be placed in the General Resources Account.

Article IV: Obligations Regarding Exchange Arrangements

Section 1 General Obligations of Members

Recognizing that the essential purpose of the international monetary system is to provide a framework that facilitates the exchange of goods, services, and capital among countries, and that sustains sound economic growth, and that a principal objective is the continuing development of the orderly underlying conditions that are necessary for financial and economic stability, each member undertakes to collaborate with the Fund and other members to assure orderly exchange arrangements and to promote a stable system of exchange rates. In particular, each member shall:

(i) endeavor to direct its economic and financial policies toward the objective of fostering orderly economic growth with reasonable price stability, with due regard to its circumstances;
(ii) seek to promote stability by fostering orderly underlying economic and financial conditions and a monetary system that does not tend to produce erratic disruptions;
(iii) avoid manipulating exchange rates or the international monetary system in order to prevent effective balance of payments adjustment or to gain an unfair competitive advantage over other members; and
(iv) follow exchange policies compatible with the undertakings under this Section.

Section 2 General Exchange Arrangements

(a) Each member shall notify the Fund, within thirty days after the date of the second amendment of this Agreement, of the exchange arrangements it intends to apply in fulfillment of its obligations under Section 1 of this Article, and shall notify the Fund promptly of any changes in its exchange arrangements.
(b) Under an international monetary system of the kind prevailing on January 1, 1976, exchange arrangements may include (i) the maintenance by a member of a value for its currency in terms of the special drawing right or another denominator, other than gold, selected by the member, or (ii) cooperative arrangements

by which members maintain the value of their currencies in relation to the value of the currency or currencies of other members, or (iii) other exchange arrangements of a member's choice.

(c) To accord with the development of the international monetary system, the Fund, by an eighty-five per cent majority of the total voting power, may make provision for general exchange arrangements without limiting the right of members to have exchange arrangements of their choice consistent with the purposes of the Fund and the obligations under Section 1 of this Article.

Section 3 Surveillance over Exchange Arrangements

(a) The Fund shall oversee the international monetary system in order to ensure its effective operation, and shall oversee the compliance of each member with its obligations under Section 1 of this Article.

(b) In order to fulfill its functions under (a) above, the Fund shall exercise firm surveillance over the exchange rate policies of members, and shall adopt specific principles for the guidance of all members with respect to those policies. Each member shall provide the Fund with the information necessary for such surveillance, and, when requested by the Fund, shall consult with it on the member's exchange rate policies. The principles adopted by the Fund shall be consistent with cooperative arrangements by which members maintain the value of their currencies in relation to the value of the currency or currencies of other members, as well as with other exchange arrangements of a member's choice consistent with the purposes of the Fund and Section 1 of this Article. These principles shall respect the domestic social and political policies of members, and in applying these principles the Fund shall pay due regard to the circumstances of members.

Section 4 Par Values

The Fund may determine, by an eighty-five per cent majority of the total voting power, that international economic conditions permit the introduction of a widespread system of exchange arrangements based on stable but adjustable par values. The Fund shall make the determination on the basis of the underlying stability of the world economy, and for this purpose shall take into account price movements and rates of expansion in the economies of members. The determination shall be made in light of the evolution of the international monetary system, with particular reference to sources of liquidity, and, in order to ensure the effective operation of a system of par values, to arrangements under which both members in surplus and members in deficit in their balances of payments take prompt, effective, and symmetrical action to achieve adjustment, as well as to arrangements for intervention and the treatment of imbalances. Upon making such determination, the Fund shall notify members that the provisions of Schedule C apply.

Section 5 Separate Currencies within a Member's Territories

(a) Action by a member with respect to its currency under this Article shall be deemed to apply to the separate currencies of all territories in respect of which the member has accepted this Agreement under Article XXXI, Section 2 (g) unless the member declares that its action relates either to the metropolitan currency alone, or only to one or more specified separate currencies, or to the metropolitan currency and one or more specified separate currencies.
(b) Action by the Fund under this Article shall be deemed to relate to all currencies of a member referred to in (a) above unless the Fund declares otherwise.

Article V: Operations and Transactions of the Fund

Section 1 Agencies Dealing with the Fund

Each member shall deal with the Fund only through its Treasury, central bank, stabilisation fund, or other similar fiscal agency, and the Fund shall deal only with or through the same agencies.

Section 2 Limitation on the Fund's Operations and Transactions

(a) Except as otherwise provided in this Agreement, transactions on the account of the Fund shall be limited to transactions for the purpose of supplying a member, on the initiative of such member, with special drawing rights or the currencies of other members from the general resources of the Fund, which shall be held in the General Resources Account, in exchange for the currency of the member desiring to make the purchase.
(b) If requested, the Fund may decide to perform financial and technical services, including the administration of resources contributed by members, that are consistent with the purposes of the Fund. Operations involved in the performance of such financial services shall not be on the account of the Fund. Services under this subsection shall not impose any obligation on a member without its consent.

Section 3 Conditions Governing Use of the Fund's General Resources

(a) The Fund shall adopt policies on the use of its general resources, including policies on stand-by or similar arrangements, and may adopt special policies for special balance of payments problems, that will assist members to solve their balance of payments problems in a manner consistent with the provisions of this Agreement and that will establish adequate safeguards for the temporary use of the general resources of the Fund.
(b) A member shall be entitled to purchase the currencies of other members from the Fund in exchange for an equivalent amount of its own currency subject to the following conditions:

(i) the member's use of the general resources of the Fund would be in accordance with the provisions of this Agreement and the policies adopted under them;

(ii) the member represents that it has a need to make the purchase because of its balance of payments or its reserve position or developments in its reserves;

(iii) the proposed purchase would be a reserve tranche purchase, or would not cause the Fund's holdings of the purchasing member's currency to exceed two hundred per cent of its quota;

(iv) the Fund has not previously declared under Section 5 of this Article, Article VI, Section 1, or Article XXVI, Section 2 (a) that the member desiring to purchase is ineligible to use the general resources of the Fund.

(c) The Fund shall examine a request for a purchase to determine whether the proposed purchase would be consistent with the provisions of this Agreement and the policies adopted under them, provided that requests for reserve tranche purchases shall not be subject to challenge.

(d) The Fund shall adopt policies and procedures on the selection of currencies to be sold that take into account, in consultation with members, the balance of payments and reserve position of members and developments in the exchange markets, as well as the desirability of promoting over time balanced positions in the Fund, provided that if a member represents that it is proposing to purchase the currency of another member because the purchasing member wishes to obtain an equivalent amount of its own currency offered by the other member, it shall be entitled to purchase the currency of the other member unless the Fund has given notice under Article VII, Section 3 that its holdings of the currency have become scarce

(i) Each member shall ensure that balances of its currency purchased from the Fund are balances of a freely usable currency or can be exchanged at the time of purchase for a freely usable currency of its choice at an exchange rate between the two currencies equivalent to the exchange rate between them on the basis of Article XIX, Section 7(a).

(ii) Each member whose currency is purchased from the Fund or is obtained in exchange for currency purchased from the Fund shall collaborate with the Fund and other members to enable such balances of its currency to be exchanged, at the time of purchase, for the freely usable currencies of other members.

(iii) An exchange under (i) above of a currency that is not freely usable shall be made by the member whose currency is purchased unless that member and the purchasing member agree on another procedure.

(iv) A member purchasing from the Fund the freely usable currency of another member and wishing to exchange it at the time of purchase for another freely usable currency shall make the exchange with the other member if requested by that member. The exchange shall be made for a freely usable currency selected by the other member at the rate of exchange referred to in (i) above.

(f) Under policies and procedures which it shall adopt, the Fund may agree to provide a participant making a purchase in accordance with this Section with special drawing rights instead of the currencies of other members.

Section 4 Waiver of Conditions

The Fund may in its discretion, and on terms which safeguard its interests, waive any of the conditions prescribed in Section 3(b)(iii) and (iv) of this Article, especially in the case of members with a record of avoiding large or continuous use of the Fund's general resources. In making a waiver it shall take into consideration periodic or exceptional requirements of the member requesting the waiver. The Fund shall also take into consideration a member's willingness to pledge as collateral security acceptable assets having a value sufficient in the opinion of the Fund to protect its interests and may require as a condition of waiver the pledge of such collateral security.

Section 5 Ineligibility to Use the Fund's General Resources

Whenever the Fund is of the opinion that any member is using the general resources of the Fund in a manner contrary to the purposes of the Fund, it shall present to the member a report setting forth the views of the Fund and prescribing a suitable time for reply. After presenting such a report to a member, the Fund may limit the use of its general resources by the member. If no reply to the report is received from the member within the prescribed time, or if the reply received is unsatisfactory, the Fund may continue to limit the member's use of the general resources of the Fund or may, after giving reasonable notice to the member, declare it ineligible to use the general resources of the Fund.

Section 6 Other Purchases and Sales of Special Drawing Rights by the Fund

(a) The Fund may accept special drawing rights offered by a participant in exchange for an equivalent amount of the currencies of other members.
(b) The Fund may provide a participant, at its request, with special drawing rights for an equivalent amount of the currencies of other members. The Fund's holdings of a member's currency shall not be increased as a result of these transactions above the level at which the holdings would be subject to charges under Section 8(b)(ii) of this Article.
(c) The currencies provided or accepted by the Fund under this Section shall be selected in accordance with policies that take into account the principles of Section 3(d) or 7(i) of this Article. The Fund may enter into transactions under this Section only if a member whose currency is provided or accepted by the Fund concurs in that use of its currency.

Section 7 Repurchase by a Member of its Currency Held by the Fund

(a) A member shall be entitled to repurchase at any time the Fund's holdings of its currency that are subject to charges under Section 8(b) of this Article.

(b) A member that has made a purchase under Section 3 of this Article will be expected normally, as its balance of payments and reserve position improves, to repurchase the Fund's holdings of its currency that result from the purchase and are subject to charges under Section 8(b) of this Article. A member shall repurchase these holdings if, in accordance with policies on repurchase that the Fund shall adopt and after consultation with the member, the Fund represents to the member that it should repurchase because of an improvement in its balance of payments and reserve position.

(c) A member that has made a purchase under Section 3 of this Article shall repurchase the Fund's holdings of its currency that result from the purchase and are subject to charges under Section 8(b) of this Article not later than five years after the date on which the purchase was made. The Fund may prescribe that repurchase shall be made by a member in installments during the period beginning three years and ending five years after the date of a purchase. The Fund, by an eighty-five per cent majority of the total voting power, may change the periods for repurchase under this subsection, and any period so adopted shall apply to all members.

(d) The Fund, by an eighty-five per cent majority of the total voting power, may adopt periods other than those that apply in accordance with (c) above, which shall be the same for all members, for the repurchase of holdings of currency acquired by the Fund pursuant to a special policy on the use of its general resources.

(e) A member shall repurchase, in accordance with policies that the Fund shall adopt by a seventy per cent majority of the total voting power, the Fund's holdings of its currency that are not acquired as a result of purchases and are subject to charges under Section 8(b)(ii) of this Article.

(f) A decision prescribing that under a policy on the use of the general resources of the Fund the period for repurchase under (c) or (d) above shall be shorter than the one in effect under the policy shall apply only to holdings acquired by the Fund subsequent to the effective date of the decision.

(g) The Fund, on the request of a member, may postpone the date of discharge of a repurchase obligation, but not beyond the maximum period under (c) or (d) above or under policies adopted by the Fund under (e) above, unless the Fund determines, by a seventy per cent majority of the total voting power, that a longer period for repurchase which is consistent with the temporary use of the general resources of the Fund is justified because discharge on the due date would result in exceptional hardship for the member.

(h) The Fund's policies under Section 3(d) of this Article may be supplemented by policies under which the Fund may decide after consultation with a member to sell under Section 3(b) of this Article its holdings of the member's currency that have not been repurchased in accordance with this Section 7, without prejudice to any action that the Fund may be authorised to take under any other provision of this Agreement.

(i) All repurchases under this Section shall be made with special drawing rights or with the currencies of other members specified by the Fund. The Fund shall adopt policies and procedures with regard to the currencies to be used by members in making repurchases that take into account the principles in Section 3(d) of this Article. The Fund's holdings of a member's currency that is used in repurchase shall not be increased by the repurchase above the level at which they would be subject to charges under Section 8(b)(ii) of this Article.

(i) If a member's currency specified by the Fund under (i) above is not a freely usable currency, the member shall ensure that the repurchasing member can obtain it at the time of the repurchase in exchange for a freely usable currency selected by the member whose currency has been specified. An exchange of currency under this provision shall take place at an exchange rate between the two currencies equivalent to the exchange rate between them on the basis of Article XIX, Section 7(a).

(ii) Each member whose currency is specified by the Fund for repurchase shall collaborate with the Fund and other members to enable repurchasing members, at the time of the repurchase, to obtain the specified currency in exchange for the freely usable currencies of other members.

(iii) An exchange under (j)(i) above shall be made with the member whose currency is specified unless that member and the repurchasing member agree on another procedure.

(iv) If a repurchasing member wishes to obtain, at the time of the repurchase, the freely usable currency of another member specified by the Fund under (i) above, it shall, if requested by the other member, obtain the currency from the other member in exchange for a freely usable currency at the rate of exchange referred to in (j)(i) above. The Fund may adopt regulations on the freely usable currency to be provided in an exchange.

Section 8 Charges

(a) (i) The Fund shall levy a service charge on the purchase by a member of special drawing rights or the currency of another member held in the General Resources Account in exchange for its own currency, provided that the Fund may levy a lower service charge on reserve tranche purchases than on other purchases. The service charge on reserve tranche purchases shall not exceed one-half of one per cent.

(ii) The Fund may levy a charge for stand-by or similar arrangements. The Fund may decide that the charge for an arrangement shall be offset against the service charge levied under (i) above on purchases under the arrangement.

(b) The Fund shall levy charges on its average daily balances of a member's currency held in the General Resources Account to the extent that they

(i) have been acquired under a policy that has been the subject of an exclusion under Article XXX(c), or

(ii) exceed the amount of the member's quota after excluding any balances referred to in (i) above.

(iii) rates of charge normally shall rise at intervals during the period in which the balances are held.

(c) If a member fails to make a repurchase required under Section 7 of this Article, the Fund, after consultation with the member on the reduction of the Fund's holdings of its currency, may impose such charges as the Fund deems appropriate on its holdings of the member's currency that should have been repurchased.

(d) A seventy per cent majority of the total voting power shall be required for the determination of the rates of charge under (a) and (b) above, which shall be uniform for all members, and under (c) above.

(e) A member shall pay all charges in special drawing rights, provided that in exceptional circumstances the Fund may permit a member to pay charges in the currencies of other members specified by the Fund, after consultation with them, or in its own currency. The Fund's holdings of a member's currency shall not be increased as a result of payments by other members under this provision above the level at which they would be subject to charges under (b)(ii) above.

Section 9 Remuneration

(a) The Fund shall pay remuneration on the amount by which the percentage of quota prescribed under (b) or (c) below exceeds the Fund's average daily balances of a member's currency held in the General Resources Account other than balances acquired under a policy that has been the subject of an exclusion under Article XXX(c). The rate of remuneration, which shall be determined by the Fund by a seventy per cent majority of the total voting power, shall be the same for all members and shall be not more than, nor less than four-fifths of, the rate of interest under Article XX, Section 3. In establishing the rate of remuneration, the Fund shall take into account the rates of charge under Article V, Section 8(b).

(b) The percentage of quota applying for the purposes of (a) above shall be:

(i) for each member that became a member before the second amendment of this Agreement, a percentage of quota corresponding to seventy-five per cent of its quota on the date of the second amendment of this Agreement, and for each member that became a member after the date of the second amendment of this Agreement, a percentage of quota calculated by dividing the total of the amounts corresponding to the percentages of quota that apply to the other members on the date on which the member became a member by the total of the quotas of the other members on the same date; plus

(ii) the amounts it has paid to the Fund in currency or special drawing rights under Article III, Section 3(a) since the date applicable under (b)(i) above; and minus

(iii) the amounts it has received from the Fund in currency or special drawing rights under Article III, Section 3(c) since the date applicable under (b)(i) above.

(c) The Fund, by a seventy per cent majority of the total voting power, may raise the latest percentage of quota applying for the purposes of (a) above to each member to:

(i) a percentage, not in excess of one hundred per cent, that shall be determined for each member on the basis of the same criteria for all members, or

(ii) one hundred per cent for all members.

(d) Remuneration shall be paid in special drawing rights, provided that either the Fund or the member may decide that the payment to the member shall be made in its own currency.

Section 10 Computations

(a) The value of the Fund's assets held in the accounts of the General Department shall be expressed in terms of the special drawing right.

(b) All computations relating to currencies of members for the purpose of applying the provisions of this Agreement, except Article IV and Schedule C, shall be at the rates at which the Fund accounts for these currencies in accordance with Section 11 of this Article.

(c) Computations for the determination of amounts of currency in relation to quota for the purpose of applying the provisions of this Agreement shall not include currency held in the Special Disbursement Account or in the Investment Account.

Section 11 Maintenance of Value

(a) The value of the currencies of members held in the General Resources Account shall be maintained in terms of the special drawing right in accordance with exchange rates under Article XIX, Section 7(a).

(b) An adjustment in the Fund's holdings of a member's currency pursuant to this Section shall be made on the occasion of the use of that currency in an operation or transaction between the Fund and another member and at such other times as the Fund may decide or the member may request. Payments to or by the Fund in respect of an adjustment shall be made within a reasonable time, as determined by the Fund, after the date of adjustment, and at any other time requested by the member.

Section 12 Other Operations and Transactions

(a) The Fund shall be guided in all its policies and decisions under this Section by the objectives set forth in Article VIII, Section 7 and by the objective of avoiding the management of the price, or the establishment of a fixed price, in the gold market.

(b) Decisions of the Fund to engage in operations or transactions under (c), (d), and (e) below shall be made by an eighty-five per cent majority of the total voting power.

(c) The Fund may sell gold for the currency of any member after consulting the member for whose currency the gold is sold, provided that the Fund's holdings of a member's currency held in the General Resources Account shall not be increased by the sale above the level at which they would be subject to charges under Section 8(b)(ii) of this Article without the concurrence of the member, and provided that, at the request of the member, the Fund at the time of sale shall exchange for the currency of another member such part of the currency received as would prevent such an increase. The exchange of a currency for the currency of another member shall be made after consultation with that member, and shall not increase the Fund's holdings of that member's currency above the level at which they would be subject to charges under Section 8(b)(ii) of this Article. The Fund shall adopt policies and procedures with regard to exchanges that take into account the principles applied under Section 7(i) of this Article. Sales under this provision to a member shall be at a price agreed for each transaction on the basis of prices in the market.

(d) The Fund may accept payments from a member in gold instead of special drawing rights or currency in any operations or transactions under this Agreement. Payments to the Fund under this provision shall be at a price agreed for each operation or transaction on the basis of prices in the market.

(e) The Fund may sell gold held by it on the date of the second amendment of this Agreement to those members that were members on August 31, 1975 and that agree to buy it, in proportion to their quotas on that date. If the Fund intends to sell gold under (c) above for the purpose of (f)(ii) below, it may sell to each developing member that agrees to buy it that portion of the gold which, if sold under (c) above, would have produced the excess that could have been distributed to it under (f)(iii) below. The gold that would be sold under this provision to a member that has been declared ineligible to use the general resources of the Fund under Section 5 of this Article shall be sold to it when the ineligibility ceases, unless the Fund decides to make the sale sooner. The sale of gold to a member under this subsection (e) shall be made in exchange for its currency and at a price equivalent at the time of sale to one special drawing right per 0.888 671 gram of fine gold.

(f) Whenever under (c) above the Fund sells gold held by it on the date of the second amendment of this Agreement, an amount of the proceeds equivalent at the time of sale to one special drawing right per 0.888 671 gram of fine gold shall be placed in the General Resources Account and, except as the Fund may decide otherwise under (g) below, any excess shall be held in the Special Disbursement Account. The assets held in the Special Disbursement Account shall be held separately from the other accounts of the General Department, and may be used at any time:

(i) to make transfers to the General Resources Account for immediate use in operations and transactions authorised by provisions of this Agreement other than this Section;

(ii) for operations and transactions that are not authorised by other provisions of this Agreement but are consistent with the purposes of the Fund. Under this subsection (f)(ii) balance of payments assistance may be made available on special terms to developing members in difficult circumstances, and for this purpose the Fund shall take into account the level of per capita income;

(iii) for distribution to those developing members that were members on August 31, 1975, in proportion to their quotas on that date, of such part of the assets that the Fund decides to use for the purposes of (ii) above as corresponds to the proportion of the quotas of these members on the date of distribution to the total of the quotas of all members on the same date, provided that the distribution under this provision to a member that has been declared ineligible to use the general resources of the Fund under Section 5 of this Article shall be made when the ineligibility ceases, unless the Fund decides to make the distribution sooner.

(iv) to use assets pursuant to (i) above shall be taken by a seventy per cent majority of the total voting power, and decisions pursuant to (ii) and (iii) above shall be taken by an eighty-five per cent majority of the total voting power.

(g) The Fund may decide, by an eighty-five per cent majority of the total voting power, to transfer a part of the excess referred to in (f) above to the Investment Account for use pursuant to the provisions of Article XII, Section 6(f).

(h) Pending uses specified under (f) above, the Fund may use a member's currency held in the Special Disbursement Account for investment as it may determine, in accordance with rules and regulations adopted by the Fund by a seventy per cent majority of the total voting power. The income of investment and interest received under (f)(ii) above shall be placed in the Special Disbursement Account.

(i) The General Resources Account shall be reimbursed from time to time in respect of the expenses of administration of the Special Disbursement Account paid from the General Resources Account by transfers from the Special Disbursement Account on the basis of a reasonable estimate of such expenses.

(j) The Special Disbursement Account shall be terminated in the event of the liquidation of the Fund and may be terminated prior to liquidation of the Fund by a seventy per cent majority of the total voting power. Upon termination of the account because of the liquidation of the Fund, any assets in this account shall be distributed in accordance with the provisions of Schedule K. Upon termination prior to liquidation of the Fund, any assets in this account shall be transferred to the General Resources Account for immediate use in operations and transactions. The Fund, by a seventy per cent majority of the total voting power, shall adopt rules and regulations for the administration of the Special Disbursement Account.

(k) Whenever under (c) above the Fund sells gold acquired by it after the date of the second amendment of this Agreement, an amount of the proceeds equivalent to the acquisition price of the gold shall be placed in the General Resources Account, and any excess shall be placed in the Investment Account for use pursuant to the provisions of Article XII, Section 6(f). If any gold acquired by the Fund after the date of the second amendment of this Agreement is sold after April 7, 2008 but prior to the date of entry into force of this provision, then, upon the entry into force of this provision, and notwithstanding the limit set forth in Article XII, Section 6(f)(ii), the Fund shall transfer to the Investment Account from the General Resources Account an amount equal to the proceeds of such sale less (i) the acquisition price of the gold sold, and (ii) any amount of such proceeds in excess of the acquisition price that may have already been transferred to the Investment Account prior to the date of entry into force of this provision.

Article VI: Capital Transfers

Section 1 Use of the Fund's General Resources for Capital Transfers

(a) A member may not use the Fund's general resources to meet a large or sustained outflow of capital except as provided in Section 2 of this Article, and the Fund may request a member to exercise controls to prevent such use of the general resources of the Fund. If, after receiving such a request, a member fails to exercise appropriate controls, the Fund may declare the member ineligible to use the general resources of the Fund.

(b) Nothing in this Section shall be deemed:

   (i) to prevent the use of the general resources of the Fund for capital transactions of reasonable amount required for the expansion of exports or in the ordinary course of trade, banking, or other business; or

   (ii) to affect capital movements which are met out of a member's own resources, but members undertake that such capital movements will be in accordance with the purposes of the Fund.

Section 2 Special Provisions for Capital Transfers

A member shall be entitled to make reserve tranche purchases to meet capital transfers.

Section 3 Controls of Capital Transfers

Members may exercise such controls as are necessary to regulate international capital movements, but no member may exercise these controls in a manner which will restrict payments for current transactions or which will unduly delay transfers of funds in settlement of commitments, except as provided in Article VII, Section 3(b) and in Article XIV, Section 2.

Article VII: Replenishment and Scarce Currencies

Section 1 Measures to Replenish the Fund's Holdings of Currencies

The Fund may, if it deems such action appropriate to replenish its holdings of any member's currency in the General Resources Account needed in connection with its transactions, take either or both of the following steps:

(i) propose to the member that, on terms and conditions agreed between the Fund and the member, the latter lend its currency to the Fund or that, with the concurrence of the member, the Fund borrow such currency from some other source either within or outside the territories of the member, but no member shall be under any obligation to make such loans to the Fund or to concur in the borrowing of its currency by the Fund from any other source;

(ii) require the member, if it is a participant, to sell its currency to the Fund for special drawing rights held in the General Resources Account, subject to Article XIX, Section 4. In replenishing with special drawing rights, the Fund shall pay due regard to the principles of designation under Article XIX, Section 5.

Section 2 General Scarcity of Currency

If the Fund finds that a general scarcity of a particular currency is developing, the Fund may so inform members and may issue a report setting forth the causes of the scarcity and containing recommendations designed to bring it to an end. A representative of the member whose currency is involved shall participate in the preparation of the report.

Section 3 Scarcity of the Fund's Holdings

(a) If it becomes evident to the Fund that the demand for a member's currency seriously threatens the Fund's ability to supply that currency, the Fund, whether or not it has issued a report under Section 2 of this Article, shall formally declare such currency scarce and shall thenceforth apportion its existing and accruing supply of the scarce currency with due regard to the relative needs of members, the general international economic situation, and any other pertinent considerations. The Fund shall also issue a report concerning its action.
(b) A formal declaration under (a) above shall operate as an authorisation to any member, after consultation with the Fund, temporarily to impose limitations on the freedom of exchange operations in the scarce currency. Subject to the provisions of Article IV and Schedule C, the member shall have complete jurisdiction in determining the nature of such limitations, but they shall be no more restrictive than is necessary to limit the demand for the scarce currency to the supply held by, or accruing to, the member in question, and they shall be relaxed and removed as rapidly as conditions permit.
(c) The authorisation under (b) above shall expire whenever the Fund formally declares the currency in question to be no longer scarce.

Section 4 Administration of Restrictions

Any member imposing restrictions in respect of the currency of any other member pursuant to the provisions of Section 3(b) of this Article shall give sympathetic consideration to any representations by the other member regarding the administration of such restrictions.

Section 5 Effect of Other International Agreements on Restrictions

Members agree not to invoke the obligations of any engagements entered into with other members prior to this Agreement in such manner as will prevent the operation of the provisions of this Article.

Article VIII: General Obligations of Members

Section 1 Introduction

In addition to the obligations assumed under other articles of this Agreement, each member undertakes the obligations set out in this Article.

Section 2 Avoidance of Restrictions on Current Payments

(a) Subject to the provisions of Article VII, Section 3(b) and Article XIV, Section 2, no member shall, without the approval of the Fund, impose restrictions on the making of payments and transfers for current international transactions.
(b) Exchange contracts which involve the currency of any member and which are contrary to the exchange control regulations of that member maintained or imposed consistently with this Agreement shall be unenforceable in the territories of any member. In addition, members may, by mutual accord, cooperate in measures for the purpose of making the exchange control regulations of either member more effective, provided that such measures and regulations are consistent with this Agreement.

Section 3 Avoidance of Discriminatory Currency Practices

No member shall engage in, or permit any of its fiscal agencies referred to in Article V, Section 1 to engage in, any discriminatory currency arrangements or multiple currency practices, whether within or outside margins under Article IV or prescribed by or under Schedule C, except as authorised under this Agreement or approved by the Fund. If such arrangements and practices are engaged in at the date when this Agreement enters into force, the member concerned shall consult with the Fund as to their progressive removal unless they are maintained or imposed under Article XIV, Section 2, in which case the provisions of Section 3 of that Article shall apply.

Section 4 Convertibility of Foreign-Held Balances

(a) Each member shall buy balances of its currency held by another member if the latter, in requesting the purchase, represents:
    (i) that the balances to be bought have been recently acquired as a result of current transactions; or
    (ii) that their conversion is needed for making payments for current transactions.
    (iii) buying member shall have the option to pay either in special drawing rights, subject to Article XIX, Section 4, or in the currency of the member making the request.
(b) The obligation in (a) above shall not apply when:
    (i) the convertibility of the balances has been restricted consistently with Section 2 of this Article or Article VI, Section 3;

(ii) the balances have accumulated as a result of transactions effected before the removal by a member of restrictions maintained or imposed under Article XIV, Section 2;
(iii) the balances have been acquired contrary to the exchange regulations of the member which is asked to buy them;
(iv) the currency of the member requesting the purchase has been declared scarce under Article VII, Section 3 (a); or
(v) the member requested to make the purchase is for any reason not entitled to buy currencies of other members from the Fund for its own currency.

Section 5 Furnishing of Information

(a) The Fund may require members to furnish it with such information as it deems necessary for its activities, including, as the minimum necessary for the effective discharge of the Fund's duties, national data on the following matters:
(i) official holdings at home and abroad of (1) gold, (2) foreign exchange;
(ii) holdings at home and abroad by banking and financial agencies, other than official agencies, of (1) gold, (2) foreign exchange;
(iii) production of gold;
(iv) gold exports and imports according to countries of destination and origin;
(v) total exports and imports of merchandise, in terms of local currency values, according to countries of destination and origin;
(vi) international balance of payments, including (1) trade in goods and services, (2) gold transactions, (3) known capital transactions, and (4) other items;
(vii) international investment position, i.e., investments within the territories of the member owned abroad and investments abroad owned by persons in its territories so far as it is possible to furnish this information;
(viii) national income;
(ix) price indices, i.e., indices of commodity prices in wholesale and retail markets and of export and import prices;
(x) buying and selling rates for foreign currencies;
(xi) exchange controls, i.e., a comprehensive Statement of exchange controls in effect at the time of assuming membership in the Fund and details of subsequent changes as they occur; and
(xii) where official clearing arrangements exist, details of amounts awaiting clearance in respect of commercial and financial transactions, and of the length of time during which such arrears have been outstanding.

(b) In requesting information the Fund shall take into consideration the varying ability of members to furnish the data requested. Members shall be under no obligation to furnish information in such detail that the affairs of individuals or corporations are disclosed. Members undertake, however, to furnish the desired information in as detailed and accurate a manner as is practicable and, so far as possible, to avoid mere estimates.

(c) The Fund may arrange to obtain further information by agreement with members. It shall act as a centre for the collection and exchange of information on monetary and financial problems, thus facilitating the preparation of studies designed to assist members in developing policies which further the purposes of the Fund.

Section 6 Consultation between Members Regarding Existing International Agreements

Where under this Agreement a member is authorised in the special or temporary circumstances specified in the Agreement to maintain or establish restrictions on exchange transactions, and there are other engagements between members entered into prior to this Agreement which conflict with the application of such restrictions, the parties to such engagements shall consult with one another with a view to making such mutually acceptable adjustments as may be necessary. The provisions of this Article shall be without prejudice to the operation of Article VII, Section 5.

Section 7 Obligation to Collaborate regarding Policies on Reserve Assets

Each member undertakes to collaborate with the Fund and with other members in order to ensure that the policies of the member with respect to reserve assets shall be consistent with the objectives of promoting better international surveillance of international liquidity and making the special drawing right the principal reserve asset in the international monetary system.

Article IX: Status, Immunities, and Privileges

Section 1 Purposes of Article

To enable the Fund to fulfill the functions with which it is entrusted, the status, immunities, and privileges set forth in this Article shall be accorded to the Fund in the territories of each member.

Section 2 Status of the Fund

The Fund shall possess full juridical personality, and in particular, the capacity:

(i) to contract;
(ii) to acquire and dispose of immovable and movable property; and
(iii) to institute legal proceedings.

Section 3 Immunity from Judicial Process

The Fund, its property and its assets, wherever located and by whomsoever held, shall enjoy immunity from every form of judicial process except to the extent that it expressly waives its immunity for the purpose of any proceedings or by the terms of any contract.

Section 4 Immunity from Other Action

Property and assets of the Fund, wherever located and by whomsoever held, shall be immune from search, requisition, confiscation, expropriation, or any other form of seizure by executive or legislative action.

Section 5 Immunity of Archives

The archives of the Fund shall be inviolable.

Section 6 Freedom of Assets from Restrictions

To the extent necessary to carry out the activities provided for in this Agreement, all property and assets of the Fund shall be free from restrictions, regulations, controls, and moratoria of any nature.

Section 7 Privilege for Communications

The official communications of the Fund shall be accorded by members the same treatment as the official communications of other members.

Section 8 Immunities and Privileges of Officers and Employees

All Governors, Executive Directors, Alternates, members of committees, representatives appointed under Article XII, Section 3(j), advisors of any of the foregoing persons, officers, and employees of the Fund:

(i) shall be immune from legal process with respect to acts performed by them in their official capacity except when the Fund waives this immunity;
(ii) not being local nationals, shall be granted the same immunities from immigration restrictions, alien registration requirements, and national service obligations and the same facilities as regards exchange restrictions as are accorded by members to the representatives, officials, and employees of comparable rank of other members; and
(iii) shall be granted the same treatment in respect of traveling facilities as is accorded by members to representatives, officials, and employees of comparable rank of other members.

Section 9 Immunities from Taxation

(a) The Fund, its assets, property, income, and its operations and transactions authorised by this Agreement shall be immune from all taxation and from all customs duties. The Fund shall also be immune from liability for the collection or payment of any tax or duty.
(b) No tax shall be levied on or in respect of salaries and emoluments paid by the Fund to Executive Directors, Alternates, officers, or employees of the Fund who are not local citizens, local subjects, or other local nationals.
(c) No taxation of any kind shall be levied on any obligation or security issued by the Fund, including any dividend or interest thereon, by whomsoever held:
    (i) which discriminates against such obligation or security solely because of its origin; or
    (ii) if the sole jurisdictional basis for such taxation is the place or currency in which it is issued, made payable or paid, or the location of any office or place of business maintained by the Fund.

Section 10 Application of Article

Each member shall take such action as is necessary in its own territories for the purpose of making effective in terms of its own law the principles set forth in this Article and shall inform the Fund of the detailed action which it has taken.

Article X: Relations with Other International Organisations

The Fund shall cooperate within the terms of this Agreement with any general international organisation and with public international organisations having specialised responsibilities in related fields. Any arrangements for such cooperation which would involve a modification of any provision of this Agreement may be effected only after amendment to this Agreement under Article XXVIII.

Article XI: Relations with Non-member Countries

Section 1 Undertakings Regarding Relations with Non-member Countries

Each member undertakes:

(i) not to engage in, nor to permit any of its fiscal agencies referred to in Article V, Section 1 to engage in, any transactions with a non-member or with persons in a non-member's territories which would be contrary to the provisions of this Agreement or the purposes of the Fund;
(ii) not to cooperate with a non-member or with persons in a non-member's territories in practices which would be contrary to the provisions of this Agreement or the purposes of the Fund; and
(iii) to cooperate with the Fund with a view to the application in its territories of appropriate measures to prevent transactions with non-members or with persons in their territories which would be contrary to the provisions of this Agreement or the purposes of the Fund.

Section 2 Restrictions on Transactions with Non-member Countries

Nothing in this Agreement shall affect the right of any member to impose restrictions on exchange transactions with non-members or with persons in their territories unless the Fund finds that such restrictions prejudice the interests of members and are contrary to the purposes of the Fund.

Article XII: Organisation and Management

Section 1 Structure of the Fund

The Fund shall have a Board of Governors, an Executive Board, a Managing Director, and a staff, and a Council if the Board of Governors decides, by an eighty-five per cent majority of the total voting power, that the provisions of Schedule D shall be applied.

Appendix

Section 2 Board of Governors

(a) All powers under this Agreement not conferred directly on the Board of Governors, the Executive Board, or the Managing Director shall be vested in the Board of Governors. The Board of Governors shall consist of one Governor and one Alternate appointed by each member in such manner as it may determine. Each Governor and each Alternate shall serve until a new appointment is made. No Alternate may vote except in the absence of his principal. The Board of Governors shall select one of the Governors as Chairman.
(b) The Board of Governors may delegate to the Executive Board authority to exercise any powers of the Board of Governors, except the powers conferred directly by this Agreement on the Board of Governors.
(c) The Board of Governors shall hold such meetings as may be provided for by the Board of Governors or called by the Executive Board. Meetings of the Board of Governors shall be called whenever requested by fifteen members or by members having one-quarter of the total voting power.
(d) A quorum for any meeting of the Board of Governors shall be a majority of the Governors having not less than two-thirds of the total voting power.
(e) Each Governor shall be entitled to cast the number of votes allotted under Section 5 of this Article to the member appointing him.
(f) The Board of Governors may by regulation establish a procedure whereby the Executive Board, when it deems such action to be in the best interests of the Fund, may obtain a vote of the Governors on a specific question without calling a meeting of the Board of Governors.
(g) The Board of Governors, and the Executive Board to the extent authorised, may adopt such rules and regulations as may be necessary or appropriate to conduct the business of the Fund.
(h) Governors and Alternates shall serve as such without compensation from the Fund, but the Fund may pay them reasonable expenses incurred in attending meetings.
(i) The Board of Governors shall determine the remuneration to be paid to the Executive Directors and their Alternates and the salary and terms of the contract of service of the Managing Director.
(j) The Board of Governors and the Executive Board may appoint such committees as they deem advisable. Membership of committees need not be limited to Governors or Executive Directors or their Alternates.

Section 3 Executive Board

(a) The Executive Board shall be responsible for conducting the business of the Fund, and for this purpose shall exercise all the powers delegated to it by the Board of Governors.
(b) Subject to (c) below, the Executive Board shall consist of twenty Executive Directors elected by the members, with the Managing Director as chairman.

(c) For the purpose of each regular election of Executive Directors, the Board of Governors, by an eighty-five per cent majority of the total voting power, may increase or decrease the number of Executive Directors specified in (ii) above.

(d) Elections of Executive Directors shall be conducted at internals of two years in accordance with regulations which shall be adopted by the Board of Governors. Such regulations shall include a limit on the total number of votes that more than one member may cast for the same candidate.

(e) Each Executive Director shall appoint an Alternate with full power to act for him when he is not present, provided that the Board of Governors may adopt rules enabling an Executive Director elected by more than a specified number of members to appoint two Alternates. Such rules, if adopted, may only be modified in the context of the regular election of Executive Directors and shall require an Executive Director appointing two Alternates to designate: (i) the Alternate who shall act for the Executive Director when he is not present and both Alternates are present and (ii) the Alternate who shall exercise the powers of the Executive Director under (f) below. When the Executive Directors appointing them are present, Alternates may participate in meetings but may not vote.

(f) Executive Directors shall continue in office until their successors are elected. If the office of an Executive Director becomes vacant more than ninety days before the end of his term, another Executive Director shall be elected for the remainder of the term by the members that elected the former Executive Director. A majority of the votes cast shall be required for election. While the office remains vacant, the Alternate of the former Executive Director shall exercise his powers, except that of appointing an Alternate.

(g) The Executive Board shall function in continuous session at the principal office of the Fund and shall meet as often as the business of the Fund may require

(h) A quorum for any meeting of the Executive Board shall be a majority of the Executive Directors having not less than one-half of the total voting power(i) Each Executive Directors hall be entitled to cast the number of votes which counted towards his election

(i) When the provisions of Section 5(*b*) of this Article are applicable, the votes which an Executive Director would otherwise be entitled to cast shall be increased or decreased correspondingly. All the votes which an Executive Director is entitled to cast shall be cast as a unit.

(ii) When the suspension of the voting rights of a member is terminated under Article XXVI, Section 2(*b*), the member may agree with all the members that have elected an Executive Director that the number of votes allotted to that member shall be cast by such Executive Director, provided that, if no regular election of Executive Directors has been conducted during the period of the suspension, the Executive Director in whose election the member had participated prior to the suspension, or his successor elected in accordance with paragraph 3(*c*)(i) of Schedule L or with (*f*) above, shall be entitled to cast the number of votes allotted to the member. The member shall be deemed to have participated in the election of the Executive Director entitled to cast the number of votes allotted to the member.

(i) The Board of Governors shall adopt regulations under which a member may send a representative to attend any meeting of the Executive Board when a request made by, or a matter particularly affecting, that member is under consideration.

Section 4 Managing Director and Staff

(a) The Executive Board shall select a Managing Director who shall not be a Governor or an Executive Director. The Managing Director shall be chairman of the Executive Board, but shall have no vote except a deciding vote in case of an equal division. He may participate in meetings of the Board of Governors, but shall not vote at such meetings. The Managing Director shall cease to hold office when the Executive Board so decides.
(b) The Managing Director shall be chief of the operating staff of the Fund and shall conduct, under the direction of the Executive Board, the ordinary business of the Fund. Subject to the general control of the Executive Board, he shall be responsible for the organisation, appointment, and dismissal of the staff of the Fund.
(c) The Managing Director and the staff of the Fund, in the discharge of their functions, shall owe their duty entirely to the Fund and to no other authority. Each member of the Fund shall respect the international character of this duty and shall refrain from all attempts to influence any of the staff in the discharge of these functions.
(d) In appointing the staff the Managing Director shall, subject to the paramount importance of securing the highest standards of efficiency and of technical competence, pay due regard to the importance of recruiting personnel on as wide a geographical basis as possible.

Section 5 Voting

(a) The total votes of each member shall be equal to the sum of its basic votes and its quota-based votes.
  (i) The basic votes of each member shall be the number of votes that results from the equal distribution among all the members of 5.502 per cent of the aggregate sum of the total voting power of all the members, provided that there shall be no fractional basic votes.
  (ii) The quota-based votes of each member shall be the number of votes that results from the allocation of one vote for each part of its quota equivalent to one hundred thousand special drawing rights.
(b) Whenever voting is required under Article V, Section 4 or 5, each member shall have the number of votes to which it is entitled under (a) above adjusted
  (i) by the addition of one vote for the equivalent of each four hundred thousand special drawing rights of net sales of its currency from the general resources of the Fund up to the date when the vote is taken, or

(ii) by the subtraction of one vote for the equivalent of each four hundred thousand special drawing rights of its net purchases under Article V, Section 3(b) and (f) up to the date when the vote is taken, provided that neither net purchases nor net sales shall be deemed at any time to exceed an amount equal to the quota of the member involved.

(c) Except as otherwise specifically provided, all decisions of the Fund shall be made by a majority of the votes cast.

Section 6 Reserves, Distribution of Net Income, and Investment

(a) The Fund shall determine annually what part of its net income shall be placed to general reserve or special reserve, and what part, if any, shall be distributed.

(b) The Fund may use the special reserve for any purpose for which it may use the general reserve, except distribution.

(c) If any distribution is made of the net income of any year, it shall be made to all members in proportion to their quotas.

(d) The Fund, by a seventy per cent majority of the total voting power, may decide at any time to distribute any part of the general reserve. Any such distribution shall be made to all members in proportion to their quotas.

(e) Payments under (c) and (d) above shall be made in special drawing rights, provided that either the Fund or the member may decide that the payment to the member shall be made in its own currency.

(i) The Fund may establish an Investment Account for the purposes of this subsection (f). The assets of the Investment Account shall be held separately from the other accounts of the General Department.

(ii) The Fund may decide to transfer to the Investment Account a part of the proceeds of the sale of gold in accordance with Article V, Section 12(g) and, by a seventy per cent majority of the total voting power, may decide to transfer to the Investment Account, for immediate investment, currencies held in the General Resources Account. The amount of these transfers shall not exceed the total amount of the general reserve and the special reserve at the time of the decision.

(iii) The Fund may use a member's currency held in the Investment Account for investment as it may determine, in accordance with rules and regulations adopted by the Fund by a seventy per cent majority of the total voting power. The rules and regulations adopted pursuant to this provision shall be consistent with (vii), (viii), and (ix) below.

(iv) The income of investment may be invested in accordance with the provisions of this subsection (f). Income not invested shall be held in the Investment Account or may be used for meeting the expenses of conducting the business of the Fund.

(v) The Fund may use a member's currency held in the Investment Account to obtain the currencies needed to meet the expenses of conducting the business of the Fund.

(vi) The Investment Account shall be terminated in the event of liquidation of the Fund and may be terminated, or the amount of the investment may be reduced, prior to liquidation of the Fund by a seventy per cent majority of the total voting power.

(vii) Upon termination of the Investment Account because of liquidation of the Fund, any assets in this account shall be distributed in accordance with the provisions of Schedule K, provided that a portion of these assets corresponding to the proportion of the assets transferred to this account under Article V, Section 12(g) to the total of the assets transferred to this account shall be deemed to be assets held in the Special Disbursement Account and shall be distributed in accordance with Schedule K, paragraph 2(a)(ii).

(viii) Upon termination of the Investment Account prior to liquidation of the Fund, a portion of the assets held in this account corresponding to the proportion of the assets transferred to this account under Article V, Section 12(g) to the total of the assets transferred to the account shall be transferred to the Special Disbursement Account if it has not been terminated, and the balance of the assets held in the Investment Account shall be transferred to the General Resources Account for immediate use in operations and transactions.

(ix) On a reduction of the amount of the investment by the Fund, a portion of the reduction corresponding to the proportion of the assets transferred to the Investment Account under Article V, Section 12(g) to the total of the assets transferred to this account shall be transferred to the Special Disbursement Account if it has not been terminated, and the balance of the reduction shall be transferred to the General Resources Account for immediate use in operations and transactions.

Section 7 Publication of Reports

(a) The Fund shall publish an annual report containing an audited Statement of its accounts, and shall issue, at intervals of three months or less, a summary Statement of its operations and transactions and its holdings of special drawing rights, gold, and currencies of members.

(b) The Fund may publish such other reports as it deems desirable for carrying out its purposes.

Section 8 Communication of Views to Members

The Fund shall at all times have the right to communicate its views informally to any member on any matter arising under this Agreement. The Fund may, by a seventy per cent majority of the total voting power, decide to publish a report made to a member regarding its monetary or economic conditions and developments which directly tend to produce a serious disequilibrium in the international balance of payments of members. If the member is not entitled to appoint an Executive Director, it shall be entitled to representation in accordance with Section 3(j) of this Article.

The Fund shall not publish a report involving changes in the fundamental structure of the economic organisation of members.

Article XIII: Offices and Depositories

Section 1 Location of Offices

The principal office of the Fund shall be located in the territory of the member having the largest quota, and agencies or branch offices may be established in the territories of other members.

Section 2 Depositories

(a) Each member shall designate its central bank as a depository for all the Fund's holdings of its currency, or if it has no central bank it shall designate such other institution as may be acceptable to the Fund.
(b) The Fund may hold other assets, including gold, in the depositories designated by the five members having the largest quotas and in such other designated depositories as the Fund may select. Initially, at least one-half of the holdings of the Fund shall be held in the depository designated by the member in whose territories the Fund has its principal office and at least forty per cent shall be held in the depositories designated by the remaining four members referred to above. However, all transfers of gold by the Fund shall be made with due regard to the costs of transport and anticipated requirements of the Fund. In an emergency the Executive Board may transfer all or any part of the Fund's gold holdings to any place where they can be adequately protected.

Section 3 Guarantee of the Fund's Assets

Each member guarantees all assets of the Fund against loss resulting from failure or default on the part of the depository designated by it.

Article XIV: Transitional Arrangements

Section 1 Notification to the Fund

Each member shall notify the Fund whether it intends to avail itself of the transitional arrangements in Section 2 of this Article, or whether it is prepared to accept the obligations of Article VIII, Sections 2, 3, and 4. A member availing itself of the transitional arrangements shall notify the Fund as soon thereafter as it is prepared to accept these obligations.

Section 2 Exchange Restrictions

A member that has notified the Fund that it intends to avail itself of transitional arrangements under this provision may, notwithstanding the provisions of any other articles of this Agreement, maintain and adapt to changing circumstances the restrictions on payments and transfers for current international transactions that were in effect on the date on which it became a member. Members shall, however, have continuous regard in their foreign exchange policies to the purposes of the Fund, and, as soon as conditions permit, they shall take all possible measures to develop such commercial and financial arrangements with other members as will facilitate international payments and the promotion of a stable system of exchange rates. In particular, members shall withdraw restrictions maintained under this Section as soon as they are satisfied that they will be able, in the absence of such restrictions, to settle their balance of payments in a manner which will not unduly encumber their access to the general resources of the Fund.

Section 3 Action of the Fund Relating to Restrictions

The Fund shall make annual reports on the restrictions in force under Section 2 of this Article. Any member retaining any restrictions inconsistent with Article VIII, Sections 2, 3, or 4 shall consult the Fund annually as to their further retention. The Fund may, if it deems such action necessary in exceptional circumstances, make representations to any member that conditions are favorable for the withdrawal of any particular restriction, or for the general abandonment of restrictions, inconsistent with the provisions of any other articles of this Agreement. The member shall be given a suitable time to reply to such representations. If the Fund finds that the member persists in maintaining restrictions which are inconsistent with the purposes of the Fund, the member shall be subject to Article XXVI, Section 2(a).

Article XV: Special Drawing Rights

Section 1 Authority to Allocate Special Drawing Rights

(a) To meet the need, as and when it arises, for a supplement to existing reserve assets, the Fund is authorised to allocate special drawing rights in accordance with the provisions of Article XVIII to members that are participants in the Special Drawing Rights Department.
(b) In addition, the Fund shall allocate special drawing rights to members that are participants in the Special Drawing Rights Department in accordance with the provisions of Schedule M.

Section 2 Valuation of the Special Drawing Right

The method of valuation of the special drawing right shall be determined by the Fund by a seventy per cent majority of the total voting power, provided, however, that an eighty-five per cent majority of the total voting power shall be required for a change in the principle of valuation or a fundamental change in the application of the principle in effect.

Article XVI: General Department and Special Drawing Rights Department

Section 1 Separation of Operations and Transactions

All operations and transactions involving special drawing rights shall be conducted through the Special Drawing Rights Department. All other operations and transactions on the account of the Fund authorised by or under this Agreement shall be conducted through the General Department. Operations and transactions pursuant to Article XVII, Section 2 shall be conducted through the General Department as well as the Special Drawing Rights Department.

Section 2 Separation of Assets and Property

All assets and property of the Fund, except resources administered under Article V, Section 2(b), shall be held in the General Department, provided that assets and property acquired under Article XX, Section 2 and Articles XXIV and XXV and Schedules H and I shall be held in the Special Drawing Rights Department. Any assets or property held in one Department shall not be available to discharge or meet the liabilities, obligations, or losses of the Fund incurred in the conduct of the operations and transactions of the other Department, except that the expenses of conducting the business of the Special Drawing Rights Department shall be paid by the Fund from the General Department which shall be reimbursed in special drawing rights from time to time by assessments under Article XX, Section 4 made on the basis of a reasonable estimate of such expenses.

Section 3 Recording and Information

All changes in holdings of special drawing rights shall take effect only when recorded by the Fund in the Special Drawing Rights Department. Participants shall notify the Fund of the provisions of this Agreement under which special drawing rights are used. The Fund may require participants to furnish it with such other information as it deems necessary for its functions.

Article XVII: Participants and Other Holders of Special Drawing Rights

Section 1 Participants

Each member of the Fund that deposits with the Fund an instrument setting forth that it undertakes all the obligations of a participant in the Special Drawing Rights Department in accordance with its law and that it has taken all steps necessary to enable it to carry out all of these obligations shall become a participant in the Special Drawing Rights Department as of the date the instrument is deposited, except that no member shall become a participant before the provisions of this Agreement pertaining exclusively to the Special Drawing Rights Department have entered into force and instruments have been deposited under this Section by members that have at least seventy-five per cent of the total of quotas.

Section 2 Fund as a Holder

The Fund may hold special drawing rights in the General Resources Account and may accept and use them in operations and transactions conducted through the General Resources Account with participants in accordance with the provisions of this Agreement or with prescribed holders in accordance with the terms and conditions prescribed under Section 3 of this Article.

Section 3 Other Holders

The Fund may prescribe:

(i) as holders, non-members, members that are non-participants, institutions that perform functions of a central bank for more than one member, and other official entities;

(ii) the terms and conditions on which prescribed holders may be permitted to hold special drawing rights and may accept and use them in operations and transactions with participants and other prescribed holders; and
(iii) the terms and conditions on which participants and the Fund through the General Resources Account may enter into operations and transactions in special drawing rights with prescribed holders.

An eighty-five per cent majority of the total voting power shall be required for prescriptions under (i) above. The terms and conditions prescribed by the Fund shall be consistent with the provisions of this Agreement and the effective functioning of the Special Drawing Rights Department.

Article XVIII: Allocation and Cancellation of Special Drawing Rights

Section 1 Principles and Considerations Governing Allocation and Cancellation

(a) In all its decisions with respect to the allocation and cancellation of special drawing rights the Fund shall seek to meet the long-term global need, as and when it arises, to supplement existing reserve assets in such manner as will promote the attainment of its purposes and will avoid economic stagnation and deflation as well as excess demand and inflation in the world.
(b) The first decision to allocate special drawing rights shall take into account, as special considerations, a collective judgment that there is a global need to supplement reserves, and the attainment of a better balance of payments equilibrium, as well as the likelihood of a better working of the adjustment process in the future.

Section 2 Allocation and Cancellation

(a) Decisions of the Fund to allocate or cancel special drawing rights shall be made for basic periods which shall run consecutively and shall be five years in duration. The first basic period shall begin on the date of the first decision to allocate special drawing rights or such later date as may be specified in that decision. Any allocations or cancellations shall take place at yearly intervals.
(b) The rates at which allocations are to be made shall be expressed as percentages of quotas on the date of each decision to allocate. The rates at which special drawing rights are to be cancelled shall be expressed as percentages of net cumulative allocations of special drawing rights on the date of each decision to cancel. The percentages shall be the same for all participants.
(c) In its decision for any basic period the Fund may provide, notwithstanding (a) and (b) above, that:
  (i) the duration of the basic period shall be other than five years; or
  (ii) the allocations or cancellations shall take place at other than yearly intervals; or
  (iii) the basis for allocations or cancellations shall be the quotas or net cumulative allocations on dates other than the dates of decisions to allocate or cancel.

(d) A member that becomes a participant after a basic period starts shall receive allocations beginning with the next basic period in which allocations are made after it becomes a participant unless the Fund decides that the new participant shall start to receive allocations beginning with the next allocation after it becomes a participant. If the Fund decides that a member that becomes a participant during a basic period shall receive allocations during the remainder of that basic period and the participant was not a member on the dates established under (b) or (c) above, the Fund shall determine the basis on which these allocations to the participant shall be made.

(e) A participant shall receive allocations of special drawing rights made pursuant to any decision to allocate unless:
   (i) the Governor for the participant did not vote in favor of the decision; and
   (ii) the participant has notified the Fund in writing prior to the first allocation of special drawing rights under that decision that it does not wish special drawing rights to be allocated to it under the decision. On the request of a participant, the Fund may decide to terminate the effect of the notice with respect to allocations of special drawing rights subsequent to the termination.

(f) If on the effective date of any cancellation the amount of special drawing rights held by a participant is less than its share of the special drawing rights that are to be cancelled, the participant shall eliminate its negative balance as promptly as its gross reserve position permits and shall remain in consultation with the Fund for this purpose. Special drawing rights acquired by the participant after the effective date of the cancellation shall be applied against its negative balance and cancelled.

Section 3 Unexpected Major Developments

The Fund may change the rates or intervals of allocation or cancellation during the rest of a basic period or change the length of a basic period or start a new basic period, if at any time the Fund finds it desirable to do so because of unexpected major developments.

Section 4 Decisions on Allocations and Cancellations

(a) Decisions under Section 2(a), (b), and (c) or Section 3 of this Article shall be made by the Board of Governors on the basis of proposals of the Managing Director concurred in by the Executive Board.

(b) Before making any proposal, the Managing Director, after having satisfied himself that it will be consistent with the provisions of Section 1(a) of this Article, shall conduct such consultations as will enable him to ascertain that there is broad support among participants for the proposal. In addition, before making a proposal for the first allocation, the Managing Director shall satisfy himself that the provisions of Section 1(b) of this Article have been met and that there is broad support among participants to begin allocations; he shall make a proposal for the first allocation as soon after the establishment of the Special Drawing Rights Department as he is so satisfied.

(c) The Managing Director shall make proposals:
   (i) not later than six months before the end of each basic period;
   (ii) if no decision has been taken with respect to allocation or cancellation for a basic period, whenever he is satisfied that the provisions of (b) above have been met;
   (iii) when, in accordance with Section 3 of this Article, he considers that it would be desirable to change the rate or intervals of allocation or cancellation or change the length of a basic period or start a new basic period; or
   (iv) within six months of a request by the Board of Governors or the Executive Board;
   (v) that, if under (i), (iii), or (iv) above the Managing Director ascertains that there is no proposal which he considers to be consistent with the provisions of Section 1 of this Article that has broad support among participants in accordance with (b) above, he shall report to the Board of Governors and to the Executive Board.

(d) An eighty-five per cent majority of the total voting power shall be required for decisions under Section 2(a), (b), and (c) or Section 3 of this Article except for decisions under Section 3 with respect to a decrease in the rates of allocation.

Article XIX: Operations and Transactions in Special Drawing Rights

Section 1 Use of Special Drawing Rights

Special drawing rights may be used in the operations and transactions authorised by or under this Agreement.

Section 2 Operations and Transactions between Participants

(a) A participant shall be entitled to use its special drawing rights to obtain an equivalent amount of currency from a participant designated under Section 5 of this Article.
(b) A participant, in agreement with another participant, may use its special drawing rights to obtain an equivalent amount of currency from the other participant.
(c) The Fund, by a seventy per cent majority of the total voting power, may prescribe operations in which a participant is authorised to engage in agreement with another participant on such terms and conditions as the Fund deems appropriate. The terms and conditions shall be consistent with the effective functioning of the Special Drawing Rights Department and the proper use of special drawing rights in accordance with this Agreement.
(d) The Fund may make representations to a participant that enters into any operation or transaction under (b) or (c) above that in the judgment of the Fund may be prejudicial to the process of designation according to the principles of Section 5 of this Article or is otherwise inconsistent with Article XXII. A participant that persists in entering into such operations or transactions shall be subject to Article XXIII, Section 2(b).

Section 3 Requirement of Need

(a) In transactions under Section 2(a) of this Article, except as otherwise provided in (c) below, a participant will be expected to use its special drawing rights only if it has a need because of its balance of payments or its reserve position or developments in its reserves, and not for the sole purpose of changing the composition of its reserves.
(b) The use of special drawing rights shall not be subject to challenge on the basis of the expectation in (a) above, but the Fund may make representations to a participant that fails to fulfill this expectation. A participant that persists in failing to fulfill this expectation shall be subject to Article XXIII, Section 2(b).
(c) The Fund may waive the expectation in (a) above in any transactions in which a participant uses special drawing rights to obtain an equivalent amount of currency from a participant designated under Section 5 of this Article that would promote reconstitution by the other participant under Section 6(a) of this Article; prevent or reduce a negative balance of the other participant; or offset the effect of a failure by the other participant to fulfill the expectation in (a) above.

Section 4 Obligation to Provide Currency

(a) A participant designated by the Fund under Section 5 of this Article shall provide on demand a freely usable currency to a participant using special drawing rights under Section 2(a) of this Article. A participant's obligation to provide currency shall not extend beyond the point at which its holdings of special drawing rights in excess of its net cumulative allocation are equal to twice its net cumulative allocation or such higher limit as may be agreed between a participant and the Fund.
(b) A participant may provide currency in excess of the obligatory limit or any agreed higher limit.

Section 5 Designation of Participants to Provide Currency

(a) The Fund shall ensure that a participant will be able to use its special drawing rights by designating participants to provide currency for specified amounts of special drawing rights for the purposes of Sections 2(a) and 4 of this Article. Designations shall be made in accordance with the following general principles supplemented by such other principles as the Fund may adopt from time to time:
    (i) A participant shall be subject to designation if its balance of payments and gross reserve position is sufficiently strong, but this will not preclude the possibility that a participant with a strong reserve position will be designated even though it has a moderate balance of payments deficit. Participants shall be designated in such manner as will promote over time a balanced distribution of holdings of special drawing rights among them.

(ii) Participants shall be subject to designation in order to promote reconstitution under Section 6(a) of this Article, to reduce negative balances in holdings of special drawing rights, or to offset the effect of failures to fulfill the expectation in Section 3(a) of this Article.
(iii) In designating participants, the Fund normally shall give priority to those that need to acquire special drawing rights to meet the objectives of designation under (ii) above.

(b) In order to promote over time a balanced distribution of holdings of special drawing rights under (a)(i) above, the Fund shall apply the rules for designation in Schedule F or such rules as may be adopted under (c) below.
(c) The rules for designation may be reviewed at any time and new rules shall be adopted if necessary. Unless new rules are adopted, the rules in force at the time of the review shall continue to apply.

Section 6 Reconstitution

(a) Participants that use their special drawing rights shall reconstitute their holdings of them in accordance with the rules for reconstitution in Schedule G or such rules as may be adopted under (b) below.
(b) The rules for reconstitution may be reviewed at any time and new rules shall be adopted if necessary. Unless new rules are adopted or a decision is made to abrogate rules for reconstitution, the rules in force at the time of review shall continue to apply. A seventy per cent majority of the total voting power shall be required for decisions to adopt, modify, or abrogate the rules for reconstitution.

Section 7 Exchange Rates

(a) Except as otherwise provided in (b) below, the exchange rates for transactions between participants under Section 2(a) and (b) of this Article shall be such that participants using special drawing rights shall receive the same value whatever currencies might be provided and whichever participants provide those currencies, and the Fund shall adopt regulations to give effect to this principle.
(b) The Fund, by an eighty-five per cent majority of the total voting power, may adopt policies under which in exceptional circumstances the Fund, by a seventy per cent majority of the total voting power, may authorise participants entering into transactions under Section 2(b) of this Article to agree on exchange rates other than those applicable under (a) above.
(c) The Fund shall consult a participant on the procedure for determining rates of exchange for its currency.
(d) For the purpose of this provision the term participant includes a terminating participant.

Article XX: Special Drawing Rights Department Interest and Charges

Section 1 Interest

Interest at the same rate for all holders shall be paid by the Fund to each holder on the amount of its holdings of special drawing rights. The Fund shall pay the amount due to each holder whether or not sufficient charges are received to meet the payment of interest.

Section 2 Charges

Charges at the same rate for all participants shall be paid to the Fund by each participant on the amount of its net cumulative allocation of special drawing rights plus any negative balance of the participant or unpaid charges.

Section 3 Rate of Interest and Charges

The Fund shall determine the rate of interest by a seventy per cent majority of the total voting power. The rate of charges shall be equal to the rate of interest.

Section 4 Assessments

When it is decided under Article XVI, Section 2 that reimbursement shall be made, the Fund shall levy assessments for this purpose at the same rate for all participants on their net cumulative allocations.

Section 5 Payment of Interest, Charges, and Assessments

Interest, charges, and assessments shall be paid in special drawing rights. A participant that needs special drawing rights to pay any charge or assessment shall be obligated and entitled to obtain them, for currency acceptable to the Fund, in a transaction with the Fund conducted through the General Resources Account. If sufficient special drawing rights cannot be obtained in this way, the participant shall be obligated and entitled to obtain them with a freely usable currency from a participant which the Fund shall specify. Special drawing rights acquired by a participant after the date for payment shall be applied against its unpaid charges and cancelled.

Article XXI: Administration of the General Department and the Special Drawing Rights Department

(a) The General Department and the Special Drawing Rights Department shall be administered in accordance with the provisions of Article XII, subject to the following provisions:
   (i) For meetings of or decisions by the Board of Governors on matters pertaining exclusively to the Special Drawing Rights Department only requests by, or the presence and the votes of, Governors appointed by members that are participants shall be counted for the purpose of calling meetings and determining whether a quorum exists or whether a decision is made by the required majority.
   (ii) For decisions by the Executive Board on matters pertaining exclusively to the Special Drawing Rights Department only Executive Directors elected by at least one member that is a participant shall be entitled to

vote. Each of these Executive Directors shall be entitled to cast the number of votes allotted to the members that are participants whose votes counted towards his election. Only the presence of Executive Directors elected by members that are participants and the votes allotted to members that are participants shall be counted for the purpose of determining whether a quorum exists or whether a decision is made by the required majority.

(iii) Questions of the general administration of the Fund, including reimbursement under Article XVI, Section 2, and any question whether a matter pertains to both Departments or exclusively to the Special Drawing Rights Department shall be decided as if they pertained exclusively to the General Department. Decisions with respect to the method of valuation of the special drawing right, the acceptance and holding of special drawing rights in the General Resources Account of the General Department and the use of them, and other decisions affecting the operations and transactions conducted through both the General Resources Account of the General Department and the Special Drawing Rights Department shall be made by the majorities required for decisions on matters pertaining exclusively to each Department. A decision on a matter pertaining to the Special Drawing Rights Department shall so indicate.

(b) In addition to the privileges and immunities that are accorded under Article IX of this Agreement, no tax of any kind shall be levied on special drawing rights or on operations or transactions in special drawing rights.

(c) A question of interpretation of the provisions of this Agreement on matters pertaining exclusively to the Special Drawing Rights Department shall be submitted to the Executive Board pursuant to Article XXIX(a) only on the request of a participant. In any case where the Executive Board has given a decision on a question of interpretation pertaining exclusively to the Special Drawing Rights Department only a participant may require that the question be referred to the Board of Governors under Article XXIX(b). The Board of Governors shall decide whether a Governor appointed by a member that is not a participant shall be entitled to vote in the Committee on Interpretation on questions pertaining exclusively to the Special Drawing Rights Department.

(d) Whenever a disagreement arises between the Fund and a participant that has terminated its participation in the Special Drawing Rights Department or between the Fund and any participant during the liquidation of the Special Drawing Rights Department with respect to any matter arising exclusively from participation in the Special Drawing Rights Department, the disagreement shall be submitted to arbitration in accordance with the procedures in Article XXIX(c).

Article XXII: General Obligations of Participants

In addition to the obligations assumed with respect to special drawing rights under other articles of this Agreement, each participant undertakes to collaborate with the Fund and with other participants in order to facilitate the effective functioning of the Special Drawing Rights Department and the proper use of special drawing rights in accordance with this Agreement and with the objective of making the special drawing right the principal reserve asset in the international monetary system.

Article XXIII: Suspension of Operations and Transactions in Special Drawing Rights

Section 1 Emergency Provisions

In the event of an emergency or the development of unforeseen circumstances threatening the activities of the Fund with respect to the Special Drawing Rights Department, the Executive Board, by an eighty-five per cent majority of the total voting power, may suspend for a period of not more than one year the operation of any of the provisions relating to operations and transactions in special drawing rights, and the provisions of Article XXVII, Section l(b), (c), and (d) shall then apply.

Section 2 Failure to Fulfill Obligations

(a) If the Fund finds that a participant has failed to fulfill its obligations under Article XIX, Section 4, the right of the participant to use its special drawing rights shall be suspended unless the Fund otherwise decides.
(b) If the Fund finds that a participant has failed to fulfill any other obligation with respect to special drawing rights, the Fund may suspend the right of the participant to use special drawing rights it acquires after the suspension.
(c) Regulations shall be adopted to ensure that before action is taken against any participant under (a) or (b) above, the participant shall be informed immediately of the complaint against it and given an adequate opportunity for stating its case, both orally and in writing. Whenever the participant is thus informed of a complaint relating to (a) above, it shall not use special drawing rights pending the disposition of the complaint.
(d) Suspension under (a) or (b) above or limitation under (c) above shall not affect a participant's obligation to provide currency in accordance with Article XIX, Section 4.
(e) The Fund may at any time terminate a suspension under (a) or (b) above, provided that a suspension imposed on a participant under (b) above for failure to fulfill the obligations under Article XIX, Section 6(a) shall not be terminated until one hundred eighty days after the end of the first calendar quarter during which the participant complies with the rules for reconstitution.
(f) The right of a participant to use its special drawing rights shall not be suspended because it has become ineligible to use the Fund's general resources under Article V, Section 5, Article VI, Section 1, or Article XXVI, Section 2(a). Article XXVI, Section 2 shall not apply because a participant has failed to fulfill any obligations with respect to special drawing rights.

Article XXIV: Termination of Participation

Section 1 Right to Terminate Participation

(a) Any participant may terminate its participation in the Special Drawing Rights Department at any time by transmitting a notice in writing to the Fund at its principal office. Termination shall become effective on the date the notice is received.
(b) A participant that withdraws from membership in the Fund shall be deemed to have simultaneously terminated its participation in the Special Drawing Rights Department.

Section 2 Settlement on Termination

(a) When a participant terminates its participation in the Special Drawing Rights Department, all operations and transactions by the terminating participant in special drawing rights shall cease except as otherwise permitted under an agreement made pursuant to (c) below in order to facilitate a settlement or as provided in Sections 3, 5, and 6 of this Article or in Schedule H. Interest and charges that accrued to the date of termination and assessments levied before that date but not paid shall be paid in special drawing rights.
(b) The Fund shall be obligated to redeem all special drawing rights held by the terminating participant, and the terminating participant shall be obligated to pay to the Fund an amount equal to its net cumulative allocation and any other amounts that may be due and payable because of its participation in the Special Drawing Rights Department. These obligations shall be set off against each other and the amount of special drawing rights held by the terminating participant that is used in the setoff to extinguish its obligation to the Fund shall be cancelled.
(c) A settlement shall be made with reasonable despatch by agreement between the terminating participant and the Fund with respect to any obligation of the terminating participant or the Fund after the setoff in (b) above. If agreement on a settlement is not reached promptly the provisions of Schedule H shall apply.

Section 3 Interest and Charges

After the date of termination the Fund shall pay interest on any outstanding balance of special drawing rights held by a terminating participant and the terminating participant shall pay charges on any outstanding obligation owed to the Fund at the times and rates prescribed under Article XX. Payment shall be made in special drawing rights. A terminating participant shall be entitled to obtain special drawing rights with a freely usable currency to pay charges or assessments in a transaction with a participant specified by the Fund or by agreement from any other holder, or to dispose of special drawing rights received as interest in a transaction with any participant designated under Article XIX, Section 5 or by agreement with any other holder.

Section 4 Settlement of Obligation to the Fund

Currency received by the Fund from a terminating participant shall be used by the Fund to redeem special drawing rights held by participants in proportion to the amount by which each participant's holdings of special drawing rights exceed its net cumulative allocation at the time the currency is received by the Fund. Special drawing rights so redeemed and special drawing rights obtained by a terminating participant under the provisions of this Agreement to meet any installment due under an agreement on settlement or under Schedule H and set off against that installment shall be cancelled.

Section 5 Settlement of Obligation to a Terminating Participant

Whenever the Fund is required to redeem special drawing rights held by a terminating participant, redemption shall be made with currency provided by participants specified by the Fund. These participants shall be specified in accordance with the principles in Article XIX, Section 5. Each specified participant shall provide at its option the currency of the terminating participant or a freely usable currency to the Fund and shall receive an equivalent amount of special drawing rights. However, a terminating participant may use its special drawing rights to obtain its own currency, a freely usable currency, or any other asset from any holder, if the Fund so permits.

Section 6 General Resources Account Transactions

In order to facilitate settlement with a terminating participant, the Fund may decide that a terminating participant shall:

(i) use any special drawing rights held by it after the setoff in Section 2(b) of this Article, when they are to be redeemed, in a transaction with the Fund conducted through the General Resources Account to obtain its own currency or a freely usable currency at the option of the Fund; or
(ii) obtain special drawing rights in a transaction with the Fund conducted through the General Resources Account for a currency acceptable to the Fund to meet any charges or installment due under an agreement or the provisions of Schedule H.

Article XXV: Liquidation of the Special Drawing Rights Department

(a) The Special Drawing Rights Department may not be liquidated except by decision of the Board of Governors. In an emergency, if the Executive Board decides that liquidation of the Special Drawing Rights Department may be necessary, it may temporarily suspend allocations or cancellations and all operations and transactions in special drawing rights pending decision by the Board of Governors. A decision by the Board of Governors to liquidate the Fund shall be a decision to liquidate both the General Department and the Special Drawing Rights Department.

(b) If the Board of Governors decides to liquidate the Special Drawing Rights Department, all allocations or cancellations and all operations and transactions in special drawing rights and the activities of the Fund with respect to the Special Drawing Rights Department shall cease except those incidental to the orderly discharge of the obligations of participants and of the Fund with respect to special drawing rights, and all obligations of the Fund and of participants under this Agreement with respect to special drawing rights shall cease except those set out in this Article, Article XX, Article XXI(d), Article XXIV, Article XXIX(c), and Schedule H, or any agreement reached under Article XXIV subject to paragraph 4 of Schedule H, and Schedule I.

(c) Upon liquidation of the Special Drawing Rights Department, interest and charges that accrued to the date of liquidation and assessments levied before that date but not paid shall be paid in special drawing rights. The Fund shall be obligated to redeem all special drawing rights held by holders, and each participant shall be obligated to pay the Fund an amount equal to its net cumulative allocation of special drawing rights and such other amounts as may be due and payable because of its participation in the Special Drawing Rights Department.

(d) Liquidation of the Special Drawing Rights Department shall be administered in accordance with the provisions of Schedule I.

Article XXVI: Withdrawal from Membership

Section 1 Right of Members to Withdraw

Any member may withdraw from the Fund at any time by transmitting a notice in writing to the Fund at its principal office. Withdrawal shall become effective on the date such notice is received.

Section 2 Compulsory Withdrawal

(a) If a member fails to fulfill any of its obligations under this Agreement, the Fund may declare the member ineligible to use the general resources of the Fund. Nothing in this Section shall be deemed to limit the provisions of Article V, Section 5 or Article VI, Section 1.

(b) If, after the expiration of a reasonable period following a declaration of ineligibility under (a) above, the member persists in its failure to fulfill any of its obligations under this Agreement, the Fund may, by a seventy per cent majority of the total voting power, suspend the voting rights of the member. During the period of the suspension, the provisions of Schedule L shall apply. The Fund may, by a seventy per cent majority of the total voting power, terminate the suspension at any time.

(c) If, after the expiration of a reasonable period following a decision of suspension under (b) above, the member persists in its failure to fulfill any of its obligations under this Agreement, that member may be required to withdraw from membership in the Fund by a decision of the Board of Governors carried by a majority of the Governors having eighty-five per cent of the total voting power.

(d) Regulations shall be adopted to ensure that before action is taken against any member under (a), (b), or (c) above, the member shall be informed in reasonable time of the complaint against it and given an adequate opportunity for stating its case, both orally and in writing.

Section 3 Settlement of Accounts with Members Withdrawing

When a member withdraws from the Fund, normal operations and transactions of the Fund in its currency shall cease and settlement of all accounts between it and the Fund shall be made with reasonable despatch by agreement between it and the Fund. If agreement is not reached promptly, the provisions of Schedule J shall apply to the settlement of accounts.

Article XXVII: Emergency Provisions

Section 1 Temporary Suspension

(a) In the event of an emergency or the development of unforeseen circumstances threatening the activities of the Fund, the Executive Board, by an eighty-five per cent majority of the total voting power, may suspend for a period of not more than one year the operation of any of the following provisions:
   (i) Article V, Sections 2, 3, 7, 8(a)(i) and (e);
   (ii) Article VI, Section 2;
   (iii) Article XI, Section 1;
   (iv) Schedule C, paragraph 5.
(b) A suspension of the operation of a provision under (a) above may not be extended beyond one year except by the Board of Governors which, by an eighty-five per cent majority of the total voting power, may extend a suspension for an additional period of not more than two years if it finds that the emergency or unforeseen circumstances referred to in (a) above continue to exist.
(c) The Executive Board may, by a majority of the total voting power, terminate such suspension at any time.
(d) The Fund may adopt rules with respect to the subject matter of a provision during the period in which its operation is suspended.

Section 2 Liquidation of the Fund

(a) The Fund may not be liquidated except by decision of the Board of Governors. In an emergency, if the Executive Board decides that liquidation of the Fund may be necessary, it may temporarily suspend all operations and transactions, pending decision by the Board of Governors.
(b) If the Board of Governors decides to liquidate the Fund, the Fund shall forthwith cease to engage in any activities except those incidental to the orderly collection and liquidation of its assets and the settlement of its liabilities, and all obligations of members under this Agreement shall cease except those set out in this Article, in Article XXIX(c), in Schedule J, paragraph 7, and in Schedule K.

(c) Liquidation shall be administered in accordance with the provisions of Schedule K.

Article XXVIII: Amendments

(a) Any proposal to introduce modifications in this Agreement, whether emanating from a member, a Governor, or the Executive Board, shall be communicated to the chairman of the Board of Governors who shall bring the proposal before the Board of Governors. If the proposed amendment is approved by the Board of Governors, the Fund shall, by circular letter or telegram, ask all members whether they accept the proposed amendment. When three-fifths of the members, having eighty-five per cent of the total voting power, have accepted the proposed amendment, the Fund shall certify the fact by a formal communication addressed to all members.
(b) Notwithstanding (a) above, acceptance by all members is required in the case of any amendment modifying:
  (i) the right to withdraw from the Fund (Article XXVI, Section 1);
  (ii) the provision that no change in a member's quota shall be made without its consent (Article III, Section 2 (d)); and
  (iii) the provision that no change may be made in the par value of a member's currency except on the proposal of that member (Schedule C, paragraph 6).
(c) Amendments shall enter into force for all members three months after the date of the formal communication unless a shorter period is specified in the circular letter or telegram.

Article XXIX: Interpretation

(a) Any question of interpretation of the provisions of this Agreement arising between any member and the Fund or between any members of the Fund shall be submitted to the Executive Board for its decision. If the question particularly affects any member, it shall be entitled to representation in accordance with Article XII, Section 3(j).
(b) In any case where the Executive Board has given a decision under (a) above, any member may require, within three months from the date of the decision, that the question be referred to the Board of Governors, whose decision shall be final. Any question referred to the Board of Governors shall be considered by a Committee on Interpretation of the Board of Governors. Each Committee member shall have one vote. The Board of Governors shall establish the membership, procedures, and voting majorities of the Committee. A decision of the Committee shall be the decision of the Board of Governors unless the Board of Governors, by an eighty-five per cent majority of the total voting power, decides otherwise. Pending the result of the reference to the Board of Governors the Fund may, so far as it deems necessary, act on the basis of the decision of the Executive Board.

(c) Whenever a disagreement arises between the Fund and a member which has withdrawn, or between the Fund and any member during liquidation of the Fund, such disagreement shall be submitted to arbitration by a tribunal of three arbitrators, one appointed by the Fund, another by the member or withdrawing member, and an umpire who, unless the parties otherwise agree, shall be appointed by the President of the International Court of Justice or such other authority as may have been prescribed by regulation adopted by the Fund. The umpire shall have full power to settle all questions of procedure in any case where the parties are in disagreement with respect thereto.

Article XXX: Explanation of Terms

In interpreting the provisions of this Agreement the Fund and its members shall be guided by the following provisions:

(a) The Fund's holdings of a member's currency in the General Resources Account shall include any securities accepted by the Fund under Article III, Section 4.
(b) Stand-by arrangement means a decision of the Fund by which a member is assured that it will be able to make purchases from the General Resources Account in accordance with the terms of the decision during a specified period and up to a specified amount.
(c) Reserve tranche purchase means a purchase by a member of special drawing rights or the currency of another member in exchange for its own currency which does not cause the Fund's holdings of the member's currency in the General Resources Account to exceed its quota, provided that for the purposes of this definition the Fund may exclude purchases and holdings under:
  (i) policies on the use of its general resources for compensatory financing of export fluctuations;
  (ii) policies on the use of its general resources in connection with the financing of contributions to international buffer stocks of primary products; and
  (iii) other policies on the use of its general resources in respect of which the Fund decides, by an eighty-five per cent majority of the total voting power, that an exclusion shall be made.
(d) Payments for current transactions means payments which are not for the purpose of transferring capital, and includes, without limitation:
  (1) all payments due in connection with foreign trade, other current business, including services, and normal short-term banking and credit facilities;
  (2) payments due as interest on loans and as net income from other investments;
  (3) payments of moderate amount for amortisation of loans or for depreciation of direct investments; and
  (4) moderate remittances for family living expenses.
  (5) The Fund may, after consultation with the members concerned, determine whether certain specific transactions are to be considered current transactions or capital transactions.

(e) Net cumulative allocation of special drawing rights means the total amount of special drawing rights allocated to a participant less its share of special drawing rights that have been cancelled under Article XVIII, Section 2(a).
(f) A freely usable currency means a member's currency that the Fund determines (i) is, in fact, widely used to make payments for international transactions, and (ii) is widely traded in the principal exchange markets.
(g) Members that were members on August 31, 1975 shall be deemed to include a member that accepted membership after that date pursuant to a resolution of the Board of Governors adopted before that date.
(h) Transactions of the Fund means exchanges of monetary assets by the Fund for other monetary assets. Operations of the Fund means other uses or receipts of monetary assets by the Fund.
(i) Transactions in special drawing rights means exchanges of special drawing rights for other monetary assets. Operations in special drawing rights means other uses of special drawing rights.

Article XXXI: Final Provisions

Section 1 Entry into Force

This Agreement shall enter into force when it has been signed on behalf of governments having sixty-five per cent of the total of the quotas set forth in Schedule A and when the instruments referred to in Section 2(a) of this Article have been deposited on their behalf, but in no event shall this Agreement enter into force before May 1, 1945.

Section 2 Signature

(a) Each government on whose behalf this Agreement is signed shall deposit with the Government of the United States of America an instrument setting forth that it has accepted this Agreement in accordance with its law and has taken all steps necessary to enable it to carry out all of its obligations under this Agreement.
(b) Each country shall become a member of the Fund as from the date of the deposit on its behalf of the instrument referred to in (a) above, except that no country shall become a member before this Agreement enters into force under Section 1 of this Article.
(c) The Government of the United States of America shall inform the governments of all countries whose names are set forth in Schedule A, and the governments of all countries whose membership is approved in accordance with Article II, Section 2, of all signatures of this Agreement and of the deposit of all instruments referred to in (a) above.
(d) At the time this Agreement is signed on its behalf, each government shall transmit to the Government of the United States of America one one-hundredth of one per cent of its total subscription in gold or United States dollars for the purpose of meeting administrative expenses of the Fund. The Government of the United States of America shall hold such funds in a special deposit account and shall transmit them to the Board of Governors of the Fund when the initial meeting has been called. If this Agreement has not come into force by December 31,

1945, the Government of the United States of America shall return such funds to the governments that transmitted them.

(e) This Agreement shall remain open for signature at Washington on behalf of the governments of the countries whose names are set forth in Schedule A until December 31, 1945.

(f) After December 31, 1945, this Agreement shall be open for signature on behalf of the government of any country whose membership has been approved in accordance with Article II, Section 2.

(g) By their signature of this Agreement, all governments accept it both on their own behalf and in respect of all their colonies, overseas territories, all territories under their protection, suzerainty, or authority, and all territories in respect of which they exercise a mandate.

(h) Subsection (d) above shall come into force with regard to each signatory government as from the date of its signature.

[The signature and depositary clause reproduced below followed the text of Article XX in the original Articles of Agreement]

Done at Washington, in a single copy which shall remain deposited in the archives of the Government of the United States of America, which shall transmit certified copies to all governments whose names are set forth in Schedule A and to all governments whose membership is approved in accordance with Article II, Section 2.

SCHEDULES

SCHEDULE A [Omitted]

SCHEDULE B: Transitional Provisions with Respect to Repurchase, Payment of Additional Subscriptions, Gold, and Certain Operational Matters

1. Repurchase obligations that have accrued pursuant to Article V, Section 7(b) before the date of the second amendment of this Agreement and that remain undischarged at that date shall be discharged not later than the date or dates at which the obligations had to be discharged in accordance with the provisions of this Agreement before the second amendment.

2. A member shall discharge with special drawing rights any obligation to pay gold to the Fund in repurchase or as a subscription that is outstanding at the date of the second amendment of this Agreement, but the Fund may prescribe that these payments may be made in whole or in part in the currencies of other members specified by the Fund. A non-participant shall discharge an obligation that must be paid in special drawing rights pursuant to this provision with the currencies of other members specified by the Fund.

3. For the purposes of 2 above 0.888 671 gram of fine gold shall be equivalent to one special drawing right, and the amount of currency payable under 2 above shall be determined on that basis and on the basis of the value of the currency in terms of the special drawing right at the date of discharge.

4. A member's currency held by the Fund in excess of seventy-five per cent of the member's quota at the date of the second amendment of this Agreement and not subject to repurchase under 1 above shall be repurchased in accordance with the following rules:

(i) Holdings that resulted from a purchase shall be repurchased in accordance with the policy on the use of the Fund's general resources under which the purchase was made.
(ii) Other holdings shall be repurchased not later than four years after the date of the second amendment of this Agreement.

5. Repurchases under 1 above that are not subject to 2 above, repurchases under 4 above, and any specification of currencies under 2 above shall be in accordance with Article V, Section 7(i).
6. All rules and regulations, rates, procedures, and decisions in effect at the date of the second amendment of this Agreement shall remain in effect until they are changed in accordance with the provisions of this Agreement.
7. To the extent that arrangements equivalent in effect to (a) and (b) below have not been completed before the date of the second amendment of this Agreement, the Fund shall

(a) sell up to 25 million ounces of fine gold held by it on August 31, 1975 to those members that were members on that date and that agree to buy it, in proportion to their quotas on that date. The sale to a member under this sub-paragraph (a) shall be made in exchange for its currency and at a price equivalent at the time of sale to one special drawing right per 0.888 671 gram of fine gold, and
(b) sell up to 25 million ounces of fine gold held by it on August 31, 1975 for the benefit of developing members that were members on that date, provided, however, that the part of any profits or surplus value of the gold that corresponds to the proportion of such a member's quota on August 31, 1975 to the total of the quotas of all members on that date shall be transferred directly to each such member. The requirements under Article V, Section 12(c) that the Fund consult a member, obtain a member's concurrence, or exchange a member's currency for the currencies of other members in certain circumstances shall apply with respect to currency received by the Fund as a result of sales of gold under this provision, other than sales to a member in return for its own currency, and placed in the General Resources Account.

Upon the sale of gold under this paragraph 7, an amount of the proceeds in the currencies received equivalent at the time of sale to one special drawing right per 0.888 671 gram of fine gold shall be placed in the General Resources Account and other assets held by the Fund under arrangements pursuant to (b) above shall be held separately from the general resources of the Fund. Assets that remain subject to disposition by the Fund upon termination of arrangements pursuant to (b) above shall be transferred to the Special Disbursement Account.

SCHEDULE C: Par Values

1. The Fund shall notify members that par values may be established for the purposes of this Agreement, in accordance with Article IV, Sections 1, 3, 4, and 5 and this Schedule, in terms of the special drawing right, or in terms of such other common denominator as is prescribed by the Fund. The common denominator shall not be gold or a currency.
2. A member that intends to establish a par value for its currency shall propose a par value to the Fund within a reasonable time after notice is given under 1 above.
3. Any member that does not intend to establish a par value for its currency under 1 above shall consult with the Fund and ensure that its exchange arrangements are consistent with the purposes of the Fund and are adequate to fulfill its obligations under Article IV, Section 1.
4. The Fund shall concur in or object to a proposed par value within a reasonable period after receipt of the proposal. A proposed par value shall not take effect for the purposes of this Agreement if the Fund objects to it, and the member shall be subject to 3 above. The Fund shall not object because of the domestic social or political policies of the member proposing the par value.
5. Each member that has a par value for its currency undertakes to apply appropriate measures consistent with this Agreement in order to ensure that the maximum and the minimum rates for spot exchange transactions taking place within its territories between its currency and the currencies of other members maintaining par values shall not differ from parity by more than four and one-half per cent or by such other margin or margins as the Fund may adopt by an eighty-five per cent majority of the total voting power.
6. A member shall not propose a change in the par value of its currency except to correct, or prevent the emergence of, a fundamental disequilibrium. A change may be made only on the proposal of the member and only after consultation with the Fund.
7. When a change is proposed, the Fund shall concur in or object to the proposed par value within a reasonable period after receipt of the proposal. The Fund shall concur if it is satisfied that the change is necessary to correct, or prevent the emergence of, a fundamental disequilibrium. The Fund shall not object because of the domestic social or political policies of the member proposing the change. A proposed change in par value shall not take effect for the purposes of this Agreement if the Fund objects to it. If a member changes the par value of its currency despite the objection of the Fund, the member shall be subject to Article XXVI, Section 2. Maintenance of an unrealistic par value by a member shall be discouraged by the Fund.
8. The par value of a member's currency established under this Agreement shall cease to exist for the purposes of this Agreement if the member informs the Fund that it intends to terminate the par value. The Fund may object to the termination of a par value by a decision taken by an eighty-five per cent majority of the total voting power. If a member terminates a par value for its currency despite the objection of the Fund, the member shall be subject to Article XXVI, Section 2. A par value established under this Agreement shall cease to exist for the purposes of this Agreement if the member terminates the par value despite the objection of the Fund, or if

the Fund finds that the member does not maintain rates for a substantial volume of exchange transactions in accordance with 5 above, provided that the Fund may not make such finding unless it has consulted the member and given it sixty days notice of the Fund's intention to consider whether to make a finding.
9. If the par value of the currency of a member has ceased to exist under 8 above, the member shall consult with the Fund and ensure that its exchange arrangements are consistent with the purposes of the Fund and are adequate to fulfill its obligations under Article IV, Section 1.
10. A member for whose currency the par value has ceased to exist under 8 above may, at any time, propose a new par value for its currency.
11. Notwithstanding 6 above, the Fund, by a seventy per cent majority of the total voting power, may make uniform proportionate changes in all par values if the special drawing right is the common denominator and the changes will not affect the value of the special drawing right. The par value of a member's currency shall, however, not be changed under this provision if, within seven days after the Fund's action, the member informs the Fund that it does not wish the par value of its currency to be changed by such action.

SCHEDULE D: Council

1.
   (a) Each member or group of members that has the number of votes allotted to it or them cast by an Executive Director shall appoint to the Council one Councillor, who shall be a Governor, Minister in the government of a member, or person of comparable rank, and may appoint not more than seven Associates. The Board of Governors may change, by an eighty-five per cent majority of the total voting power, the number of Associates who may be appointed. A Councillor or Associate shall serve until a new appointment is made or until the next regular election of Executive Directors, whichever shall occur sooner.
   (b) Executive Directors, or in their absence their Alternates, and Associates shall be entitled to attend meetings of the Council, unless the Council decides to hold a restricted session. Each member and each group of members that appoints a Councillor shall appoint an Alternate who shall be entitled to attend a meeting of the Council when the Councillor is not present, and shall have full power to act for the Councillor.
2.
   (a) The Council shall supervise the management and adaptation of the international monetary system, including the continuing operation of the adjustment process and developments in global liquidity, and in this connection shall review developments in the transfer of real resources to developing countries.
   (b) The Council shall consider proposals pursuant to Article XXVIII(a) to amend the Articles of Agreement.
3.

(a) The Board of Governors may delegate to the Council authority to exercise any powers of the Board of Governors except the powers conferred directly by this Agreement on the Board of Governors.
(b) Each Councillor shall be entitled to cast the number of votes allotted under Article XII, Section 5 to the member or group of members appointing him. A Councillor appointed by a group of members may cast separately the votes allotted to each member in the group. If the number of votes allotted to a member cannot be cast by an Executive Director, the member may make arrangements with a Councillor for casting the number of votes allotted to the member.
(c) The Council shall not take any action pursuant to powers delegated by the Board of Governors that is inconsistent with any action taken by the Board of Governors and the Executive Board shall not take any action pursuant to powers delegated by the Board of Governors that is inconsistent with any action taken by either the Board of Governors or the Council.

4. The Council shall select a Councillor as chairman, shall adopt regulations as may be necessary or appropriate to perform its functions, and shall determine any aspect of its procedure. The Council shall hold such meetings as may be provided for by the Council or called by the Executive Board.
5.
(a) The Council shall have powers corresponding to those of the Executive Board under the following provisions: Article XII, Section 2(c), (f), (g), and (j); Article XVIII, Section 4(a) and Section 4(c)(iv); Article XXIII, Section 1; and Article XXVII, Section l(a).
(b) For decisions by the Council on matters pertaining exclusively to the Special Drawing Rights Department only Councillors appointed by a member that is a participant or a group of members at least one member of which is a participant shall be entitled to vote. Each of these Councillors shall be entitled to cast the number of votes allotted to the member which is a participant that appointed him or to the members that are participants in the group of members that appointed him, and may cast the votes allotted to a participant with which arrangements have been made pursuant to the last sentence of 3(b) above.
(c) The Council may by regulation establish a procedure whereby the Executive Board may obtain a vote of the Councillors on a specific question without a meeting of the Council when in the judgment of the Executive Board an action must be taken by the Council which should not be postponed until the next meeting of the Council and which does not warrant the calling of a special meeting.
(d) Article IX, Section 8 shall apply to Councillors, their Alternates, and Associates, and to any other person entitled to attend a meeting of the Council.
(e) When an Executive Director is entitled to cast the number of votes allotted to a member pursuant to Article XII, Section 3(i)(iii), the Councillor appointed by the group whose members elected such Executive Director shall be entitled to vote and cast the number of votes allotted to such

member. The member shall be deemed to have participated in the appointment of the Councillor entitled to vote and cast the number of votes allotted to the member.

6. The first sentence of Article XII, Section 2(a) shall be deemed to include a reference to the Council.

SCHEDULE E: Transitional Provisions with Respect to Executive Directors

1. Upon the entry into force of this Schedule:

(a) Each Executive Director who was appointed pursuant to former Article XII, Sections 3(*b*)(i) or 3(*c*), and was in office immediately prior to the entry into force of this Schedule, shall be deemed to have been elected by the member who appointed him; and

(b) Each Executive Director who cast the number of votes of a member pursuant to former Article XII, Section 3(i)(ii) immediately prior to the entry into force of this Schedule, shall be deemed to have been elected by such a member.

SCHEDULE F: Designation

During the first basic period the rules for designation shall be as follows:

(a) Participants subject to designation under Article XIX, Section 5(a)(i) shall be designated for such amounts as will promote over time equality in the ratios of the participants' holdings of special drawing rights in excess of their net cumulative allocations to their official holdings of gold and foreign exchange.

(b) The formula to give effect to (a) above shall be such that participants subject to designation shall be designated:

  (i) in proportion to their official holdings of gold and foreign exchange when the ratios described in (a) above are equal; and

  (ii) in such manner as gradually to reduce the difference between the ratios described in (a) above that are low and the ratios that are high.

SCHEDULE G: Reconstitution

1. During the first basic period the rules for reconstitution shall be as follows:

(a)

  (i) A participant shall so use and reconstitute its holdings of special drawing rights that, five years after the first allocation and at the end of each calendar quarter thereafter, the average of its total daily holdings of special drawing rights over the most recent five-year period will be not less than thirty per cent of the average of its daily net cumulative allocation of special drawing rights over the same period.

  (ii) Two years after the first allocation and at the end of each calendar month thereafter the Fund shall make calculations for each participant so as to ascertain whether and to what extent the participant would need to acquire special drawing rights between the date of the calculation and the end of any five-year period in order to comply with the requirement in (a)(i) above. The Fund shall adopt regulations with respect to the bases on which these calculations shall be made and with respect to the timing of the designation of participants under Article XIX, Section 5(a)(ii), in order to assist them to comply with the requirement in (a)(i) above.

(iii) The Fund shall give special notice to a participant when the calculations under (a)(ii) above indicate that it is unlikely that the participant will be able to comply with the requirement in (a)(i) above unless it ceases to use special drawing rights for the rest of the period for which the calculation was made under (a)(ii) above.

(iv) A participant that needs to acquire special drawing rights to fulfill this obligation shall be obligated and entitled to obtain them, for currency acceptable to the Fund, in a transaction with the Fund conducted through the General Resources Account. If sufficient special drawing rights to fulfill this obligation cannot be obtained in this way, the participant shall be obligated and entitled to obtain them with a freely usable currency from a participant which the Fund shall specify.

(b) Participants shall also pay due regard to the desirability of pursuing over time a balanced relationship between their holdings of special drawing rights and their other reserves.

2. If a participant fails to comply with the rules for reconstitution, the Fund shall determine whether or not the circumstances justify suspension under Article XXIII, Section 2(b).

SCHEDULE H: Termination of Participation

1. If the obligation remaining after the setoff under Article XXIV, Section 2(b) is to the terminating participant and agreement on settlement between the Fund and the terminating participant is not reached within six months of the date of termination, the Fund shall redeem this balance of special drawing rights in equal half-yearly installments within a maximum of five years of the date of termination. The Fund shall redeem this balance as it may determine, either (a) by the payment to the terminating participant of the amounts provided by the remaining participants to the Fund in accordance with Article XXIV, Section 5, or (b) by permitting the terminating participant to use its special drawing rights to obtain its own currency or a freely usable currency from a participant specified by the Fund, the General Resources Account, or any other holder.
2. If the obligation remaining after the setoff under Article XXIV, Section 2(b) is to the Fund and agreement on settlement is not reached within six months of the date of termination, the terminating participant shall discharge this obligation in equal half-yearly installments within three years of the date of termination or within such longer period as may be fixed by the Fund. The terminating participant shall discharge this obligation, as the Fund may determine, either (a) by the payment to the Fund of a freely usable currency, or (b) by obtaining special drawing rights, in accordance with Article XXIV, Section 6, from the General Resources Account or

in agreement with a participant specified by the Fund or from any other holder, and the setoff of these special drawing rights against the installment due.
3. Installments under either 1 or 2 above shall fall due six months after the date of termination and at intervals of six months thereafter.
4. In the event of the Special Drawing Rights Department going into liquidation under Article XXV within six months of the date a participant terminates its participation, the settlement between the Fund and that government shall be made in accordance with Article XXV and Schedule I.

SCHEDULE I: Administration of Liquidation of the Special Drawing Rights Department

1. In the event of liquidation of the Special Drawing Rights Department, participants shall discharge their obligations to the Fund in ten half-yearly installments, or in such longer period as the Fund may decide is needed, in a freely usable currency and the currencies of participants holding special drawing rights to be redeemed in any installment to the extent of such redemption, as determined by the Fund. The first half-yearly payment shall be made six months after the decision to liquidate the Special Drawing Rights Department.
2. If it is decided to liquidate the Fund within six months of the date of the decision to liquidate the Special Drawing Rights Department, the liquidation of the Special Drawing Rights Department shall not proceed until special drawing rights held in the General Resources Account have been distributed in accordance with the following rule:

> After the distributions made under 2(a) and (b) of Schedule K, the Fund shall apportion its special drawing rights held in the General Resources Account among all members that are participants in proportion to the amounts due to each participant after the distribution under 2(b). To determine the amount due to each member for the purpose of apportioning the remainder of its holdings of each currency under 2(d) of Schedule K, the Fund shall deduct the distribution of special drawing rights made under this rule.

3. With the amounts received under 1 above, the Fund shall redeem special drawing rights held by holders in the following manner and order:

(a) Special drawing rights held by governments that have terminated their participation more than six months before the date the Board of Governors decides to liquidate the Special Drawing Rights Department shall be redeemed in accordance with the terms of any agreement under Article XXIV or Schedule H.
(b) Special drawing rights held by holders that are not participants shall be redeemed before those held by participants, and shall be redeemed in proportion to the amount held by each holder.
(c) The Fund shall determine the proportion of special drawing rights held by each participant in relation to its net cumulative allocation. The Fund shall first redeem special drawing rights from the participants with the highest proportion until this proportion is reduced to that of the second highest proportion; the

Fund shall then redeem the special drawing rights held by these participants in accordance with their net cumulative allocations until the proportions are reduced to that of the third highest proportion; and this process shall be continued until the amount available for redemption is exhausted.

4. Any amount that a participant will be entitled to receive in redemption under 3 above shall be set off against any amount to be paid under 1 above.
5. During liquidation the Fund shall pay interest on the amount of special drawing rights held by holders, and each participant shall pay charges on the net cumulative allocation of special drawing rights to it less the amount of any payments made in accordance with 1 above. The rates of interest and charges and the time of payment shall be determined by the Fund. Payments of interest and charges shall be made in special drawing rights to the extent possible. A participant that does not hold sufficient special drawing rights to meet any charges shall make the payment with a currency specified by the Fund. Special drawing rights received as charges in amounts needed for administrative expenses shall not be used for the payment of interest, but shall be transferred to the Fund and shall be redeemed first and with the currencies used by the Fund to meet its expenses.
6. While a participant is in default with respect to any payment required by 1 or 5 above, no amounts shall be paid to it in accordance with 3 or 5 above.
7. If after the final payments have been made to participants each participant not in default does not hold special drawing rights in the same proportion to its net cumulative allocation, those participants holding a lower proportion shall purchase from those holding a higher proportion such amounts in accordance with arrangements made by the Fund as will make the proportion of their holdings of special drawing rights the same. Each participant in default shall pay to the Fund its own currency in an amount equal to its default. The Fund shall apportion this currency and residual claims among participants in proportion to the amount of special drawing rights held by each and these special drawing rights shall be cancelled. The Fund shall then close the books of the Special Drawing Rights Department and all of the Fund's liabilities arising from the allocations of special drawing rights and the administration of the Special Drawing Rights Department shall cease.
8. Each participant whose currency is distributed to other participants under this Schedule guarantees the unrestricted use of such currency at all times for the purchase of goods or for payments of sums due to it or to persons in its territories. Each participant so obligated agrees to compensate other participants for any loss resulting from the difference between the value at which the Fund distributed its currency under this Schedule and the value realised by such participants on disposal of its currency.

SCHEDULE J: Settlement of Accounts with Members Withdrawing

1. The settlement of accounts with respect to the General Resources Account shall be made according to 1 to 6 of this Schedule. The Fund shall be obligated to pay to a member withdrawing an amount equal to its quota, plus any other amounts due to it from the Fund, less any amounts due to the Fund, including charges accruing after the date of its withdrawal; but no payment shall be made until six months after the date of withdrawal. Payments shall be made in the currency of the withdrawing

member, and for this purpose the Fund may transfer to the General Resources Account holdings of the member's currency in the Special Disbursement Account or in the Investment Account in exchange for an equivalent amount of the currencies of other members in the General Resources Account selected by the Fund with their concurrence.
2. If the Fund's holdings of the currency of the withdrawing member are not sufficient to pay the net amount due from the Fund, the balance shall be paid in a freely usable currency, or in such other manner as may be agreed. If the Fund and the withdrawing member do not reach agreement within six months of the date of withdrawal, the currency in question held by the Fund shall be paid forthwith to the withdrawing member. Any balance due shall be paid in ten half-yearly installments during the ensuing five years. Each such installment shall be paid, at the option of the Fund, either in the currency of the withdrawing member acquired after its withdrawal or in a freely usable currency.
3. If the Fund fails to meet any installment which is due in accordance with the preceding paragraphs, the withdrawing member shall be entitled to require the Fund to pay the installment in any currency held by the Fund with the exception of any currency which has been declared scarce under Article VII, Section 3.
4. If the Fund's holdings of the currency of a withdrawing member exceed the amount due to it, and if agreement on the method of settling accounts is not reached within six months of the date of withdrawal, the former member shall be obligated to redeem such excess currency in a freely usable currency. Redemption shall be made at the rates at which the Fund would sell such currencies at the time of withdrawal from the Fund. The withdrawing member shall complete redemption within five years of the date of withdrawal, or within such longer period as may be fixed by the Fund, but shall not be required to redeem in any half-yearly period more than one-tenth of the Fund's excess holdings of its currency at the date of withdrawal plus further acquisitions of the currency during such half-yearly period. If the withdrawing member does not fulfill this obligation, the Fund may in an orderly manner liquidate in any market the amount of currency which should have been redeemed.
5. Any member desiring to obtain the currency of a member which has withdrawn shall acquire it by purchase from the Fund, to the extent that such member has access to the general resources of the Fund and that such currency is available under 4 above.
6. The withdrawing member guarantees the unrestricted use at all times of the currency disposed of under 4 and 5 above for the purchase of goods or for payment of sums due to it or to persons within its territories. It shall compensate the Fund for any loss resulting from the difference between the value of its currency in terms of the special drawing right on the date of withdrawal and the value realised in terms of the special drawing right by the Fund on disposal under 4 and 5 above.
7. If the withdrawing member is indebted to the Fund as the result of transactions conducted through the Special Disbursement Account under Article V, Section 12(f)(ii), the indebtedness shall be discharged in accordance with the terms of the indebtedness.
8. If the Fund holds the withdrawing member's currency in the Special Disbursement Account or in the Investment Account, the Fund may in an orderly manner exchange in any market for the currencies of members the amount of the currency

of the withdrawing member remaining in each account after use under 1 above, and the proceeds of the exchange of the amount in each account shall be kept in that account. Paragraph 5 above and the first sentence of 6 above shall apply to the withdrawing member's currency.
9. If the Fund holds obligations of the withdrawing member in the Special Disbursement Account pursuant to Article V, Section 12(h), or in the Investment Account, the Fund may hold them until the date of maturity or dispose of them sooner. Paragraph 8 above shall apply to the proceeds of such disinvestment.
10. In the event of the Fund going into liquidation under Article XXVII, Section 2 within six months of the date on which the member withdraws, the accounts between the Fund and that government shall be settled in accordance with Article XXVII, Section 2 and Schedule K.

SCHEDULE K: Administration of Liquidation [Omitted]

1. In the event of liquidation the liabilities of the Fund other than the repayment of subscriptions shall have priority in the distribution of the assets of the Fund. In meeting each such liability the Fund shall use its assets in the following order:

(a) the currency in which the liability is payable;
(b) gold;
(c) all other currencies in proportion, so far as may be practicable, to the quotas of the members.

2. After the discharge of the Fund's liabilities in accordance with 1 above, the balance of the Fund's assets shall be distributed and apportioned as follows:

(a) (i) The Fund shall calculate the value of gold held on August 31, 1975 that it continues to hold on the date of the decision to liquidate. The calculation shall be made in accordance with 9 below and also on the basis of one special drawing right per 0.888 671 gram of fine gold on the date of liquidation. Gold equivalent to the excess of the former value over the latter shall be distributed to those members that were members on August 31, 1975 in proportion to their quotas on that date.
(ii) The Fund shall distribute any assets held in the Special Disbursement Account on the date of the decision to liquidate to those members that were members on August 31, 1975 in proportion to their quotas on that date. Each type of asset shall be distributed proportionately to members.
(b) The Fund shall distribute its remaining holdings of gold among the members whose currencies are held by the Fund in amounts less than their quotas in the proportions, but not in excess of, the amounts by which their quotas exceed the Fund's holdings of their currencies.
(c) The Fund shall distribute to each member one-half the Fund's holdings of its currency but such distribution shall not exceed fifty per cent of its quota.
(d) The Fund shall apportion the remainder of its holdings of gold and each currency

(i) among all members in proportion to, but not in excess of, the amounts due to each member after the distributions under (b) and (c) above, provided that distribution under 2(a) above shall not be taken into account for determining the amounts due, and
(ii) any excess holdings of gold and currency among all the members in proportion to their quotas.

3. Each member shall redeem the holdings of its currency apportioned to other members under 2(d) above, and shall agree with the Fund within three months after a decision to liquidate upon an orderly procedure for such redemption.
4. If a member has not reached agreement with the Fund within the three-month period referred to in 3 above, the Fund shall use the currencies of other members apportioned to that member under 2(d) above to redeem the currency of that member apportioned to other members. Each currency apportioned to a member which has not reached agreement shall be used, so far as possible, to redeem its currency apportioned to the members which have made agreements with the Fund under 3 above.
5. If a member has reached agreement with the Fund in accordance with 3 above, the Fund shall use the currencies of other members apportioned to that member under 2(d) above to redeem the currency of that member apportioned to other members which have made agreements with the Fund under 3 above. Each amount so redeemed shall be redeemed in the currency of the member to which it was apportioned.
6. After carrying out the steps in the preceding paragraphs, the Fund shall pay to each member the remaining currencies held for its account.
7. Each member whose currency has been distributed to other members under 6 above shall redeem such currency in the currency of the member requesting redemption, or in such other manner as may be agreed between them. If the members involved do not otherwise agree, the member obligated to redeem shall complete redemption within five years of the date of distribution, but shall not be required to redeem in any half-yearly period more than one-tenth of the amount distributed to each other member. If the member does not fulfill this obligation, the amount of currency which should have been redeemed may be liquidated in an orderly manner in any market.
8. Each member whose currency has been distributed to other members under 6 above guarantees the unrestricted use of such currency at all times for the purchase of goods or for payment of sums due to it or to persons in its territories. Each member so obligated agrees to compensate other members for any loss resulting from the difference between the value of its currency in terms of the special drawing right on the date of the decision to liquidate the Fund and the value in terms of the special drawing right realised by such members on disposal of its currency.
9. The Fund shall determine the value of gold under this Schedule on the basis of prices in the market.
10. For the purposes of this Schedule, quotas shall be deemed to have been increased to the full extent to which they could have been increased in accordance with Article III, Section 2(b) of this Agreement.

SCHEDULE L: Suspension of Voting Rights

In the case of a suspension of voting rights of a member under Article XXVI, Section 2(b), the following provisions shall apply:
1. The member shall not:

(a) participate in the adoption of a proposed amendment of this Agreement, or be counted in the total number of members for that purpose, except in the case of an amendment requiring acceptance by all members under Article XXVIII(b) or pertaining exclusively to the Special Drawing Rights Department;
(b) appoint a Governor or Alternate Governor, appoint or participate in the appointment of a Councillor or Alternate Councillor, or elect or participate in the election of an Executive Director.

2. The number of votes allotted to the member shall not be cast in any organ of the Fund. They shall not be included in the calculation of the total voting power, except for purposes of: (a) the acceptance of a proposed amendment pertaining exclusively to the Special Drawing Rights Department and (b) the calculation of basic votes pursuant to Article XII, Section 5(a)(i)
3.

(a) The Governor and Alternate Governor appointed by the member shall cease to hold office.
(b) The Councillor and Alternate Councillor appointed by the member, or in whose appointment the member has participated, shall cease to hold office, provided that, if such Councillor was entitled to cast the number of votes allotted to other members whose voting rights have not been suspended, another Councillor and Alternate Councillor shall be appointed by such other members under Schedule D, and, pending such appointment, the Councillor and Alternate Councillor shall continue to hold office, but for a maximum of thirty days from the date of suspension.
(c) The Executive Director elected by the member, or in whose election the member has participated, shall cease to hold office, unless such Executive Director was entitled to cast the number of votes allotted to other members whose voting rights have not been suspended. In the latter case:
    (i) if more than ninety days remain before the next regular election of Executive Directors, another Executive Director shall be elected for the remainder of the term by such other members by a majority of the votes cast; pending such election, the Executive Director shall continue to hold office, but for a maximum of thirty days from the date of suspension;
    (ii) if not more than ninety days remain before the next regular election of Executive Directors, the Executive Director shall continue to hold office for the remainder of the term.
(d) The member shall be entitled to send a representative to attend any meeting of the Board of Governors, the Council, or the Executive Board, but not any meeting of their committees, when a request made by, or a matter particularly affecting, the member is under consideration.

SCHEDULE M: Special One-Time Allocation of Special Drawing Rights

1. Subject to 4 below, each member that, as of September 19, 1997, is a participant in the Special Drawing Rights Department shall, on the 30th day following the effective date of the fourth amendment of this Agreement, receive an allocation of special drawing rights in an amount that will result in its net cumulative allocation of special drawing rights being equal to 29.315788813 per cent of its quota as of September 19, 1997, provided that, for participants whose quotas have not been adjusted as proposed in Resolution No. 45-2 of the Board of Governors, calculations shall be made on the basis of the quotas proposed in that resolution.
2.

(a) Subject to 4 below, each country that becomes a participant in the Special Drawing Rights Department after September 19, 1997 but within three months of the date of its membership in the Fund shall receive an allocation of special drawing rights in an amount calculated in accordance with (b) and (c) below on the 30th day following the later of: (i) the date on which the new member becomes a participant in the Special Drawing Rights Department, or (ii) the effective date of the fourth amendment of this Agreement.
(b) For the purposes of (a) above, each participant shall receive an amount of special drawing rights that will result in such participant's net cumulative allocation being equal to 29.315788813 per cent of its quota as of the date on which the member becomes a participant in the Special Drawing Rights Department, as adjusted:
    (i) first, by multiplying 29.315788813 per cent by the ratio of the total of quotas, as calculated under 1 above, of the participants described in (c) below to the total of quotas of such participants as of the date on which the member became a participant in the Special Drawing Rights Department, and
    (ii) second, by multiplying the product of (i) above by the ratio of the total of the sum of the net cumulative allocations of special drawing rights received under Article XVIII of the participants described in (c) below as of the date on which the member became a participant in the Special Drawing Rights Department and the allocations received by such participants under 1 above to the total of the sum of the net cumulative allocations of special drawing rights received under Article XVIII of such participants as of September 19, 1997 and the allocations received by such participants under 1 above.
(c) For the purposes of the adjustments to be made under (b) above, the participants in the Special Drawing Rights Department shall be members that are participants as of September 19, 1997 and (i) continue to be participants in the Special Drawing Rights Department as of the date on which the member became a participant in the Special Drawing Rights Department, and (ii) have received all allocations made by the Fund after September 19, 1997.

3.

(a) Subject to 4 below, if the Federal Republic of Yugoslavia (Serbia/Montenegro) succeeds to the membership in the Fund and the participation in the Special Drawing Rights Department of the former Socialist Federal Republic of Yugoslavia in accordance with the terms and conditions of Executive Board Decision No. 10237-(92/150), adopted December 14, 1992, it shall receive an allocation of special drawing rights in an amount calculated in accordance with (b) below on the 30th day following the later of: (i) the date on which the Federal Republic of Yugoslavia (Serbia/Montenegro) succeeds to membership in the Fund and participation in the Special Drawing Rights Department in accordance with the terms and conditions of Executive Board Decision No. 10237-(92/150), or (ii) the effective date of the fourth amendment of this Agreement.
(b) For the purposes of (a) above, the Federal Republic of Yugoslavia (Serbia/ Montenegro) shall receive an amount of special drawing rights that will result in its net cumulative allocation being equal to 29.3157888 13 per cent of the quota proposed to it under paragraph 3(c) of Executive Board Decision No. 10237-(92/150), as adjusted in accordance with 2(b)(ii) and (c) above as of the date on which the Federal Republic of Yugoslavia (Serbia/Montenegro) qualifies for an allocation under (a) above.

4. The Fund shall not allocate special drawing rights under this Schedule to those participants that have notified the Fund in writing prior to the date of the allocation of their desire not to receive the allocation.
5.

(a) If, at the time an allocation is made to a participant under 1, 2, or 3 above, the participant has overdue obligations to the Fund, the special drawing rights so allocated shall be deposited and held in an escrow account within the Special Drawing Rights Department and shall be released to the participant upon discharge of all its overdue obligations to the Fund.
(b) Special drawing rights being held in an escrow account shall not be available for any use and shall not be included in any calculations of allocations or holdings of special drawing rights for the purposes of the Articles, except for calculations under this Schedule. If special drawing rights allocated to a participant are held in an escrow account when the participant terminates its participation in the Special Drawing Rights Department or when it is decided to liquidate the Special Drawing Rights Department, such special drawing rights shall be canceled.
(c) For purposes of this paragraph, overdue obligations to the Fund consist of overdue repurchases and charges in the General Resources Account, overdue principal and interest on loans in the Special Disbursement Account, overdue charges and assessments in the Special Drawing Rights Department, and overdue liabilities to the Fund as trustee.
(d) Except for the provisions of this paragraph, the principle of separation between the General Department and the Special Drawing Rights Department and the unconditional character of special drawing rights as reserve assets shall be maintained.

Selected Bibliography

Adinolfi, Giovanna. *Poteri e interventi del Fondo Monetario Internazionale.* Padova: Cedam, 2012.

Andrews, David M. (ed.). *Orderly Change: International Monetary Relations since Bretton Woods.* Ithaca: Cornell University Press, 2008.

Bahram, Ghazi. *The IMF, The World Bank Group and the Question of Human Rights.* New York: Transnational Publishers, 2005.

Bergthaler, Wolfgang & Andrew Giddings. 'Recent Quota and Governance Reforms at the International Monetary Fund'. In *European Yearbook of International Economic Law 2013*, edited by Herrmann, Christoph & Markus Krajewski, Jorg Terhechte. Heidelberg: Springer, 2013, 371–389.

Bergthaler, Wolfgang & Wouter Bossu. 'Recent Legal Developments in the International Monetary Fund'. In *European Yearbook of International Economic Law 2010*, edited by Herrmann, Christoph & Jörg Philipp Terhechte. Heidelberg: Springer, 2010, 391–404.

Boughton, J. M. *Silent Revolution: The International Monetary Fund 1979–1989.* Washington D.C.: IMF, 2001.

Boughton, J. M. *Tearing Down Walls: The International Monetary Fund 1990–1999.* Washington D.C.: IMF, 2012.

Bradlow, Daniel. *The Law of International Financial Institutions.* Oxford: Oxford University Press, 2023.

Bradlow, Daniel & Hunter, David (eds). *International Financial Institutions and International Law.* Austin: Kluwer Press, 2010.

Buira, Ariel. *Reforming the Governance of the IMF and the World Bank.* London: Anthem Press, 2005.

Carreau, Dominique. *Le Fonds monétaire international.* Paris: Pedone, 2009.

Clift, Ben. *The IMF and the Politics of Austerity in the Wake of the Global Financial Crisis.* Oxford: Oxford University Press, 2018

Copelovitch, Mark S. *The International Monetary Fund in the Global Economy: Banks, Bonds, and Bailouts.* London: Cambridge University Press, 2010.

Dam, K. *The Rules of the Game: Reform and Evolution of the International Monetary System.* Chicago: The University of Chicago Press, 1982.

Darrow, Mac. *Between Light and Shadow, The World Bank, The International Monetary Fund and International Human Rights Law.* Oxford: Oxford University Press, 2003.

Dell, Sidney (ed.). *The International Monetary System and Its Reform.* Parts 1, 2 and 3. Amsterdam etc.: Elsevier Science Publishers, 1987.

Dell, Sidney. 'The Future of the International Monetary System'. In *The Future Role of the United Nations in an Interdependent World*, edited by John P. Renninger. Dordrecht: Martinus Nijhoff Publishers, 1989, 101–135.

Denters, Erik. *Law and Policy of IMF Conditionality.* The Hague etc.: Kluwer Law International, 1996.

ECB. *IMF Surveillance in Europe*, Occasional Paper No. 158, January 2015.

Edwards, Richard W. Jr. *International Monetary Collaboration.* Dobbs Ferry, New York: Transnational Publishers, Inc., 1985.

Effros, Robert C. (ed.). *Current Legal Issues Affecting Central Banks.* Vols I–V. Washington, D.C.: IMF, 1992–1998.

Garritsen de Vries, Margaret. *Balance of Payments Adjustment, 1945–1986: The IMF Experience.* Washington D.C.: IMF, 1987.

Garritsen de Vries, Margaret. *The IMF in a Changing World.* Washington D.C.: IMF, 1986.

Garritsen de Vries, Margaret. *The International Monetary Fund 1966–1971.* Vols 1 and 2. Washington D.C.: IMF, 1976.

Garritsen de Vries, Margaret. *The International Monetary Fund 1972–1978.* Vols 1, 2 and 3. Washington D.C.: IMF, 1985.

Giovanoli, Mario & Diego Devos (eds). *International Monetary and Financial Law: The Global Crisis.* Oxford: Oxford University Press, 2010.

Gold, Joseph. *Exchange Rates in International Law and Organisation.* American Bar Association, 1988.

Gold, Joseph. *Interpretation: The IMF and International Law.* London etc.: Kluwer Law International, 1996.

Gold, Joseph. *Legal and Institutional Aspects of the International Monetary System: Selected Essays.* Vol. 2. Washington D.C.: IMF, 1984.

Gold, Joseph. *Legal and Institutional Aspects of the International Monetary System: Selected Essays.* Washington D.C.: IMF, 1979.

Hagan, Sean. 'Reforming the IMF'. In IMF, *Current Developments in Monetary and Financial Law: Restoring Financial Stability – The Legal Response.* Vol. 6. Washington, D.C.: IMF, 2012, 253 ff.

Helleiner, Eric. *Forgotten Foundations of Bretton Woods: International Development and the Making of the Postwar Order*, Ithaca: Cornell University Press, 2014.

Herdegen, Matthias. *Principles of International Economic Law.* Oxford: Oxford University Press, 2024.

Herrmann Christoph & Dornacher, *Corinna. International and European Monetary Law: An Introduction.* Cham: Springer, 2017.

Horsefield, J. Keith (ed.). *The International Monetary Fund 1945–1965.* Vols 1, 2 and 3. Washington D.C.: IMF, 1969.

IMF. *Current Developments in Monetary and Financial Law.* Vols 1–6. Washington, D.C.: IMF, 1999–2013.

IMF. *IMF History: A Digital Collection.* Washington, D.C.: IMF, 2014.

Jackson, John H., William J. Davey & Alan O. Sykes Jr. *Legal Problems of International Economic Relations.* 3rd edn. St. Paul, Minn.: West Publishing Co., 1995.

James, Harold. *International Monetary Cooperation Since Bretton Woods.* New York etc.: Oxford University Press, 1996.
Lastra, Rosa Maria. *International Financial and Monetary Law.* Oxford: Oxford University Press, 2015.
Lastra, Rosa Maria & Lee Buchheit. Sovereign Debt Management. Oxford: Oxford University Press, 2014.
Lastra, Rosa Maria. *Legal Foundations of International Monetary Stability.* Oxford: Oxford University Press, 2006.
Louka, Elli. *The Global Economic Order: The International Law and Politics of the Financial and Monetary System.* Cheltenham, UK: Edward Elgar, 2020
Lowenfeld, Andreas F. 'The International Monetary System: A Look Back Over Seven Decades'. *Journal of International Economic Law* 13, no. 3 (2010): 575–595.
Lowenfeld, Andreas F. *International Economic Law.* Oxford: Oxford University Press, 2008.
Lowenfeld, Andreas F. *The International Monetary System.* 2nd edn. New York: Matthew Bender, 1984.
Mann, F. A. *The Legal Aspects of Money.* 5th edn. Oxford: Oxford University Press, 1992.
Norton, Joseph J. & Mads Andenas (eds). *International Monetary and Financial Law Upon Entering the New Millennium: A Tribute to Sir Joseph and Ruth Gold.* London: British Institute of International and Comparative Law, 2003.
Palombino, Fulvio Maria (ed.). *Introduction to International Economic Law.* Torino: Giappichelli, 2025.
Proctor, Charles. *Mann on the Legal Aspect of Money.* Oxford: Oxford University Press, 2005.
Proctor, Charles. *Mann and Proctor on the Law of Money.* Oxford: Oxford University Press, 2022.
Qureshi, Asif & Andreas Ziegler. *International Economic Law: International Monetary and Financial Law.* London: Routledge, 2010.
Riesenhuber, Eva. *The International Monetary Fund under Constraint: Legitimacy of Its Crisis Management.* The Hague: Kluwer Law International, 2001.
Sciso, Elena (ed.). *Accountability, Transparency and Democracy in the Functioning of Bretton Woods Institutions.* Cham: Springer, 2017.
Southard, Frank Allan. 'The Evolution of the International Monetary Fund'. *Essays in International Finance.* Princeton University, No. 135, 1979.
Steil, Benn. *The Battle of Bretton Woods: John Maynard Keynes, Harry Dexter White and the Making of a New World Order.* Princeton: Princeton University Press, 2013.
Steinki, Bernhard & Wolfgang Bergthaler. 'Recent Reforms of the Finances of the International Monetary Fund: An Overview'. In *European Yearbook of International Economic Law* 3 (EYIEL), edited by C. Herrmann & J. P. Terhechte (2012), 635–666.
Treasurers Department (of IMF). 'Financial Organisation and Operations of the IMF'. *Pamphlet Series*, no. 45. Washington D.C.: IMF, 1991.
Truman, Edwin (ed.). *Reforming the IMF for the 21st Century.* Washington, D.C.: Peterson Institute for International Economics, 2006.

Selected Bibliography

Viterbo, Annamaria. *International Economic Law and Monetary Measures: Limitations to States' Sovereignty and Dispute Settlement.* Cheltenham, UK – Northampton, MA, USA: Edward Elgar, 2012.
Viterbo, Annamaria. *Sovereign Debt Restructuring: The Role and Limits of Public International Law.* Torino: Giappichelli, 2020.
Zimmermann, Claus. *A Contemporary Concept of Monetary Sovereignty*. Oxford: Oxford University Press, 2013.
Wilkie, Christopher. *Special Drawing Rights (SDRs): The First International Money*. Oxford: Oxford University Press, 2012.

Index

The numbers here refer to paragraph numbers.

Index

www.ingramcontent.com/pod-product-compliance
Ingram Content Group UK Ltd.
Pitfield, Milton Keynes, MK11 3LW, UK
UKHW020142290926
15471UKWH00004B/654

9 789403 501567